Rethinking globalizations
Edited by Barry K. Gills
University of Newcastle, United Kingdom

This series is designed to break new ground in the literature on globalization and its academic and popular understanding. Rather than perpetuating or simply reacting to the economic understanding of globalization, this series seeks to capture the term and broaden its meaning to encompass a wide range of issues and disciplines and convey a sense of alternative possibilities for the future.

Limits to Globalization

North–South divergence

William R. Thompson
and Rafael Reuveny

Routledge
Taylor & Francis Group

LONDON AND NEW YORK

UCB

First published 2010
by Routledge
2 Park Square Milton Park Abingdon Oxon OX14 4RN

Simultaneously published in the USA and Canada
by Routledge
270 Madison Avenue, New York, NY 10016

Routledge is an imprint of the Taylor & Francis Group, an informa business.

© 2010 William R. Thompson and Rafael Reuveny

Typeset in Sabon by Keyword Group Ltd.
Printed and bound in Great Britain by TJ International Ltd,
Padstow, Cornwall

British Library Cataloguing in Publication Data
A catalogue record for this book is available from the British Library

Library of Congress Cataloging in Publication Data
Thompson, William R.
Limits to globalization : North-South divergence / William R.
Thompson and Rafael Reuveny.
p. cm. – (Rethinking globalizations ; 21)
Includes bibliographical references and index.
1. International economic relations. 2. Globalization–Economic
aspects. 3. Developing countries–Economic conditions. I. Reuveny,
Rafael. II. Title.
HF1359.T467 2009
337–dc22
2009006107

ISBN10: 0-415-77672-4 (hbk)
ISBN10: 0-415-77673-2 (pbk)
ISBN10: 0-203-87279-7 (ebk)

ISBN13: 978-0-415-77672-1 (hbk)
ISBN13: 978-0-415-77673-8 (pbk)
ISBN13: 978-0-203-87279-6 (ebk)

Contents

Figures

Tables

Acknowledgments

Parts of Chapter 3 first appeared in "Exploring the North–South Gap Longitudinally." *Japanese Journal of Political Science* 4 (2003): 77–102. A portion of Chapter 4 was published as "Uneven Economic Growth and the World Economy's North–South Stratification." *International Studies Quarterly* 52 (2008): 579–605. Earlier versions of Chapter 5 appeared as "The Limits of Economic Globalization: Still Another North–South Cleavage? *World Society Focus Paper* (Zurich, Switzerland, 2006) and in *International Journal of Comparative Sociology* 48, 2 (Spring, 2007): 107–135 as well as with the title "How 'Global' is Economic Globalization?" in Mark Herkenrath, ed., *The Regional and Local Shaping of World Society*. Muenster, Germany: LIT Verlag, 2007. Much of Chapter 6 was published as "World Economic Growth, Systemic Leadership and Southern Debt Crises." *Journal of Peace Research* 41 (2004): 5–24. Parts of Chapter 7 are found in earlier forms in "The Extent of the Kondratieff Wave's Effect on Violence in the North–South Context," in Tessaleno Devezas, ed., *Kondratieff Waves, Warfare and World Security*. Amsterdam: IOS Press (2006) and "World Economic Growth, Northern Antagonisms, and North–South Conflict." *Journal of Conflict Resolution* 46 (August, 2002): 484–514. Some of Chapter 8 appeared as "Systemic Leadership, World Economic Growth, and Southern Democratization in the Long Run." *International Interactions* 34 (2008): 1–24. Our thanks, respectively, to Cambridge University Press, Blackwell-Wiley, Sage Publications, LIT Verlag, IOS Press, and Taylor and Francis for permission to republish the earlier material in revised form.

1 Unreal and unflat worlds

A popular book in the 1990s, Singer and Wildavsky's (1993) *The Real World Order,* divided the post-Cold War world into two zones – one of peace and the other of turmoil. The peaceful one was composed of wealthy and democratic states located in Western Europe, North America, Japan, and the South Pacific, and comprised about 15 percent of the world's population. The other zone encompassed the rest of the world's population, living in lesser developed states, often authoritarian, and occasionally embroiled in internal and external conflicts. The emergence of such a segmented world, accompanied by the anomaly of a single surviving superpower, was expected to give rise to a new form of international politics. Even so, the authors of this perspective believed that such a world had to be transitional. While the peaceful zone would continue to remain wealthy and democratic, states in the zone of turmoil would gradually develop, democratize, and join the peaceful zone. Every 20 years or so, the size of the peaceful zone was expected to expand. Just how long it would take to eliminate the zone of turmoil was not predicted, but eliminated it would be and without wealth transfers from the rich to the poor. The poor states would emulate the rich and bring their economies up to modern speed, progressively removing any barriers to the natural propensity toward development and democratization, as portrayed in Figure 1.1.

The book's popularity can be explained in part by its capturing a liberal view of the future just as the Soviet Union was disintegrating and the old Cold War prisms were being shattered. The view was highly optimistic, to say the least. The gradual contraction of the zone of turmoil assumes movement toward economic convergence. Guatemala might not become as wealthy as Switzerland, but its economy is expected to become more like the Swiss economy. But, do we have any evidence that movement toward convergence has taken place already? Or, does the evidence point toward widening divergence characterized by a very clear stratification? Assuming that there is a division of the world into rich and poor states, is the world likely to remain characterized by a rich minority and a poor majority? Or, is there some likelihood of a significant number of escapes from Singer and Wildavsky's zone of turmoil? These questions are central to liberalism, its

Figure 1.1 The real world order model.

neoclassical economics offspring, a number of international relations theories, and, quite frankly, the future of the planet.

As a matter of fact, there is not a great deal of evidence for economic convergence (except among the more affluent states). There is very clearly a bimodal division between rich and poor states, despite widespread views to the contrary. States have escaped the "turmoil zone," but, so far, they have not been all that numerous. Nor is it clear that many states are likely to escape in the relatively near future. We think we can explain the root of this problem fairly parsimoniously even though we do not think that there is a single cause. Long-term economic growth is fueled by the intermittent introduction of radically new technology which eventually diffuses, but most unevenly. The constraints on diffusion are multiple but can be simplified by noting that the ability to absorb new technology is variable and itself dependent on a package encompassing such things as technology transmission channels that connect local economies to the outside world, human skills, governmental receptivity, and entrepreneurial and financial facilitators. Many states score poorly on the presence of these factors. Technological diffusion, therefore, is and has been limited for some time.

This state of affairs is not likely to change overnight or any time soon. We do not insist that all lesser developed states remain underdeveloped forever because of the restricted nature of technological diffusion. A handful of states have improved their ability to absorb novel technology, and there is no reason to assume that this process will not continue. Yet, it will continue to be a fairly slow process, and there may prove to be sizeable parts of the world that go untouched by improved technological absorptive capacities. One dimension of the problem is that some parts of the world would have to do a great deal to overcome the barriers restricting the importation of new ways of doing things. Removing these barriers relatively quickly also probably could not be done without considerable societal and political turbulence. Hence, some part of the problem is a lack of eagerness to embrace the costs of major and extensive reforms on the part of both elites and masses.

Yet another dimension of the problem is that numerous analysts seem reluctant to embrace fully the implications of technology-driven economic growth and diffusion. Some economists still hold out hope for universal economic convergence, while others have moved toward some form of conditional convergence. Policy makers still talk about universal democratization and continue to promote liberal economic strategies, as if all economies and political systems have already converged to a single template – or might do so fairly soon. Globalization has its partisans and foes, yet the highly selective or segmented nature of globalization processes does not seem to be fully recognized. Debt crises come and go. Yet, observers seem reluctant to acknowledge that these recurring problems are built into the structure of North–South interactions. They are not random policy problems due to occasional shocks. They are likely to persist as Southern reverberations of Northern economic turndowns. While Singer and Wildavsky (1993) talked about two worlds of peace and turmoil, the reality of global conflict patterns is that the North has become more pacific while the South has become more conflictual. Part of this transformation is an increase in North–South conflict, ranging from invasions of Iraq to Cold War facilitation of Southern internal wars to jihadi attacks on US and European targets, that also go less than fully recognized for what they are – that is, as manifestations of North–South conflict.[1]

As authors, we cannot improve Southern technological absorptive capacities with a snap of our fingers or expand technological diffusion through wishful thinking. We cannot wave a magic wand and expect economic realities to change overnight. We can address, however, the conceptualization and empirical analysis of North–South policy problems – problems that, we think, are not always accurately interpreted. In this book, we focus on some of the relationships among the six processes identified in Figure 1.2. We develop a continuous measure of North–South inequality stretching from 1870 to 2005 that facilitates asking and answering whether the extent of inequality is increasing, decreasing, or staying about the same. We elaborate how technological diffusion and North–South inequality are linked. We also seek to show how globalization contributes to inequality and how

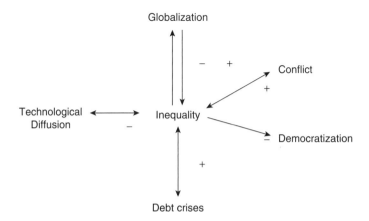

Figure 1.2 The North–South gap and some implications.

the future of globalization is constrained by the extent of inequality. We are able to reinforce the contention that debt crises, whatever else they may be, are cyclical manifestations of downturns in world economic growth.

Given our commitment to systemic modeling in these particular analyses, there are limitations to what we can do with conflict and democratization interrelationships but we can at least underline some of the ways in which they are related to macro-inequalities and shaped by external influences. Throughout all of our chapters, we choose to stress systemic explanations. This bias is not due to a belief on our part that non-systemic perspectives have no value. Rather, we choose to explore and develop systemic analyses in part because they remain underexplored and underdeveloped in the field. We think this is undesirable because systemic approaches have much to tell us about processes such as global structural inequalities, globalization, and development. Ultimately, though, we fully accept the counter-charge that systemic explanations must be limited if they are not linked to sub-systemic behavior.

In short, we do not deny that economic development is linked in some ways to democratization or that substantial changes in economic development and democratization levels can lead to reductions in the levels of societal conflict, à la the Real World Order model. But, models such as this do not fully appreciate what is required to achieve substantial economic development or the barriers to achieving substantial economic development. What we question, accordingly, is how much economic development can be anticipated in the next few decades. If we are right, a major North–South gap is here to stay for a considerable period of time. We do not need to accept the gap as inevitable as much as we need to come to terms with its existence, the reasons for its existence, the steps that might be most fruitful in narrowing the gap, and the implications of a structural divide that cannot help but strongly influence the nature of twenty-first century international relations.[2] If nothing else, it implies that processes of globalization, democratization, and the escape from zones of turmoil will move much more slowly than was anticipated a decade and a half ago.

In the remainder of this chapter, we sketch our basic argument as a foundation for the exploration of links among inequality, technological diffusion, globalization, debt crises, conflict, and democratization in the following chapters. We begin the overview with an evaluation of the metaphor of a world economy that is becoming more "flat," and some of its problems, as information technology transforms working places around the globe.

Flat versus unflat worlds

A popular thesis about globalization, invoked by the journalist Thomas Friedman (2007), focuses on the three eras summarized in Table 1.1. In the first era, roughly spanning from Columbus (1492) to the Industrial Revolution (latter eighteenth century for the British system leader), states

Table 1.1 Friedman's flat world thesis

Era	Time period	Dynamic focus of globalization
1.0	1492–1800	The power and creativity of countries to break down barriers
2.0	1800–2000	Multinational corporations fueled by falling transportation and telecommunication costs
3.0	2000–	Individuals empowered by personal computers connected worldwide by fiber optic cable

used force to knock down barriers to increased interdependence. In the second era, running from the Industrial Revolution to the advent of the Internet, multinationals, advantaged by a long sequence of cost-cutting hardware for faster transportation of goods and communications, were the principal agents. In the current, early twenty-first century era, it is individuals connected around the globe by computers that will lead the way because technological innovations are flattening or equalizing the capabilities and opportunities open to people. In the process, the first era, globalization 1.0 "shrank the world from a size large to a size medium (p. 9)." Globalization era 2.0 "shrank the world from a size medium to a size small (p. 9)." The era 3.0 that we have only recently entered, "is shrinking the world from a size small to size tiny and flattening the playing field at the same time (p. 10)."[3]

Friedman knows the world is not really flat and that there are a very large number of people living in what he calls the "unflat world." For our part, we agree that the world is not flat but we are a bit skeptical about the pace and extent of the world's shrinkage and ultimate flattening. Friedman is a globalization optimist, in the sense that he thinks the technological forces at play will persevere and make the whole world more "flat." That may occur, and we would all be delighted if it did come to pass. Yet far more likely, we think, is that the world will shrink and become more flat; that is, more globalized, for some and less so for others. In the process of flattening part of the world, moreover, the divide between the flat and unflat – to maintain the metaphor – will become greater. That should constrain to some extent how far globalization will progress in the flatter world. It most definitely will make the unflat part of the world even more unflat. As globalization pessimists, we see the cup neither half full nor half empty. Rather, we see at least two cups that are imperfectly linked together. In one cup, globalization processes seem to be accelerating while the other cup is left much less affected. The more the first cup globalizes, the more the other cup has to make up if it wants to resemble the first cup. We do not insist that the globalizing "cup" or part of the world must remain smaller in terms of the number of populations and countries affected – although the globalizing segment of the world does not currently encompass the majority of the planet. What we do insist on is that there are very strong constraints on how far globalization can proceed if a sizeable proportion of the world remains outside the full force of the "shrinking" dynamics at work.

We do not come by this view of globalization pessimism lightly. It is based on rather strong evidence that the current era's leading technology, as in past eras, is highly concentrated. To be sure, more technological diffusion can be anticipated – but only within severe limits if the past is any judge. To illustrate the most contemporary extent of concentration, we have three key types of evidence. The worldwide Internet is the virtual highway for Freidman's individual empowerment. Access to it is supposed to be the great equalizer. But, who actually uses this highway? Regardless of the answer, the Internet can be used for all sorts of activities, ranging from research to communication to game playing. But, who best uses information technology (IT) for economic productivity purposes? Finally, even if the production of information technology is highly concentrated, it does not mean that the ability to absorb and receive the benefits of IT innovation is highly concentrated – or does it?

It should come as no surprise that Internet usage was highly concentrated in 1990 (see Table 1.2). Few people had access anywhere to this novelty then. In the last 15 years or more, access/usage/technological "penetration" has increased greatly, but the lion's share of this increase remains concentrated in the more affluent parts of the world. The number of users per thousand population is often used as an index of technological penetration. The United States is one of the leaders in Internet usage, with some 63 percent of the population having been online.[4] The other most affluent parts of the world, as suggested by OECD membership, lag somewhat behind on average at about 45 percent. Less affluent parts of

Table 1.2 Internet users (per 1000 people)

	1990	1998	2000	2005
United States	8	69	543	630
OECD	3	69*	282*	445
Eastern Europe/ CIS	0	8	39	185
Latin America/ Caribbean	0	8	32	156
East Asia/Pacific	0	5	23	106
Arab States	0	2	6	88
South Asia	0	0.4	4	52
Sub-Saharan Africa	0	1	4	26

*excludes the United States

Source: Based on United Nations Development Programme (2001, 2007).

the world – in descending order: Eastern Europe, Latin America, East Asia, Arab states, South Asia, and sub-Saharan Africa – can be said to have increased their utilization of the Internet dramatically from a zero starting point. Yet, they all remain far behind the United States and OECD world.

No doubt, Internet usage will continue to expand in all of the less well-connected regions but probably more slowly and subject to some serious constraints in the less developed world. Even so, the Internet is not the singular crown jewel of the information technology era. More problematic is the concentration in technology producing hubs. These hubs bring together a number of critical ingredients for developing innovations in digital technology, including university training, corporate support, risk taking, and venture capital. A survey designed to identify the location of these hubs rank ordered 46 sites, arrayed in Table 1.3, according to the relative availability of all the different types of ingredients for innovation success. A quick glance at the places listed suggests that they are found all over the world. That is good news for globalization optimists. Less comforting perhaps is the realization that as many as 30 (about 65 percent) are located in North America and Europe. All but one of the nine Asian hubs (about 20 percent of the total) are found in the more developed coastal zone of East/Southeast Asia (Korea, Japan, Taiwan, Hong Kong, Singapore). Add the two Australian and the one Israeli sites to the list and we end up with about 89 percent of the sites situated in the most affluent parts of the world.

Table 1.3 Subjective ranking of technology hubs

Score	Technology hubs
16	Silicon Valley, United States
15	Boston, United States
15	Stockholm-Kista, Sweden
15	Israel
14	Raleigh-Durham-Chapel Hill, United States
14	London, United Kingdom
14	Helsinki, Finland
13	Austin, United States
13	San Francisco, United States
13	Taipei, Taiwan
13	**Bangalore, India**
12	New York City, United States
12	Albuquerque, United States
12	Montreal, Canada
12	Seattle, United States
12	Cambridge, United Kingdom
12	Dublin, Ireland
11	Los Angeles, United States
11	Malmo, Sweden-Copenhagen, Denmark

Continued

Table 1.3 Cont'd

Score	Technology hubs
11	Bavaria, Germany
11	Flanders, Belgium
11	Tokyo, Japan
11	Kyoto, Japan
11	Hsinchu, Taiwan
10	Virginia, United States
10	Thames Valley, United Kingdom
10	Paris, France
10	Baden-Wurttenberg, Germany
10	Oulu, Finland
10	Melbourne, Australia
9	Chicago, United States
9	Hong Kong, China
9	Queensland, Australia
9	**Sao Paulo, Brazil**
8	Salt Lake City, United States
8	Santa Fe, United States
8	Glasgow-Edinburgh, United Kingdom
8	Sophia Antipolis, France
8	Inchon, Korea
8	**Kuala Lumpur, Malaysia**
8	**Campinas, Brazil**
7	Singapore
6	Trondheim, Norway
4	**El Ghazala, Tunisia**
4	**Guateng, South Africa**

Note: Lesser developed sites in bold.

Source: Based on United Nations Development Programme (2001).

Another way of gauging the extent of concentration is to count not merely the number of sites but also the weights associated with the complements of ingredients available at each site. If we were to add the subjective weights associated with the North American, European, Australian, Israeli, and developed Asian sites, the more affluent world controls approximately 93 percent of the technological hub resources in the world. That type of concentration is probably less likely to change than is the number of Internet users.

Does it make a difference? While we cannot state without qualification that technological hubs are directly and exclusively responsible for high-tech production, there is bound to be a reasonably strong correlation. Table 1.4 lists the 30 leading exporters of high-tech commodities at the end of the twentieth century. Thirty-five of the forty-six (76 percent) technological hubs are located in the leading high-tech exporting economies.

Table 1.4 Thirty leading exporters of high-tech products
(billions of dollars, 1998–99)

Rank	Exporter	Exports
1	United States	206
2	Japan	126
3	Germany	95
4	United Kingdom	77
5	Singapore	66
6	France	65
7	Korea	48
8	The Netherlands	45
9	**Malaysia**	44
10	**China**	40
11	**Mexico**	38
12	Ireland	29
13	Canada	26
14	Italy	25
15	Sweden	22
16	Switzerland	21
17	Belgium	19
18	**Thailand**	17
19	Spain	11
20	Finland	11
21	Denmark	9
22	**Philippines**	9
23	Israel	7
24	Austria	7
25	Hungary	6
26	Hong Kong	5
27	Brazil	4
28	**Indonesia**	3
29	Czech Republic	3
30	**Costa Rica**	3

Note: Lesser developed states in bold.

Source: Based on United Nations Development Programme (2001: 42).

Everybody does not need to be online. Nor is it likely that every part of the world will ever be linked closely to a technology hub. However, for the benefits of IT to be realized maximally, a respectable proportion of the world must be able to absorb the new technology and put it to local use. One index of IT receptiveness is the Technological Achievement Index, which is described in Table 1.5. It combines information on the ability to create new technology, how well recent innovations have been absorbed, how well older but related innovations have been absorbed, and whether the local population is likely to have the necessary skills to manipulate IT applications. Each of these four criteria have two indicators, and all eight indicators are given equal weight in an aggregated index.

Table 1.5 Ingredients for the technological achievement index

Categories	Indicators
Creation of technology	Patents granted per capita
	Receipts of royalty and license fees from abroad per capita
Diffusion of recent innovations	Internet hosts per capita
	High and medium technology exports as share of all exports
Diffusion of old innovations	Logarithm of telephones per capita (mainline and cellular combined)
	Logarithm of electricity consumption per capita
Human skills	Mean years of schooling (age 15 and above)
	Gross enrollment ratio at tertiary level in science, mathematics, and engineering

Source: Based on United Nations Development Programme (2001).

To whom does IT diffuse? The answer should not be too surprising by now. The highest scorers (above 0.5) on the Technological Achievement Index are listed in the first column of Table 1.6. By and large, they are the most important producers of IT. The next group, column two, with scores ranging between 0.481 and 0.357, tend to be either producers or states located near producers. More than half of the second column is located in Europe. The third group, labeled "dynamic adapters" by the authors of the Technological Achievement Index, encompasses another 26 states, including China, India, Iran, South Africa, and a number of Latin American states, among others. All other states are considered to be marginal or substantially off the IT grid. If we have roughly 190 states in the world, this means that about 9 percent (the 17 in column 1) are well situated to adapt IT innovations. Another 10 percent (the 19 in column 2) can be expected to do almost as well. The third group (column 3), another 14 percent, can absorb some IT but certainly not at the level of the first two groups. That leaves two-thirds of the world currently marginal to IT advancements.

Information technology is one type of technology that is currently quite important. However, the problems with its diffusion are not novel. The limitations on the diffusion of advanced technology go back in history as long as there has been technology. Yet, we do not feel any great need to go back to Stone Age technology to develop a theoretical understanding of some of its implications. Nor is our inclination to turn to models of economic growth and development. We turn instead to a perspective on international relations – the leadership long cycle research program – that is centered on technological innovation and its effects on world politics.

Table 1.6 Technological achievement index rankings

Leaders	Potential leaders	Dynamic adapters
Finland	Spain	Uruguay
United States	Italy	South Africa
Sweden	Czech Republic	Thailand
Japan	Hungary	Trinidad & Tobago
Korea	Slovenia	Panama
The Netherlands	Hong Kong	Brazil
United Kingdom	Slovakia	Philippines
Canada	Greece	China
Australia	Portugal	Bolivia
Singapore	Bulgaria	Colombia
Germany	Poland	Peru
Norway	Malaysia	Jamaica
Belgium	Croatia	Iran
New Zealand	Mexico	Tunisia
Austria	Cyprus	Paraguay
France	Argentina	Ecuador
Israel	Romania	El Salvador
	Costa Rica	Dominican Rep.
	Chile	Syria
		Egypt
		Algeria

Source: Based on United Nations Development Programme (2001).

The leadership long cycle perspective

The leadership long cycle perspective observes that, increasingly over the past millennium, systemic leadership and world economic growth have consistently followed a twin-peaked wave pattern, each wave lasting roughly 50 years.[5] During the first – *ascent* – wave, one country rises to leadership in the world system. During the second – *catch-up* – wave, the leader is established but then begins a relative decline as competitors emerge. In *upswing* phases of each wave, leadership and growth are expanding. In *downswing* phases of each wave, they are contracting. In the ascent wave, political relationships among the most powerful states are desta-bilized by uneven growth. In the downswing phase of the ascent wave, a global competition follows the destabilization, which historically (between 1494 and 1945 in any event) involved global combat between coalitions led by the leader and by a challenger. One state, denoted as the system leader, emerges as the principal political–military winner, thanks in large part to its lead in technological innovation. However, leadership is a dynamic force. A catch-up wave follows in which the competitors of the leader begin to challenge the leader's position. The leader gradually loses its economic and political edge, and a new ascent wave is initiated with the next system leader emerging.

Even so, the leader and its challengers are restricted to a subset of elite actors that are most capable of absorbing, emulating, and outdoing the radical innovations introduced by the system leader. The rest of the world encompasses a mixture of states with more and less advanced economies. The more advanced economies (the rich or the North) tend to be capable of catching up with the leader eventually. Most of the less advanced economies (the poor or the South) cannot bridge the technological gap between the early and late developers.

A number of generalizations related to this interpretation have been developed and tested empirically elsewhere.[6] Most critical for our purposes, the key to global ascent, is the successful monopolization of radical innovations in leading sectors of commerce and industry, outlined in Table 1.7.[7] The introduction of leading sectors leads to the growth of the pioneering lead economy and, in turn, the growth of the lead economy stimulates world growth. The monopoly profits finance the buildup of the leader's global reach military forces, which are critical for maintaining its global economic and security concerns. At its peak, the system leader maintains a commanding lead in global reach power. Then, as its economic centrality dissipates, so too does its lead in global reach military capabilities. World economic growth and shifting concentrations in radical innovation eventually reduce the economic lead of the pioneer. Yet, again, only some economies are able to converge on the leader's position of affluence and technological sophistication.

One primary feature of this process is its discontinuous nature. Economic growth and radical innovations have been manifested as long waves that decay when the innovational novelties lose their ability to accelerate growth.

Table 1.7 Leaders and leading sectors

Global leader	Global lead industries	Observed growth peak
Portugal	Guinea gold	1480s
	Indian pepper	1510s
The Netherlands	Baltic trade	1560s
	Asian trade	1630s
Britain I	Tobacco, sugar, Indian textiles	1670s
	Tobacco, sugar, tea, Indian textiles	1710s
Britain II	Cotton textiles, iron production	1780s
	railroads	1830s
United States	Steel, chemicals, electricity	1870s/1900s
	Motor vehicles, aerospace, semiconductors	1950s

As old innovations become routine components of the world economy, new spurts in economic growth hinge on the advent of the next cluster of radical technological change. A second strong feature, therefore, is alternating periods of fast growth (stimulated by new technology) and slow growth (brought on by the routinization of now old technology) – to the extent that new technology is slow to emerge or encounters various infrastructural inadequacies, or political restrictions on change, slow or negative economic growth (world economic depression) is likely to persist until at least some of these barriers are overcome.

Economic globalization is also about overcoming international barriers. It is an old process of increased interaction and integration between and among populations located initially within Afro-Eurasia and, much later, incorporating the Americas and Australia. Interaction and integration have not proceeded inexorably or continuously. Instead, interaction and integration, aligned with the timing of technological innovation and economic growth, pulsate or come in accelerated spurts. But, if the world economy is composed of zones with much different prospects for generating economic growth and trade, it is reasonable to expect that: (a) contemporary globalization will proceed unevenly, and that (b) Northern participation in contemporary globalization processes should outpace Southern participation. Technological development, led by the world system's lead economy, with implications for the emergence of new products, new ways of production, and faster, less expensive transportation modes, should be more intensely registered within the North than within the South. Northern economies are better prepared to accommodate successive changes in best practices. They are also more inclined to both create products for export that reflect their advanced technology and to trade with other similar advanced economies that can afford and absorb their exports. The contemporary globalization of trade should thus proceed with a marked intra-Northern bias and driven by waves of economic growth and leadership generated by the system leader.

One empirical question is just how marked that bias is. Is it moderate or extremely strong? If the bifurcation of growth and trade prospects into two zones is quite pronounced, as we think it is and has been for some time, we should expect to find that the unevenness of globalization propensities is also quite strong. It may even be that the often-discussed threat to indigenous cultures and traditions emanating from globalization pressures may prove to be less worrisome since the Southern participation in contemporary trade globalization is simply too limited.

But, we need to examine the underlying empirical questions before we jump to possible conclusions – just how biased, if at all, are contemporary trade globalization processes? Are they virtually monopolized by a vibrant North? Or, are we exaggerating the bi-zonal division of the world economy and the expectation of very different trade globalization propensities? Moreover, our assertion that the system leader's edge in technological growth and global reach capabilities, coupled with discontinuous long waves of growth stemming from technological spurts, are important drivers of globalization also needs empirical assessment. We also want to take the opportunity to examine linkages to other processes, including debt, conflict, and democratization.

Before following up on these particular questions, we need to first establish a theoretical and empirical foundation for comparing North and South. Chapter 2 further elaborates our understanding of long-term economic growth patterns, some of the factors that influence the patterns, and, in particular, the role of limited technological diffusion. We do not see limited technological diffusion as a one-variable explanation of everything else. Rather, we see a number of interpretations advanced by other observers complementing and feeding into limited technological diffusion as one of the more significant processes contributing to a North–South developmental gap. We also believe that the technological diffusion problem has not been given sufficient attention. We portray it as a, if not the, central factor in the development and maintenance of the North–South gap.

Chapter 3 is dedicated to the existential task of documenting the emergence of a North–South gap. Is it feasible to simplify the acknowledged complexities of world development patterns in a bimodal way? If so, who qualifies for the North, and who is relegated to the South? How often have states moved from the South to the North, and vice versa? While we are at it, we can also pose the question of just how great the income gap is between the North and the South. Is it increasing, decreasing, or staying about the same?

Once these foundations are established, we can move on to our other questions. Chapter 4 examines our assertion that the main problem in North–South inequality is uneven technological diffusion. If the main stimulus for technological innovation is highly concentrated in system leader economies, can we trace how far the original stimuli diffuse? We think that radical technological diffusion is largely restricted to the North. Each subsequent iteration of radical economic change thereby further contributes to widening the gap between North and South.

Contemporary globalization, for some, is the harbinger of economic equalization. As more states participate in the world economy's trading and investment networks, poorer and less developed states should have opportunities to catch up with states that became wealthier and more developed earlier. We do not deny that some states benefit from globalization processes. Southern states, however, benefit far less than Northern states because many Southern states are left out of the ongoing expansion of trade. We examine this problem in Chapter 5.

We recognize 1.5 exceptions to our generalization that technological diffusion has been highly uneven. The partial exception is nineteenth-century migration patterns that favored the western offshoots of the United States, Canada, Australia, and New Zealand. Not only did the migration contribute significantly to the economic development of some, initially Southern, areas with surplus land and relatively limited population, they also made a contribution to the economic development of the European states from which they came.[8] If nothing else, they probably helped to reduce "excess" labor problems in states undergoing the transition from agrarian to industrial economies. Yet, if nineteenth-century migration proved an exception to the rule of Northern favoritism, twentieth-century migration patterns, which tend to flow from the South to the North, are no longer exceptional. Twentieth century and, so far, twenty-first-century migration patterns have contributed to the concentration of wealth and technological development in the North at the expense of the South. We note these facets of migration in Chapter 5.

The other exception is the diffusion of public health technology and information. There are constraints, of course, on this diffusion as well, but medicinal, medical, and sanitation improvements have spread quite far. People in the South are less likely to die at birth and more likely to live longer than they once were. Yet, these improvements, combined with slowly declining fertility rates, mean that Southern populations have and are expanding faster than do their Northern counterparts. The sad irony of this exception, of course, is that higher growth rates translate into less per capita economic wealth. Once again, the North is favored and the South is "penalized" in this particular respect by the advent of public health technology. Chapter 5 also touches upon this exception.

As noted earlier, Southern states are highly vulnerable to external market fluctuations. If states (or their economies) specialize in providing raw materials for Northern consumption and the demand/prices for these commodities fluctuate, it stands to reason that Southern economic prospects are held hostage to variable extents by processes over which their own economies have little control. We think this generalization can be taken one step further. Southern economies periodically and repetitively undergo debt crises that reflect a number of things but certainly encompass structured relations between North and South. When Northern economies falter, Southern economies suffer even more. Historically, they have experienced reduced trade demand, restricted investment capital, and gunboat diplomacy sometimes leading to outright military occupation by Northern states. Our point is not that all of these behaviors continue to recur, but that the basic structural interdependencies do persist. Southern economic growth prospects, as a consequence, are handicapped by this vulnerability and cyclical roadblocks to further development. Chapter 6 explores this problem empirically in order to establish its existence as a recurring feature of North–South interactions.

Conflict is not conducive to Southern economic development. We accept this generalization as a reasonably safe assumption. Rather than dwell on how conflict makes development more difficult, we continue in Chapter 7 our emphasis, consistently betrayed in earlier chapters, on the external influences on Southern development prospects. Chapter 6 argues that Southern debt is closely related to Northern prosperity and depression.

To what extent is conflict in the South or between North and South a function of fluctuations in Northern growth and systemic leadership? Compared to the debt crisis problem, patterns of conflict are much more complicated. Specifically, in Chapter 7, we compare the expectations of lateral pressure and world-system schools of thought to hypotheses generated by our own perspective. There does appear to be some relationship(s), but North–South conflict patterns appear to work differently than many scholars have thought.

The Wildavsky-Singer recipe for expanding zones of peace is predicated on economic development and democratization. While we are pessimistic about the extent and scope of economic development in the twenty-first century, democratization is likely to fare better – again, up to a point. We show that democratization, often thought to be a largely domestic process of either middle-class expansion and/or elite pacts, is systematically influenced by external influences – as in the case of conflict, world economic growth, and systemic leadership. Chapter 8 is dedicated to this exercise. However, ongoing democratization does not necessarily mean that the world is going to become entirely democratic any time soon – nor does it necessarily mean that zones of turmoil will become pacified or that zones of peace will follow. If the democratization of the South is not founded on a strong economic base, we can anticipate continued reversals and less expansion of the "democratic peace" than might otherwise be anticipated.

Chapter 9 summarizes our arguments and findings on inequality, technological diffusion, debt, conflict, and democratization. The notion that the world will become increasingly developed and pacific seems improbable to us. More likely is a widening rich–poor gap that will be with us for some time to come. Some states, no doubt, will manage to escape the global South, but most will not do so in the near or perhaps even the more distant future. Why this is likely to be the case is not or should not be mysterious. Yet, many people continue to see a much more optimistic, globalizing future in the offing in which the poor ultimately become more like the rich. Would that it were so but if the optimistic future is not probable, thinking it is will only make things worse.

In sum, we think that the prospects for the expanding effects of economic development, globalization, and democratization are constrained by a widening North–South divide that is fueled primarily by uneven technological diffusion. The North can be expected to continue advancing in technological development, globalization, and democratization. The North may become flatter, but in doing so they only make the rest of the world less flat. This unflat world is the real world order that we need to come to terms with, as it will provide a fundamental structural constraint and context for international relations throughout the twenty-first century, if not beyond.

2 Interpreting economic growth and development

In this chapter, we combine leadership long cycle principles with some selected observations made by economic historians about what might be called the nineteenth- and twentieth-century channels of world economic growth and trade. We retain the assertion of the leadership long cycle perspective that systemic leadership and the long waves of discontinuous economic growth, for which system leaders are primarily responsible, drives long-term fluctuations in world economic activity. Economic innovation in the lead economy of the system leader creates technological spurts that drive long waves of economic growth and fund systemic leadership foundations and capabilities. Yet, economic growth and trade never operate on a level playing field. Some parts of the world economy are always favored over other parts, and we need to build this fact of life into our models of growth and trade.

From our perspective, economic growth and trade are especially dependent on the intermittent surges in technological change introduced by the system's lead economy. As a consequence, new products and industries emerge in discontinuous fashion. So, too, do new ways of distributing commodities faster and cheaper. Radical innovations and lowered transaction costs do not simply fall from the sky; they are introduced and developed primarily by system leaders. In the seventeenth century, it was the Dutch. The eighteenth and nineteenth centuries were dominated by British technological change. In the twentieth and perhaps the twenty-first centuries, the US economy has served as the principal pioneer of changes in the way people produce and exchange goods.

Surges in globalization, therefore, are fueled by waves of long-term growth stimuli emanating primarily from the system leader's economy. These spikes in economic growth drive economic productivity and lowered transaction costs in the system leader's economy that, in turn, drive growth, productivity and lowered transaction costs in the rest of the world. In order to obtain the new products, some reductions in barriers to trade will ensue. Technological diffusion will enhance the ability of some other economies to produce the new products, and these expanded competencies will also encourage lowered trade barriers. In the process, the system leader also serves as a principal source of investment and finance, thereby providing further encouragement for positive growth spirals.

Order in long-distance commerce is another contribution traceable to system leaders. Technological growth and predominance in leading sectors of commerce and industry give the system leader an added incentive to develop specialized capabilities of global reach. Trade routes must be kept open and made relatively secure from interference and piracy.[1] For this reason, a concentration in economic technological innovation tends to be accompanied by a concentration in global reach capabilities that historically have been predominately naval, given the maritime medium favored by long-distance trade throughout much of the past five centuries. Not only does the system leader have a strong incentive to develop such power, it also has the wherewithal – thanks to the rents from technological leadership – to fund it.

Globalization is thus stimulated fundamentally by a package of technological change, lowered transaction costs (including costs pertaining to security), lowered trade barriers, expanded investment, and economic growth diffusion – all of which are attributable to some great extent to the economic and political–military actions of system leaders. If the source of these changes is highly concentrated, it should come as no surprise that the impacts of the changes are apt to be less than universal. Some parts of the world are likely to benefit more while others benefit less, depending on various factors such as resource endowment, location, and receptivity to technological diffusion.[2]

We are certainly aware that other things than technology can matter to economic development. For instance, Figure 2.1 outlines Rodrik and Subramanian's (2008) interpretation of the complexities of causality in long-term economic development. Health, productivity, institutions, resources, distance, demand – all can make some difference. There is no reason to dispute the significance of these factors, but we strongly suspect that all of the paths sketched in Figure 2.1 are not of equal importance. We choose to emphasize the technology path (path b in Figure 2.1) over the others because we think it is one of the most important tracks (but certainly not the only track), and because cases can be made for many of the other paths encouraging or discouraging technology diffusion. Put another way, many economists these days seem to be giving first place to institutions. We demur and put technological innovation and diffusion at the top of our list of factors, without seeking to write off institutions altogether.

If we continue with the assertions that technological innovation is critical to modern economic growth, discontinuous in time, and initially concentrated in space, we find, according to leadership long cycle theory, that Britain in the nineteenth century and the United States in the twentieth century have been the most favored locations in the world economy and the lead economies of the past two centuries. But, what about the rest of the world? Is it reasonable to argue that all other parts of the world economy

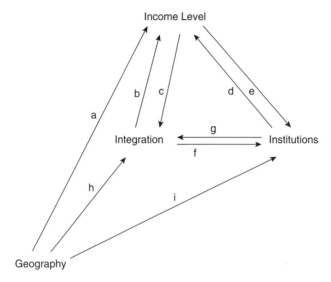

Where:

a = health of population and agricultural productivity
b = efficiency and dissemination of technology
c = demand for foreign goods and services
d = property rights and rule of law
e = demand for good institutions
f = openness and transparency
g = capacity to trade
h = distance from markets
i = natural resources and institutions

Figure 2.1 Development and its "deep" determinants according to Rodrik and Subramanian.
Source: Based on Rodrik and Subramanian (2008: 80).

had equal chances to either produce their own leader or to catch up to the technological leaders? We think not.

Angus Maddison (1995), following the lead of Adam Smith (1776/1937), argues that, from an 1820 perspective, a combination of various criteria (per capita income, resource endowment, population, and institutional/ societal characteristics likely to influence economic performance) would have yielded the following regional hierarchy of zones within the world economy that were most likely to do well in the future (where 1 stands for most likely and 7 stands for least likely): (1) Western Europe (including Britain); (2) Western offshoots (e.g., Canada, the United States, Australia, New Zealand); (3) Southern Europe; (4) Eastern Europe (including Russia); (5) Latin America; (6) Asia; and (7) Africa. To a considerable extent, we argue, as do others, that their prospects were also affected by the degree to which they were to become integrated to the world economy through migration, investment, and trade.

The first two zones (Western Europe and its offshoots) performed best in terms of growth and trade in the nineteenth and twentieth centuries. Southern Europe, for the most part, began to catch up with Western Europe in the second half of the twentieth century. Eastern Europe has had mixed success, thanks in part to an extended period of unsuccessful experimentation with highly centralized economic production decisions and deliberate efforts to reduce the degree of integration with Western Europe. The last three zones, Latin America, Asia, and Africa, have also experienced considerably mixed outcomes ranging from the remarkable catching up by Japan, and other Asian tigers (realized and still emerging), respectively, to the stagnation and worse fate of a number of African economies. Overall, however, the point is that the 1820 regional hierarchy has by and large been maintained into the twenty-first century.[3]

Why might this be the case? Part of the answer is that the Western European and offshoots zones have so far retained world technological leadership. Diffusion from, and imitation of, the British and US industrialization leads was most likely to occur within these two zones because of the criteria suggested by Maddison (essentially relative affluence and facilitative environments for economic growth and trade). As a consequence, Belgium, France, Germany, and the United States were among the first places to follow the British industrial lead in the first half of the nineteenth century. Moreover, nineteenth- and twentieth-century flows of skilled labor and investment demonstrated a bias in moving from Western Europe to its offshoots. British investors, by far the single most important source of foreign investment in the nineteenth century, clearly favored the United States, Canada, Australia, and South Africa – as demonstrated in Table 2.1. O'Brien (2006) adds that the external security costs of the offshoots were augmented in a major way by the nineteenth century services of the British navy. Later, in the second half of the twentieth century, Western Europe was the region that was the most successful in converging on the US lead in per capita income. This convergence can also be attributed non-controversially in part to the external security subsidies provided by US military capabilities after 1945 (see, for instance, Gilpin, 1975, among many others).

At the other end of the regional hierarchy, different stories characterized specific locales within the heterogeneous "Third World" of Asia, Latin America, and Africa. Yet, for a long time, there were also some common denominators in terms of relatively high population growth, subsistence-oriented economic production, marked income inequalities, and institutions that were less than conducive to economic growth. To a great extent, these three zones have also specialized in exporting undiversified primary products (as demonstrated in Table 2.2) to the more technologically advanced zones, and, to a lesser extent, importing their manufactured goods.

Table 2.1 Principal recipients of British foreign investment, 1850s–1914

Decades	Principal recipients
1850s–1860s	United States, Australia, India, France, Russia
1870s–1880s	United States, Australia, Argentina
1890s–1900s	Canada, United States, Australia, South Africa, Argentina

Source: Based on the discussion in Edelstein (1982: 288–311).

Table 2.2 Less developing area exports (million dollars)

Exported commodity	1840	1860	1880	1900	1913
Cocoa		2.1	2.9	17	84
Coffee	32.2	53.7	114.5	153.6	336
Copper	5	16.1	12.7	12.5	44
Cotton	11.6	35.8	96.9	107.7	300
Cotton manufactures		3.8	7	26.4	n.a.
Fertilizers	0.8	16.2	25.5	45.6	n.a.
Hemp		2.5	n.a.	13	n.a.
Hides and skins	1	7.9	25.3	37.3	170
Indigo	16.7	14.1	18.9	11.2	2
Jute		1.5	2.2	26.2	105
Jute manufactures		1.5	5.8	20.2	n.a.
Nuts		1.8	7.1	19.3	30
Oilseeds		7.7	29.5	42.6	220
Opium	6.1	47.7	79.3	31.5	11
Rice	2	20.1	55.3	88.5	242
Rubber		2	8.5	73.1	210
Silk	9.9	39.8	34.2	29.3	n.a.
Sugar	49	75.5	99.8	85	132
Tea	25.7	26.4	65.2	67.4	133
Tin	1.1	4.3	10.8	36.1	104
Tobacco leaf	1.5	7.6	10.3	25.4	40
Wheat	4.5	3	16.5	13.7	n.a.
Total	167.1	391.1	748.8	982.6	2163
All less developing country exports	238	543.2	1107	1529.7	3028
Total/All LDC exports	70%	72 %	68%	64%	72%

Source: Based on Hanson (1980: 36).

Nor has it helped that a number of the "first world's" technological innovations have created manufactured substitutes for many of the "third
world's" raw materials. The fact that much of the nineteenth- to twentieth-
century pool of movable investment capital and skilled labor migrated
elsewhere is another negative contribution to Southern economic growth.

Another part of the explanation, however, has already been suggested above – namely, that advanced technology is distributed unevenly in part because the ability to absorb new technology is also subject to unevenness. The initial innovation of radically new technology is highly centralized. It eventually diffuses to other economies that are in a position to make use of the new technology. Two important factors underlying being in a position to make use of new technology, as diagrammed in Figure 2.2, are connections to the world economy and technological absorptive capacity.

The degree of integration to the rest of the world economy makes some difference. Better-integrated states are more involved in trade and investment flows than are less integrated states. Their populations are better connected to outside agents through migration, diasporic, and other types of networks. We see these interdependency biases emerging very early on, as was suggested in Table 2.2. Table 2.3 focuses on a measure of trade interdependence (exports per capita) in the nineteenth century. The geographical terms of reference are not identical to the ones used by Maddison but they are very close. In the nineteenth century, Britain was at the center of a trade

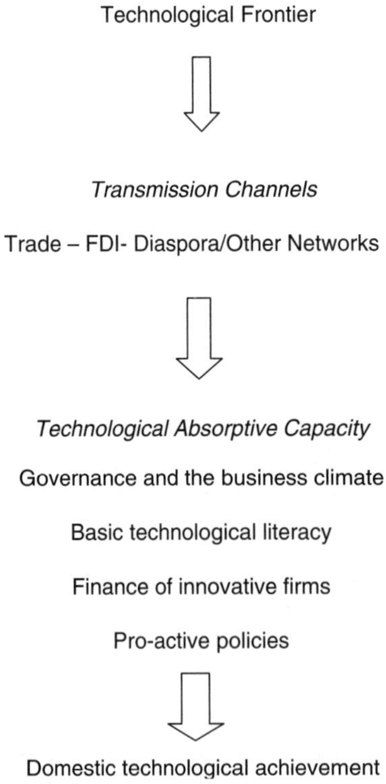

Technological Frontier

Transmission Channels

Trade – FDI- Diaspora/Other Networks

Technological Absorptive Capacity

Governance and the business climate

Basic technological literacy

Finance of innovative firms

Pro-active policies

Domestic technological achievement

Figure 2.2 A technological diffusion model.
Source: Simplified from World Bank (2008: 8).

Table 2.3 Degree of economic interdependence (per capita exports in constant dollars, 1880=100)

Area	1820	1840	1860	1880	1900
United Kingdom	3.65	7.25	20.7	31	36.25
Other Western Europe	1.70	2.90	7.3	14.8	25.9
Other Europe	0.85	1.25	2.8	4.3	5.95
North America	3	5.15	8.85	18.95	26.8
South America	1.05	2	5.60	9.10	15.05
Central America	n.a.	5.55	n.a.	n.a.	8.85
Asia	0.05	0.15	0.35	0.80	1.30
Africa	0.05	0.10	0.45	1.55	2.40
Oceania	n.a.	2.50	n.a.	n.a.	46.35
World average	0.45	0.80	2.60	4.40	7.55

n.a. signifies data not available.

Source: Based on Hanson (1980: 21).

interaction matrix, with Western Europe, North America, and Oceania (mainly Australia and New Zealand) also fairly central. This lineup is quite similar to Maddison's Western Europe and Western offshoots categorization. Next in line are South and Central America, followed by other parts of Europe. Asia and Africa remained poorly connected and well below the world average by the beginning of the twentieth century.

We have already seen that the pattern of nineteenth-century investment and migration flows resembled the flow of trade. Britain, the predominant source of foreign investment in that century, favored its own colonies or former colonies as targets of investment, as did other European sources of capital. However, as colonial metropoles went out of fashion in the twentieth century, their investment in their former colonies diminished. Figure 2.3 suggests that investment in the Third World has diminished in general throughout the twentieth century.

If one wishes to explain why the Western offshoots have done so well, an obvious rationale can be linked to the people who moved to the offshoots. Krieckhaus (2006) argues persuasively, in this context, that many Southern development problems are neither simply random effects or coincidence but are linked directly and indirectly to the effects of colonialism and international processes in general. We do not subscribe to all aspects of his interpretation, but much of it is quite compatible with our own perspective. Most of all, we appreciate his emphasis on international effects. Krieckhaus begins by noting that economic growth is influenced by a variety of domestic and external factors but that most analysts give too much credit to internal processes and not enough to processes that operate beyond national boundaries. He groups external factors pertinent to economic growth in three categories: (1) modern economic growth has distinctly

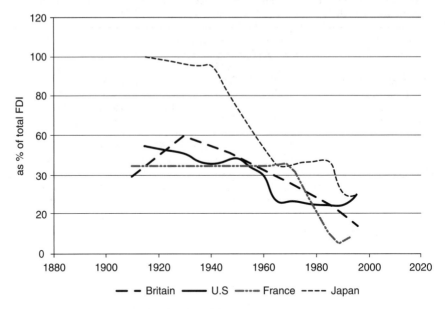

Figure 2.3 Investment in the third world.

European origins and, wherever European migration was great, economic success was nearly guaranteed but European colonialism was often predatory and exploitative and were best avoided altogether from the perspective of future economic growth prospects; (2) many ostensibly domestic factors in the South (such as sociopolitical cleavages, human skills, and state institutions) are legacies of colonial rule; and (3) international shocks have strong influences on economic growth, and these influences are especially likely to register in the weak economies and states often found in the South.

Examining a sample of 90 non-European states, Krieckhaus (2006) found a strong correlation between the number of European settlers and descendants as of 1900 and subsequent economic growth through at least 1960. Table 2.4 displays his evidence. All of the states in his wealthy cluster had a high level of European settlement (>50 percent) history. All of the states with a 10–50 percent settlement pattern possessed economies of at least intermediate-level wealth. States with a less than 10 percent European settler history were most likely to be clustered in the poor category. Of the 50 states that were not extensively settled by Europeans, 72 percent are located in the poor category.

Krieckhaus explained this finding in terms of the proclivities of the European settlers. They are said to have brought a healthy respect for property rights, which helped lead to the creation of constitutionally limited states that were reluctant to intervene in economic processes. They also

Table 2.4 Krieckhaus correlation of European settlers and development

	Poor (<US$1650)		Intermediate (between US$1650 and US$3400)	Wealthy (>US$3400)
Settler colonies (>50%)				Argentina Australia Canada New Zealand United States Uruguay
Partial settler colonies (10–50%)			Algeria Bolivia Brazil Chile Colombia Costa Rica Dominican Rep. Ecuador El Salvador Guatemala Honduras Mexico Nicaragua Panama Paraguay Peru South Africa	Israel Venezuela
Not extensively settled by Europeans (<10%)	Bangladesh Benin Burkina Faso Burundi Cameroon Chad China Congo, Dem. Republic of Cote d'Ivoire Egypt Ethiopia Ghana India Indonesia Kenya Korea, Republic of Madagascar Malawi	Mali Morocco Mozambique Nepal Niger Nigeria Pakistan Rwanda Sierra Leone Sri Lanka Syria Taiwan Tanzania Thailand Togo Uganda Zambia Zimbabwe	Angola Central African Republic Guinea Hong Kong Iran Jamaica Japan Malaysia Papua New Guinea Philippines Senegal Singapore Tunisia Turkey	

Source: Based on Krieckhaus (2006: 36).

brought with them relatively high levels of education and health. Once they arrived, they also worked to ensure that their children's education and health were protected by the state. Thus, Krieckhaus explains the higher growth manifested in Table 2.4 with liberal European settlers who had high levels of human skills that they were prepared to maintain. The more settlers that came, the better were the prospects for economic growth.

Krieckhaus (2006) does not actually provide any evidence on the education, health, or liberal attitudes of European settlers. We are dubious that it is possible to generalize about heterogeneous waves of settlement from different parts of Europe encompassing some 500 years.[4] It probably took a while (and perhaps a few wars), moreover, for the demands for state provisions of education and health to take effect. From our perspective, we are somewhat agnostic on how critical property rights, liberal states, and early health and education actually were in specific comparison to factors such as geography/climate, natural endowments, government protection of infant industries, and distance from European and Asian battlefields. Yet, at a bare minimum, we suspect that a case can be made for the Western offshoots (using Maddison's term) in the large settler population category being well connected to the world economy and most receptive and capable of adopting and adapting new technology. The trade, investment, and migration channels for diffusion were certainly evident. So, too, was the absorptive capacity compared to much of the rest of the world.

Some proportion of the European settler economic growth record can be attributed to favorable geography. One of the complications of unevenness in the world economy is that some geographical locations happen to be favored over others. Sachs, Mellinger, and Gallup (2001) emphasize three sets of locational impacts, as summarized in Table 2.5. If the least expensive way to move commodities (and people and ideas) is by sea, access to the sea can make some difference in which economies are able to make strong connections with the rest of the world. Infectious disease is also more likely to be prevalent in tropical/sub-tropical areas which lack severe winters that regularly kill infectious carriers such as mosquitoes. The consequences include high levels of mortality in infants and children and corresponding attempts to counter this tendency with high fertility rates. The ironic outcome is more children than might otherwise be expected and subsequent problems in educating and employing them. Temperate areas, moreover, tend to be much more productive in terms of food output, which, in the long-term, facilitates urbanization and technological development because larger non-food-growing populations can be supported.[5]

That coastal access and temperate climate make some difference to economic growth seems undeniable. Using GIS techniques, Sachs, Mellinger, and Gallup (2001) have been able to estimate proportional distributions of area, population, and GNP. They found, as reported partially in Table 2.6, that temperate regions encompassing a little over one-third of the world's population accounted for a little over two-thirds of the world's total GNP.

Table 2.5 Why geographical location matters

Major Impacts	Explanation
Connectivity	Coastal areas have greater access to less costly sea trade that is advantageous for transporting goods, people and ideas.
Disease and population effects	Tropical and subtropical areas facilitate the prevalence of infectious disease that are much less likely in areas with cold winters. High disease incidence can lead to high levels of child mortality and, therefore, high levels of fertility. As a result, populations may be characterized by large proportions of young children straining societal capabilities to educate and employ them as they mature. Women tend to spend much of their most productive years raising children.
Food availability and constraints on development	Temperate zone agricultural output per hectare, on average, is about 2.8 times the size of agricultural output per hectare in tropical zones due to high temperatures, precipitation variation, and pest infestations. Low food output constrains urbanization and encourages continuing focus on low-technology agriculture, as opposed to high-technology manufacturing and services.

Source: Based on Sachs, Mellinger, and Gallup (2001: 73–75).

Table 2.6 Climate, geography, and wealth concentration

	% of world total	% Coastal	% Hinterland
Temperate			
Land area	39.2	8.4	30.9
Population	34.9	22.8	12.1
GNP	67.2	52.9	14.3
Tropical			
Land area	19.9	5.5	14.4
Population	40.3	21.8	18.5
GNP	17.4	10.5	6.9
Desert			
Land area	29.6	3	26.6
Population	18	4.4	13.6
GNP	10.1	3.2	6.8

Note: Coastal designates regions located within 100 kilometers of a sea coast or sea-navigable waterway.

Source: Based on Sachs, Mellinger, and Gallup (2001: 74).

Nearly 80 percent of this two-thirds proportion was produced in coastal regions. In contrast, tropical and desert regions have 58 percent of the world's population but manage to generate only slightly over one-fourth of the world's GNP. An impressive proportion of the tropical and desert land area (about 82 percent) is located more than 100 kilometers from a coast or sea-navigable waterway.

Our point here, however, is not simply that geography also makes some difference to economic development. That observation should not be particularly controversial. Rather, we suggest that European settlement was most likely in coastal–temperate areas. We do not have precise numbers on this propensity, but North American settler populations were certainly initially highly concentrated on the Atlantic seaboard, and the Australian population pattern remains extensively coastal in location. Thus, we need to be careful in giving too much credit to whatever attitudes European settlers might have brought to areas that were already geographically prone to favor economic development. Nor was this propensity coincidental. Europeans avoided tropical and sub-tropical areas in large numbers because they could not survive the diseases or grow the types of crops to which they were already accustomed. It literally took them centuries to penetrate the Americas and Africa from their coastal starting points.

There is also a difference between Northwestern and Southern Europe that might be worth exploring. Economies created by settlers from Northwestern Europe, the epicenter of modern economic growth, had much better luck with economic growth than did those from Southern Europe who went to Latin America. Certainly, the first wave of Southern European transplants in the Americas (beginning in the late fifteenth century) were about as predatory as they come. Spanish conquistadors were neither especially liberal nor well educated. Just how liberal and educated subsequent waves of migration from Southern Europe to South and Central America were is certainly debatable and deserves closer scrutiny.[6]

Acemoglu, Johnson, and Robinson (2001, 2002) add something useful here. Their basic argument is that two fundamental colonial strategies were pursued. Europeans tended to develop institutions that either favored maximum extraction of resources and taxation from populations engaged in mining and/or agriculture, or institutions that favored investment and property rights. The first strategy was authoritarian and coercive in that it concentrated political power within a small elite that could control labor and taxation. The second strategy was more democratic and assumed widespread participation in political institutions and markets.

Which strategy was pursued hinged on relative profitability calculations. If there was an abundant labor supply to be exploited, the extractive strategy was likely to be adopted. If the area was sparsely settled and conducive to large-scale European settlement (meaning the relative absence of malaria and yellow fever), the development of institutions favoring investment and property rights was more probable. Settlers insisted on rights that were comparable or superior to what they had enjoyed in the metropole. Since they also desired economic success, they were likely to develop institutions and practices that favored long-term performance, including industrialization.

Acemoglu, Johnson, and Robinson (2002) emphasize that colonialism imposed bad institutions on areas that were once prosperous and good institutions on areas that were once poor, leading to a reversal of economic fortunes. Areas that were rich in 1500 had become less developed by the nineteenth century by failing to industrialize. Areas that had been poor in 1500 became rich in the nineteenth century by industrializing. Their empirical analyses certainly support this observation but, of course, it leaves somewhat open-ended just what intermediating role institutions played in the industrialization process.[7]

For Acemoglu, Johnson, and Robinson, the institutions, especially property rights, are what matter most.[8] For Krieckhaus, it is liberal attitudes. Sachs, Mellinger, and Gallup emphasize geography, but not exclusively. Whether one emphasizes the healthiness of the European migrants (as does Krieckhaus) or suggests that Europeans preferred to avoid areas that were unhealthy for them (as do Acemoglu, Johnson, and Robinson) may be simply a matter of choice. We think, however, it is safe to say that large-scale European settlement in the Western offshoots created better and more conducive opportunities for ultimately adopting and adapting new technology than did the situations found in areas that did not experience large-scale European migration. We also find the emphasis on extraction and authoritarian, extractive institutions elsewhere compelling, even if European colonialists sometimes only continued pre-colonial practices. Yet, one should keep in mind that the authoritarian practices were the norm while the large-scale European settler offshoots were few in number.

But, we leave the specifics of these questions for academic battles to be waged elsewhere. The finding reported in Table 2.4 is certainly suggestive. Still, there are some puzzles associated with it. Krieckhaus notes that the neatness of the pattern does not persist after 1960, largely because the growth of early developers slowed down and later developers accelerated. Latin American states also experimented with what are described as autarkic development strategies that proved to be less attractive by the 1980s.[9] That may be but there appear to be other things going on. For instance, Argentina and Uruguay do not represent the same sort of economic growth successes as the United States and Canada. Israel, which technically was not colonized by Europeans, does not have the same type of economy as the oil-rich Venezuela. More generally, there is also the question of what happened after 1960. For these reasons, Table 2.7 re-examines the settler question with the same sample but relying instead on power parity purchasing GDP per capita data in 1960 and 2000. We establish our three wealth/development categories by comparing them to the most advanced economy of the 1960–2000 period, the United States. The wealthier/more developed

Table 2.7 Settlers in 1900 and wealth stratification, 1960 and 2000

	Low	*Intermediate*	*High*
Settler colonies (>50%)			← Argentina Australia Canada New Zealand United States ← Uruguay
Partial settler "colonies" (10–50%)		← Algeria ← Bolivia Brazil	
			Chile
		Colombia Costa Rica	
	Dominican Republic →		
		← Ecuador ← El Salvador ← Guatemala	
	Honduras		Israel
		← Nicaragua Panama ← Paraguay	Mexico
			←Peru ←South Africa Venezuela
Not extensively settled by Europeans (<10%)	Angola Bangladesh Benin Burkina Faso Burundi Cameroon Central African Republic Chad China Cote d'Ivoire Egypt Ethiopia Ghana Guinea India Indonesia Kenya Madagascar Malawi Mali Morocco Mozambique Nepal	← Congo Iran ← Jamaica Malaysia → ← Philippines ← Senegal Singapore → Syria → Taiwan → Turkey	Hong Kong Japan

Table 2.7 Cont'd

	Low	Intermediate	High
	Niger		
	Nigeria		
	Pakistan		
	Rwanda		
	Sierra Leone		
	Sri Lanka →		
	South Korea →		
	Tanzania		
	Thailand →		
	Togo		
	Tunisia →		
	Uganda		
	Zambia		
	Zimbabwe		

Note: States are placed according to their 1960 wealth stratification status. An arrow (→) signifies movement into the next lower or higher category by 2000 (with the exception of South Korea which moved from low to high). Low wealth in 1960 = < 1416 in 1990 international Geary-Khamis dollars, in 2000 = < 3516; High wealth in 1960 = > 2832, in 2000 = >7032. The low wealth threshold is determined by calculating 12.5% of the United States' 1960 GDP per capita, using Maddison (2003) data. The high wealth threshold is set at 25% or higher of the United States' 2000 GDP per capita.

group possesses a GDP per capita equal to or greater than 25 percent of the United States GDP per capita. The least wealthy/less developed group falls below a 12.5 percent threshold.[10]

Our 1960 findings look much like those reported by Krieckhaus. What is most interesting is what happened between 1960 and 2000. Two of the six states in the greater than 50 percent settler category fell back into the intermediate wealth/development class. Slightly more than half of the entries in the partial settler category were pushed back into the next lowest wealth/development category. We find somewhat more variance in the non-European-settled third category than Krieckhaus did, but the more interesting development is the movement of a number of largely Asian states into higher wealth/development classes by 2000.[11]

Thus, our re-examination reinforces the notion that European settlement patterns have made some difference but the impact is not quite as strong as it looks if the examination is restricted to an analysis of the 1960 distribution. The economic decline of a number of Latin American states, in contrast to Krieckhaus' emphasis on the growth rates of richer states slowing down, may support our observation that all European settlers did not arrive with the same proclivities, skills, and individual absorptive capacities. The improvements registered by a number of largely Asian states suggests that there are clearly other things going on than simply who was colonized, and to what extent this occurred.[12]

The colonization story clearly retains some explanatory value. Northwest European settlers did transplant British values and technological know-how to the United States, Canada, Australia, and New Zealand, in particular. That is one part of the settler equation. Another part, however, is the type of investment attention these four states received. The "Western offshoots" were the favored beneficiaries of one-fourth to one-third of foreign investment prior to World War II, as reflected in Table 2.8.[13] Just what proportion of the attractiveness of these investments one attributes to property rights institutions or the economic profitability we cannot say. What we can say is that some parts of the world have been better connected to the world economy than other parts. European settlement patterns had something to do with this prior to the twentieth century. So, too, did investment and trade choices.

Krieckhaus and Acemoglu, Johnson, and Robinson are on stronger ground with the argument that colonial regimes, in general, were not usually designed to maximize independent economic growth. Colonial administrations, in most cases, were more oriented to facilitating resource extraction than improving the education and health of their populations. Even, or perhaps especially, colonies acquired after 1885 were expected to function as cheaply as possible because they were not regarded as valuable as earlier colonial acquisitions. These European colonial regimes then represented opportunities foregone as much as they constituted exercises in predatory exploitation. Moreover, the extent of predatory exploitation is also said (by Krieckhaus) to have encouraged the adoption of post-colonial socialist policies that signified a rejection of the liberal thought and selective practices of the exploiters. A post-independence generation later, many of those policies have been abandoned as unproductive. Here again, we would emphasize, however, that European colonial regimes, in general, did very little to prepare their populations for subsequent technological achievement.[14]

Other legacies of the colonial era include notoriously arbitrary boundaries that separated some ethnic groups while creating often heterogeneous

Table 2.8 Distribution of capital invested abroad by major sources

Regions	1914	1938
Europe	30.7%	18.9%
Western Offshoots	25.5	31.7
Latin America	19.2	19.9
Asia	13.9	19.2
Africa	10.7	8.4

Source: Maddison (2001: 99).

societies in which some groups, favored in the colonial era, were most likely to inherit political power once the colonial power left but not necessarily to hold on to the reins of power indefinitely. These types of considerations easily translate into one of Krieckhaus' (2006: 80–81) emphases on external factors. War, especially wars fought with foreign states, are bad for economic growth. States in the Krieckhaus sample that fought either internal or external wars did less well in terms of 1960–2000 economic growth than did states that fought no wars (see Table 2.9). Wars fought with external powers, often more developed states, were much more damaging economically than internal warfare.[15]

The other types of external influences on economic growth emphasized by Krieckhaus are fluctuations in the world economy and foreign aid. One point is that world market fluctuations are more strongly felt as shocks by weaker economies than by stronger economies.[16] The second point is that foreign aid, while often less important than is imagined, is sometimes critical to economic growth success stories. We have no argument with either of these observations. The international system and a variety of external influences clearly have favored some states and regions over others, and these historical biases help explain the persistence of stratification in the world system.

The "in-between" zones (in Maddison's rank order) of Southern and Eastern Europe enjoyed or suffered different fates that may even out in the long run, but in the intermediate run has led to a more rapid integration of Southern and Western Europe. To the extent that the imposition of communist economic planning led to barriers against the adoption of new technology and poor economic performance, not entirely unlike European colonialism, the dismantling of the barriers means that some parts of Eastern Europe will emulate this convergence fairly rapidly while other parts will do so much more slowly.[17]

Table 2.9 Impact of war on economic growth, 1960–2000 (average annual growth rates)

Types of impact	Growth rates
No war	2 %
War	0
Economically relevant warfare*	–0.9
With external foe	–2.4
With domestic foe	–0.1

*Economically irrelevant wars are defined as wars that "do not take place on a country's home territory, border wars, or wars of less than one week's duration."

Source: Based on Krieckhaus (2006: 80–81).

Our current concern, nevertheless, is not with forecasting possible outcomes within or between Maddison's seven zones. We suggest instead that the regional hierarchy can be simplified further into two macro-zones. Western Europe and the Western offshoots are the core of a global North that has been augmented by adherents from Southern and Eastern Europe, as well as by a small number of Asian states.[18] Latin America, Asia, and Africa historically have constituted the core of a global South, incorporating as well, at various times, parts of Eastern and Southern Europe. Neither macro-zone assignment guarantees permanent success or failure in economic growth and trade. Nor is membership in one zone a terminal categorization. It is conceivable that Northern states can become Southern and certainly the opposite type of status mobility exists.[19] But the prospects for economic growth and trade, along with other imaginable outcomes, have been in the nineteenth and twentieth centuries and will probably continue to be more benign in the global North than in the global South.

We have already made a number of references to the global North and South. Where are Northern and Southern states located? Which states fall into which categorization? How stable are the categorizations? Do states move back and forth between the South and North with some frequency? Or, is there any movement at all? Is the gap between North and South widening or diminishing? These questions are addressed in the next chapter.

3 Exploring the North–South gap longitudinally

Has the absolute and relative gap between the North and the South narrowed appreciatively? Is there evidence of convergence on a global scale? To answer these questions, we assemble continuously aggregated information on the last century and a third of the size and relative wealth of the world economy's rich states, or the North, and poor states, or the South. While other studies have addressed these questions, the longer analyses have been restricted to richer states and the broader analyses have been restricted to relatively short time frames. When we began our longitudinal analyses, it was possible to generate, with the aid of some interpolation, a 56-state sample thanks to Maddison's (1995) well-respected data collection of yearly, real gross domestic product (GDP) and population figures. With additional data subsequently taken from Maddison (2007), we are able to encompass 133 years (1870–2003) and the overwhelming majority of the world's economic output and population.[1] There is also sufficient heterogeneity within the data to monitor annual fluctuations in economic growth and membership of North and South.

We find that a few Southern states have moved to the North but, so far, the identities of the North and the South have not changed much since the late nineteenth century. Based on these results, and subject to the usual other things remaining equal, the likelihood of substantial convergence within the next century seems slim. If Singer and Wildavsky (1993) are right about planetary bipolar tendencies toward peace and turmoil, the zone of turmoil is likely to be with us for some time to come. Future convergence is unlikely without some major changes in the distribution of wealth across nations. Such redistribution seems unlikely to be forthcoming in the absence of radical policy intervention.

In this chapter, we first discuss the literature on convergence, followed by our theoretical perspective. We then explain our new database. Finally, the database is pressed into service to answer our existential questions about convergence and divergence.

Convergence in the mainstream economic growth literature

Our point of departure is the convergence controversy in the mainstream economic growth literature. We discuss this controversy not because we wish to engage it fully, but rather to suggest a different approach to understanding convergence. In the mainstream literature, there are two main theories. Neoclassical growth theory (Cooper, 2007) assumes that technological progress is exogenous, whereas in new growth theory progress is endogenous.[2] The neoclassical model predicts that, in the absence of technological progress, countries with similar parameters (e.g., population growth rate, technology) will converge on the same steady-state income per capita, regardless of initial wealth (absolute convergence). Among countries with the same parameters, poorer countries should grow faster along the transition path leading to the same steady state. Countries with different parameters do not converge absolutely, however their growth rates will be larger the further away they are from their own steady states (conditional convergence). In the case with technological progress, the neoclassical model predicts that all countries will grow at the rate of progress. In contrast, some new growth theory models expect that countries with a higher saving rate and better institutions will exhibit higher growth.[3] In these models, the growth rates of countries do not converge as long as their institutions and saving rates differ.

Empirical studies of convergence in the mainstream literature often employ national data from 1960 to 1990.[4] In the typical regression, the growth rate inspected as the dependent variable is computed as an average over the period, and the independent variables include initial wealth and other variables (that differ across studies) to "condition" the convergence. Studies have found partial support for convergence within some heterogeneous or federal states (Barro and Sala-I-Martin, 1992; Mankiw, Romer, and Weil, 1992) but not in others (Cashin and Sahay, 1996). Evidence in support of conditional convergence across a small number of nations also is available (Dollar, 2007; Heshmati, 2007; Sachs and Warner, 1995).

Studies that looked at growth over relatively long periods of time have focused on wealthier states. Abramowitz (1986) and Baumol (1986) found supporting evidence for convergence among rich states. But, as DeLong (1986; Dowrick and DeLong, 2003) noted, such samples obviously are biased. Maddison (1995) argues that the studies finding convergence among the richest states overlook the fact that most of these states were not catching up with the economic leader until after 1950, a point to which we will return.

Not all analysts focus on the richest states, but their non-rich state data are often limited. Kuznets (1972) argued that the absolute gap between rich and poor had widened slowly before World War II and then accelerated. Bairoch (1993) claimed that there was no gap between today's developed and developing states at the beginning of the nineteenth century, but that the gap has widened since that time. Pritchett (1997) uses logic and a simple computation of selected country growth values for 1870 in comparison with 1960 and 1980–94 data, to argue for divergence.

Others have argued that the post-World War II data support divergence, subject to various qualifications.[5] Morawetz (1977), for example, does so based on an analysis of 1950–75 growth data. Maddison (1995: 22, 25) presents calculations on long-term, individual rates of convergence/ divergence with US GDP per capita for a number of states without really providing a detailed examination. His conclusion (Maddison, 1995: 22) is that "although the global long-term picture is one of divergence, there has been a substantial degree of catch-up since 1950." Explaining 1960–85 data, Passe-Smith (1996, 1998) finds that the rich and middle-income states became richer, while the poor became poorer. Yet, this result disappears when nine then-communist states are removed from the examination. Passe-Smith (1996) also finds support for the idea that convergence is more likely in periods of economic expansion and divergence is more acute in periods of contraction. This idea assumes that richer states are better able to cope with economic crisis than poor states. However, this finding is limited to a comparison of the 1960–74 and 1975–85 experiences, and Passe-Smith notes the need for a longer examination.

Thus, the empirical results are not conclusive. As one scholar puts it, "the consensus now emerging [on whether economies converge or not] is one of uncertainty" (Temple, 1999: 134). We propose to gain insights on economic convergence by addressing the problem of insufficient longitudinal data and by suggesting a new theoretical approach to analyze them.

Measuring the North–South gap longitudinally

The notions of technological diffusion and national receptivity to innovations, put forward in the last chapter, are complex. In this chapter, we do not study the causes of diffusion and receptivity, but rather explore some implications of our theoretical perspective for convergence.

The data

Since the processes discussed here are relatively slow, we need long time series on development. However, the most common index of development – real GDP per capita – is a relatively recent concept. Data on GDP per capita typically date to about 1950. To be sure, some rich states have longer series, but this is of limited assistance if one wishes to compare collectively the rich and the poor.

There is one exception to this empirical lacuna. Maddison (1995, 2007) provides historical population and real GDP data on 56 and ultimately many more states. The GDP data are expressed in constant dollars, purchasing power parity-adjusted terms that are unlikely to be improved upon in the very near future. Many small states are omitted in the early samples, but Maddison (1995) notes that his initial sample accounted for 93 percent of world output and 87 percent of world population in 1992.[6] We utilize these data to compute real GDP per capita for each country, from 1870 to 2003.[7]

Maddison's data have some missing points.[8] We fill in the data gaps between any two given points in Maddison's data by using linear interpolation. Of course, the interpolated portions of the series may not be accurate. However, since we aggregate the data to create systemic indices, some distortion is naturally acceptable at this level of aggregation. Moreover, the series that are available are already the most complete account for most of the world economy. Thus, we think that our interpolations do not distort the big picture for which we are looking.

Assigning states to North and South

The assignment of states to North and South proceeds from our theoretical position that economic growth has been characterized by successive technological revolutions. It is possible to push this interpretation further back in time, but for present purposes it suffices to say that one of these technological revolutions focused on the late-eighteenth-century advances in the production of cotton textiles and iron. A second revolution was led by advances in steam engines and railroads, a third by developments in steel, chemicals, and electricity, while a fourth one was closely geared to automobile and jet engine production. A fifth and ongoing revolution seems to focus on computers, information technology, and biomedical engineering.

Each technological revolution is led by a single pioneering economy – Britain in the first two and the United States in the last three. The revolutionary aspects of these innovations are not restricted to singular products. The identifications with cotton textiles or automobiles, while real, are symptomatic of more encompassing changes that improve the production of novel and old products. After a period of monopoly, the new processes diffuse to economies capable of absorbing, and often improving upon, the techniques. The ones that can absorb these innovations qualify as "Northern" economies. The ones that cannot do so qualify as "Southern" economies. In this respect, long-term economic development is very much a moving target with some Northern states setting new bars periodically that other states struggle to attain or exceed.

How can we measure this conceptual distinction between North and South? We do not have a comprehensive schedule of the movement away from agrarian economies and national industrialization timing that might be employed for this purpose. Even if we did, it would not necessarily distinguish between industrialization that is cutting-edge as opposed to industrialization that has long since become routine. For instance, building railroads in the early nineteenth century meant that the economies in which this capability existed could lead the rest of the world in industrialization. Building railroads in the late twentieth century is a different matter. It is part of a process of catching up to the leaders, but, as in the case of rail-roads, the leader–follower temporal gap can be more than one century long. So, not just any industrialization will count if we wish to assess economic inequalities based on industrial capability.

We do not have convenient access to systematic information on who produces which particular high-tech product in any given year. We might be able to develop such a data archive in the future, assuming we could also develop some consensus on which products were appropriately high-tech and how much participation in their multilateral production is required to qualify.[9] We prefer to avoid these complicated empirical issues at this time.

An alternative approach involves specifying real per capita GDP thresholds for poor, middle-income, and rich economies. The presumption would be that the rich and more developed economies, subject to some obvious caveats for oil producers, are most likely to have developed the production base necessary to absorb and profit from successive waves of radical technological revolution. Such thresholds have been advanced in the literature as single levels to be used for all time periods.[10] However, the simple number threshold method may not be adequate when serial data encompassing more than 100 years are used. A fallback strategy involves developing a threshold that is pegged to the state with the highest GDP per capita. In this method, a state with an economy that meets some proportion of the leader's wealth would qualify as Northern; otherwise, it would be classified as Southern.

Choosing a threshold

There is no obvious threshold that can distinguish between North and South. Yet, the very nature of the innovation and diffusion process we are describing as fundamental to modern economic development does suggest an important clue. The level of economic development attained by an economy is always relative to the levels attained by other economies that are either more or less complex. Since we trace the principal source of radical innovations to the lead economy, and argue as well that this economy is also the principal beneficiary of these waves of radical technological innovation, it makes sense that we key our economic development assessments on the lead economy. How developed an economy is then becomes a question of how far behind it is from the level attained by the world economy's leading economy. Is it close (i.e., Northern) or far behind (i.e., Southern)? Accordingly, we have experimented with three benchmark thresholds –50, 33, and 25 percent of the leader's real GDP per capita – as crude markers of how far countries have to go to catch up with the leader. Eventually, we settled on the 25 percent threshold for reasons to be elaborated below.[11]

GDP per capita, of course, is an imperfect indicator for this purpose. Some economies have great wealth in raw materials and very small populations. Their relatively high GDPs per capita would be misleading in this respect because their wealth is due more to raw material extraction and not modern economic development. Thus, we would have been forced to exclude Middle Eastern oil producers if their data had been in our sample, but none are.[12] We also exclude South American states from the North, because, in some cases, their moderate real GDP per capita figures, we think, suggest that their economies are more complex and modern than they really are.[13] To be sure, some South American states have moved out of the pure raw material provider category, but they are still grappling with absorbing earlier innovation waves, while most Northern economies are already in the process of mastering the latest innovation wave. We do not make these categorical exceptions lightly. We are aware that indicators, once adopted, are not meant to be tampered with selectively. We do so in order that our simple indexing system will agree with our theoretical approach.

A number of industrialization histories give us some overall sense of the pattern of technological leader–followership in the nineteenth and twentieth centuries. However, these studies often lack the specificity we need. One partial exception that employs similar assumptions to ours about economic growth is Freeman and Perez (1988). Table 3.1 lists their impressions of which states counted most prominently as the technological leader, other leaders, and other industrial and newly industrializing states, during each of the five eras of technological revolution beginning in the 1770s.

As far as we know, Table 3.1 is not based on any formal criteria. The entries for the fifth era are particularly acknowledged by the authors to be guesses. But, by and large, all of these entries constitute informed guesses. The first four columns are hardly surprising. We would expect countries such as Britain, France, and the United States to qualify as Northern states at some point prior to World War II. Some East European states also might be expected to qualify at some point. Whether all of the newly industrializing states put forward by Freeman and Perez should qualify as Northern is doubtful, but states such as Taiwan should probably qualify in the last quarter of the twentieth century.

Table 3.2 arrays the outcome of our per capita GDP threshold matching. The entries are the years when states qualified as Northern for each threshold. Twelve of the 27 states that might be considered elite meet all three thresholds in 1870. These states constitute a hard-core elite group concentrated in Western Europe and North America, plus Australia and New Zealand. One might have anticipated the early inclusion of these cases. Their qualification by all three thresholds reinforces our approach, but fails to help us in picking among the three thresholds (50, 33, and 25) that we were considering as possible benchmarks.

The lower half of Table 3.2 indicates that the lowest threshold is the most liberal, while the highest threshold is the most conservative. Using the

Table 3.1 Freeman and Perez: Identification of industrial and industrializing states

1770s–40s	1830s–90s	1880s–40s	1930s–90s	1980s–
Britain	Britain	Germany	United States	Japan
—	—	United States	Germany	United States
France	France	—	—	Germany
Belgium	Belgium	Britain	Other EEC	Sweden
----------	Germany	France	Japan	—
German States	United States	Belgium	Sweden	Other EEC
The Netherlands	—	Switzerland	Switzerland	EFTA
	Italy	The Netherlands	USSR	USSR and other East European
	The Netherlands	—	Other EFTA	Taiwan
	Switzerland	Italy	Canada	Korea
	Austria-Hungary	Austria-Hungary	Australia	Canada
		Canada	—	Australia
		Sweden	Other East European	—
		Denmark	Korea	Brazil
		Japan	Brazil	Mexico
		Russia	Mexico	Argentina
			Venezuela	Venezuela
			Argentina	China
			China	India
			India	Indonesia
			Taiwan	Turkey
				Egypt
				Pakistan
				Nigeria
				Algeria
				Tunisia
				Other Latin American

Note: Dotted lines separate three sub-categories: (1) the leader(s), (2) other leaders, (3) other industrial and newly industrializing states.

Source: Freeman and Perez (1988).

50 percent threshold, Russia and South Korea never qualify. The other two thresholds delineate the same group (with the exception of Poland), although not at the same time. As many as 20 states qualify in 1870. Otherwise, one main difference between the two assignments can be reduced to whether states such as Greece, Portugal, and Taiwan qualify in one decade or the next. Another main difference is that Japan and Russia qualify as Northern states in 1894 and 1931, respectively, if the 25 percent

Table 3.2 Northern identifications with alternative thresholds

State	25%	33%	50%
Australia	1870	1870	1870
Austria	1870	1870	1870
Belgium	1870	1870	1870
Denmark	1870	1870	1870
France	1870	1870	1870
Germany	1870	1870	1870
The Netherlands	1870	1870	1870
New Zealand	1870	1870	1870
Sweden	1870	1870	1870
Switzerland	1870	1870	1870
United Kingdom	1870	1870	1870
United States	1870	1870	1870
Canada	1870	1870	1882
Norway	1870	1870	1930
Finland	1870	1870	1961
Italy	1870	1870	1962
Spain	1870	1870	1974
Ireland	1870	1870	1990
Czechoslovakia	1870	1870	–
Hungary	1870	1870	–
Japan	1894	1932	1968
Poland	1929	–	–
Russia	1931	1960	–
Greece	1956	1966	1978
Portugal	1957	1967	1991
Taiwan	1977	1983	1991
S. Korea	1983	1987	–

threshold is employed, and in 1932 and 1960, respectively, if the 33 percent threshold is used. The year 1894 may be a bit early for Japanese economic elite status, but 1932 seems a bit too late. The year 1931 seems plausible for the Soviet Union, but 1960, 2 years after Sputnik, seems much too late. We prefer to be overly generous than overly stingy in our assignments because a more liberal categorization works in favor of finding convergence – an outcome that we do not think is too likely. A less liberal categorization might ensure that convergence is impossible. On the basis of these considerations, we have chosen the 25 percent threshold as possessing more face validity and utility. Table 3.3 lists the members of our sample.

Our measurement procedures are relatively crude. While no state assigned to the South seems out of place, some of the Northern assignments seem to occur prematurely.[14] However, no state identified as Northern in Table 3.2 ultimately seems out of place. We suspect that any conceivable index will yield some individual outcomes that make analysts uncomfortable. The question is whether we can live with the overall outcome. We think the 25 percent threshold listed in Table 3.2 provides a reasonable foundation

Table 3.3 North–South identifications, 1870–2003

Lower South	Upper South	North
		United Kingdom
		United States
		Belgium
		The Netherlands
		Switzerland
		Denmark
		Germany
		Austria
		France
		Sweden
		(Canada)
		(Australia)
		(New Zealand)
		(Ireland)
		Czechoslovakia
		Hungary
		(Norway)
		Spain
		Italy
	Argentina	
	Brazil	
	Chile	
	Colombia	
	Mexico	
	Peru	
	Venezuela	
	Turkey	
	Japan	– > 1894
	Finland	– > 1919
	Poland	– > 1929
	Russia	– > 1931
	Turkey	
	Bulgaria	
	Yugoslavia	
1942–51 < –	Rumania	
	Greece	– > 1956
	Portugal	– > 1957
(1945–67) < –	South Korea	– > 1983
	(1944; 1968–82)	
(1965–) < –	Philippines	
Taiwan	– > (1968–76)	– > 1977
Thailand	– > 1980	
China	– > 1991	
India		
Burma		
Indonesia		
Pakistan		
Bangladesh		

Continued

Table 3.3 Cont'd

Lower South	Upper South	North
Ethiopia		
Egypt		
Morocco		
Nigeria		
Zaire		
Ivory Coast		
Kenya		
Tanzania		

Notes: The thresholds for the lower South, upper South, and North are listed in the text. Latin American states are restricted to the South. Northern states in parentheses met the qualifying threshold prior to independence from a Northern state and are therefore counted from 1870 as Northern.

for a North–South categorization, at least for the 1995 data base. Table 3.3 adds the Southern states relying on the 25 percent threshold. "Our" South misses the poorest of the poor.[15] Thus, our assessments will underestimate the full extent of interstate inequality. If we were to find little inequality, such a bias would be troubling. Yet, as will be demonstrated shortly, finding little evidence for inequality is hardly a problem.

Table 3.4 divides the Southern group into an upper group and a lower group, based on a 50:50 split at 12.5 percent of the Northern leader's GDP per capita. States in the lower South have GDP per capita less than this threshold, while the states in the upper South possess GDP per capita that exceed the threshold. We are of course seeking primarily to address whether states have moved from the South to the North. But, we also should look for movement toward this possibility. Thus, we are also interested in whether states have been able to move from the lower South to the upper South.

Movement from the lower South to the upper South has occurred, but it cannot be considered the norm. In our sample, only four states have made this intra-Southern transition so far: Taiwan, South Korea, Thailand, and China. The first two continued to transit out of the South altogether. The last two may as well. Note, though, that it is also possible for states to move in the opposite direction. Romania and South Korea moved into the lower South for temporary periods. The Philippines also made this same move, but it is not clear how temporary the movement may turn out to be.

Contrast this record with the movement within the North captured in Table 3.5. In the North, the tendency has been for states in the lower stratum to move into the upper tier. Eight states have accomplished this feat. It is certainly conceivable that most, if not all, of the states in the lower North might be expected to make this same intra-categorical transition. Only one state has failed to maintain its Northern status (Russia) and, presumably, this loss of status reflects a temporary outcome, as well as a rather distinctive history of imperial disintegration.

Table 3.4 Movement within the South, 1870–2003

Upper South	Lower South
Argentina	
Brazil	
Chile	
Colombia	
Mexico	
Peru	
Venezuela	
Turkey	
Japan (to North in 1894)	
Finland (North in 1919)	
Poland (to North in 1929)	
Russia (to North in 1931)	
Bulgaria	
Yugoslavia (disintegrated in early 1990s)	
Romania	Romania (1942–51)
Greece (to North in 1956)	
Portugal (to North in 1957)	
Taiwan (to North in 1977)	Taiwan (1870–1967)
South Korea (to North in 1983)	South Korea (1945–67)
Philippines	Philippines (1965–)
Thailand (from 1980)	Thailand (1870–1979)
China (from 1991)	China (1870–1990)
	India
	Burma/Myanmar
	Indonesia
	Pakistan
	Bangladesh
	Ethiopia
	Egypt
	Morocco
	Nigeria
	Zaire
	Ivory Coast
	Kenya
	Tanzania

Nothing about our theoretical argument implies that North and South need be fixed entities. At the same time, states are unlikely to move back and forth very frequently. Thus, we admit states to the North in any year in which they qualify, as long as they continue to qualify in subsequent years. The alternative would be to identify North and South either at the beginning or ending of our examination period and then hold the identities as fixed for the entire longitudinal analysis. While we do not find these strategies especially attractive, we will employ them in subsequent sensitivity analyses toward the end of this chapter, along with others, that check whether our assumptions are to some extent responsible for the empirical outcomes that we observe.

Table 3.5 Movement within the North, 1870–2003

Upper North	Lower North
United Kingdom	Greece
United States	Czechoslovakia*
Australia	Hungary
Switzerland	Poland
New Zealand	Russia**
The Netherlands	
Sweden	
Belgium	
Denmark	
France	
Germany	
Ireland	
Canada (1880)	
Norway (1930)	
Finland (1959)	
Italy (1960)	
Japan (1967)	
Spain (1971)	
Taiwan (1994)	
South Korea (2001)	

*Czechoslovakia's decomposition into the Czech Republic and Slovakia has not affected their ability to meet the minimal qualifications for Northern membership.

**The Soviet Union's demise led to the Russian core's failure to meet the minimal Northern membership threshold from 1993 onwards. Presumably, this loss of economic status will prove to be a temporary phenomenon.

Empirical analysis

We first present a basic data analysis, assessing the extent that the North–South per capita incomegap has been growing since 1870. We then explain the observed growing North–South income gap based on our theoretical perspective. Our empirical analysis is relatively simple, focusing on computing our measure of convergence, visually inspecting the data, and smoothing their growth rates over time. This basic and simple approach is used by many studies of political economic history. As shown next, however, the current analysis nevertheless yields powerful results that support our interpretation.

Basic data analysis

Computing real GDP per capita for each group (North versus South) in each year, the real GDP figures of all the countries that belong to a group in each year are aggregated. Similarly, we aggregate the population figures of all the countries in that group, in each year. Finally, we divide the GDP of each group by the population of that group, in each year.

Given these data, the next operational issue is what constitutes convergence and divergence. For present purposes, we straightforwardly define economic convergence as a visual tendency of GDP per capita for the North and South to move toward a common value. If the visual distance between these series is growing over time, we define the situation as divergence.

Figure 3.1 presents the yearly population of the North and South. The majority of the world's population is in the South. In 1870, the population of the North was about 207 million and the sample Southern population totaled 728 million. In relative terms, about 22 percent of the world's population inhabited the North, and 78 percent was found in the South. In 2003, the Northern population numbered approximately 1 billion, and the sample Southern population encompassed some 4.2 billion. Thus, after 133 years, the North had shrunk to encompass 19.1 percent of the world. Hence, the proportional breakdown of the world population into our components was relatively stable over time.

In 2003, the size of the North–South population gap was 3.24 billion. In 1870, the gap had only been 624 million people. The gap grew faster after the 1930s compared with the period prior to the 1930s. From 1870 to 1929, the Northern and Southern populations grew at roughly similar rates.

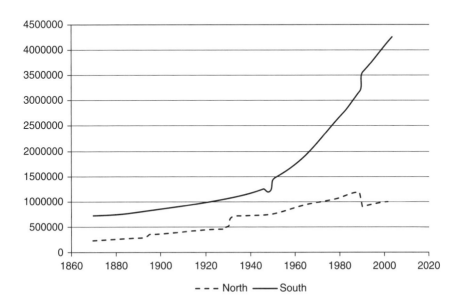

Figure 3.1 North and South populations.

Between 1930 and 2003, the Southern population expanded four-fold while the Northern population roughly doubled.

Figure 3.2 presents the real GDP per capita for the North and the South. In 1870, the North's real GDP per capita was around US$2100. The Southern GDP per capita was US$624. In relative terms, the North's real GDP per capita was 3.52 times larger than the South's real GDP per capita. From 1870 to 1930, the North–South absolute income gap grew slowly.[16] The 1930s world depression affected Northern income per capita more than it did the Southern income, resulting in a brief movement toward convergence. From the 1930s on, the absolute North–South gap has been expanding, and at an even faster rate after the 1950s. In 1950, the Northern real GDP per capita was about US$4930 and the Southern real GDP per capita was US$860. In relative terms, the Northern GDP per capita was about 5.7 times larger than the Southern level. By 2003, the Northern GDP per capita levels had climbed to US$21874. The Southern position had improved as well, attaining an average figure of US$3682. But, in relative terms, the Northern income level was 5.94 times larger than the Southern level. One can only conclude that the relative North–South gap has diverged. It is not a novel phenomenon, even though it has expanded more quickly in the last half of the twentieth century.

We think the empirical answers to our questions about longitudinal tendencies toward convergence are reasonably clear. Still, our answers are based on a number of assumptions about who belongs to the North and

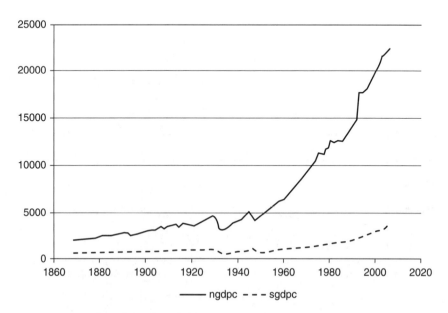

Figure 3.2 North and South real GDP per capita.

South, on what basis, and whether the identities of the categories should be allowed to change over time. The question remains whether something similar emerges when we relax or drop these assumptions. This is the query pursued in the next section on sensitivity analysis.

Sensitivity analysis

Our conceptualization of North and South employs a relative threshold scheme, which is driven by our theoretical approach. If we place system leader economic innovation at the center of long-term growth processes, it follows that the development status of all other states needs to be indexed in terms of the leader, especially since economic development is a continuing process characterized by intermittent surges of radically new technology. However, it is possible to argue that this conceptualization, while appropriate for our goal, may distort the North–South convergence picture, since it allows countries to move from North to South and from South to North as their real GDP per capita changes over time. However, we have examined a number of alternative approaches to see whether how we proceeded to calculate North–South inequality made much difference. In an earlier analysis (Reuveny and Thompson, 2002), we set the North–South sample according to Goldstein's (2002: 16–18) categorization of nations in regions. For Goldstein's purposes, all countries located in North America, Western Europe, Japan/Pacific, and Russia/Eastern Europe are classified as Northern. China and all states located in the Middle East, Latin America, South Asia, and Africa are classified as Southern.[17] In this approach, one decides on the structure of the North and the South in an ending year and maintains this division unchanged for the whole post-1870 period.

Another approach involves taking the list of countries to be included in the North and the South and setting their categorization according to their real GDP per capita in 1870. The categorical classifications are then kept unchanged for the entire period under examination. Since we are unaware of any literature that indicates the structure of the North and the South in 1870 and requiring some threshold, we fell back on the one used in our earlier analyses. In neither case (either the regional identification at the end of the series or freezing the categorical identifications at the beginning of the series) did it make any discernible difference to the movement of inequality across time (see Reuveny and Thompson, 2002).

Finally, we look at still another aggregation of the data in Figure 3.3. In this figure, the sample approach is abandoned and the reservations about Latin American economies are dropped (Rasler and Thompson, 2009). That is, the country N in Figure 3.5 is 170 representing all of the states in Maddison's 2007 compilation.[18] Any state satisfying the threshold for inclusion in the Northern group is accepted, with the sole exclusion of oil producers.

The dynamics shown in Figures 3.2 and 3.3 are similar in appearance. We infer that our portrayal of the lack of convergence is not contingent on

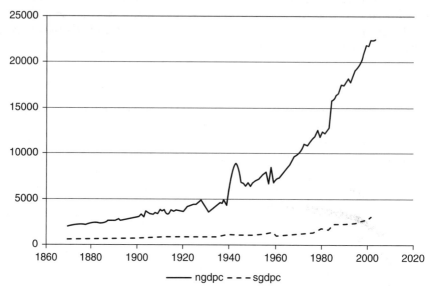

Figure 3.3 The North–South gap with data on 170 states.

how we calculate the gap between North and South. All of these figures indicate that there is no North–South convergence and that, over time, the income per capita distance between North and South is growing. In all cases, there also are very brief periods of convergence, as shown in the early 1930s and immediately following World War II. We conclude, therefore, that the results presented in Figure 3.2 are reasonably robust.

It is certainly possible to argue that all North and South aggregations are to some extent subjective. We also conducted another set of sensitivity analyses (Reuveny and Thompson, 2002) designed to check if convergence occurs when the data are not aggregated in any categorical way, but rather are inspected at the country level. One way to analyze the national data for convergence is to compute the standard deviation at each point in time. If the standard deviation from national real GDP per capita grows over time, there is no convergence (as countries GDP per capita are further dispersed from one another) and vice versa. The problem with this approach is that national real GDP per capita data are growing over time for all countries in our period due to technological progress. This means that the standard deviations from the real GDP per capita of all countries would also grow over time.

We dealt with the issue of growing standard deviations over time in two ways. First, we computed the statistics of coefficient of determination in each year, which is defined as the standard deviation of real GDP per capita divided by the average real GDP per capita. Second, we computed the natural logarithm of the real GDP per capita for each year. The standard deviation is then computed from the logged data. This is a familiar method used to deal with situations involving data characterized by various orders of magnitudes, which can influence the calculation of standard deviations.

The results from the coefficient of determination and the standard deviation from the logged data also confirmed our categorical results. The coefficient of variation generally grew over time. Periods of large growth rates were shown in the early 1900s, early 1940s, 1950s, and 1980s. In part, these step-level changes reflect the availability of data for generally poorer countries. Adding more relatively poor countries thus increases the variation. Nonetheless, there is no downward trend within each step level and, hence, no suggestion of convergence.

The standard deviation of the logged real GDP per capita also grew over time, again suggesting no convergence tendencies. Periods of increased rates of divergence were noticeable in the early 1900s, early 1940s and 1950s, and the 1980s. We assume that these findings further buttress the contention that convergence is simply not happening.

One last sensitivity question concerns the BRIC question. BRIC stands for Brazil, Russia, India, and China – countries that are considered the most prominent "newly emerging" economies in the early twenty-first century. Their rapid growth, especially China's, seems to make questions of North–South gaps obsolete for a number of observers. Obviously, some parts of the South are doing well currently and may continue to do well in the future, even if their growth rates almost have to slow down somewhat. What might happen to our figures depicting North–South gaps if the BRIC states were to become Northern?

There are at least two considerations here. One is that counting Russia as a newly emerging economy is at the very least awkward in our accounting scheme. Its predecessor, the Soviet Union, had qualified for the North more than half a century before self-destructing. Russia's economy fell back into the South temporarily and is currently making something of a comeback based largely on selling raw materials at high prices. Putting Russia aside, Figures 3.4, 3.5, and 3.6 compare the respective GDP per capita trajectories of Brazil, India, and China with those of the North and the South. The question is whether any of these "newly emerging" growth patterns are noticeably different from the longitudinal track of the average Southern GDP per capita.

Brazil's trajectory began to diverge from the average Southern path in the 1930s and has maintained a stronger relative position since then. However, the upward progress of Brazilian GDP per capita seems to have flattened out somewhat over the past 25 years or so.[19] It would be hard to say that Brazilian GDP per capita was converging on the Northern track based on the data through 2003. The Indian record (Figure 3.5) is actually less strong than the average Southern path, although it seems to be on a reasonably parallel track. The Chinese trajectory has been accelerating over the past

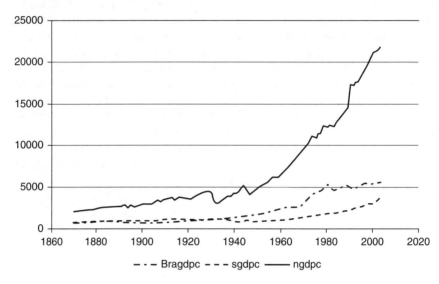

Figure 3.4 Southern, Northern, and Brazilian GDP per capita.

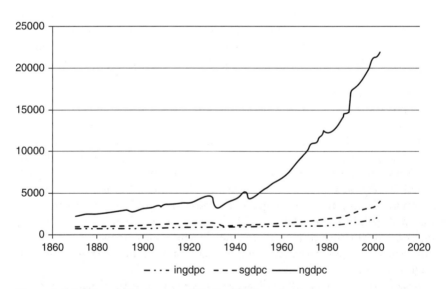

Figure 3.5 Southern, Northern, and Indian GDP per capita.

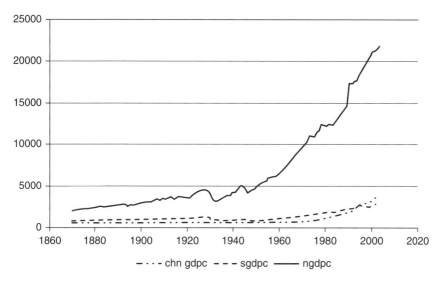

Figure 3.6 Southern, Northern, and Chinese GDP per capita.

few decades and has surpassed the average Southern line. In a number of decades, it might catch up to the Northern trajectory. It could qualify for Northern status long before that – assuming the rapid growth can be sustained into the future.

Two of the BIC states have done better than the average Southern GDP per capita. Yet, none of the BIC economic histories seem radically different in terms of their trajectories. A Brazilian or Chinese ascent into the Northern column would be encouraging, and it could also alter rather dramatically the number of people that could claim Northern status if China continued moving upwards in status. It would not, however, eliminate the North–South gap or the very large number of states that would remain in the Southern column if or when a few more states manage to move up the technological gradient.

Finally, we note somewhat parenthetically that Passe-Smith (1996) hypothesizes that divergence (convergence) is more likely in periods of contraction (expansion) because richer states are more capable of weathering contraction than poorer states. Southern growth rates, on average, have not dipped quite as low as Northern growth rates in periods of contraction. In periods of expansion, Northern growth rates exceed Southern growth rates. Such an outcome suggests the reverse of Passe-Smith's prediction. Growth slows down faster in depressed times in the North than in the South, thereby allowing some convergence, as demonstrated in the 1930s in Figure 3.2. However, these downturns are relatively short-lived. The potential for movement toward North–South convergence in contracting eras should not be exaggerated.

It is of course certainly conceivable that China or India might eventually move into the North. Such a transition would have a significant effect on the North–South gap in view of the large Chinese and Indian populations. However, if either or both of these states were to improve substantially their economic standing, there could also be repercussions in the major power hierarchy. Historically, accommodating new major powers has always proven to be a difficult proposition. The older, established powers have been reluctant to surrender their position. The newer powers have been eager to supplant the older states that appear to thwart their upward mobility. This type of structural context has proven explosive in the past (e.g., Germany in World War I, and both Germany and Japan in World War II). Yet, major power conflict also could come about without a movement out of the Southern category for either China or India.[20]

Then too there is another dimension of China's rapid growth that needs to be kept in mind, and it is a dimension that should not be restricted to China.[21] A significant proportion of China's recent improvement has been felt very unevenly. Galbraith, Krytynskaia, and Wang (2003) note that Chinese income gains have been largely restricted to Beijing, Shanghai, and Guangdong province. These areas certainly involve a sizeable number of people, but they still represent something less than the whole of China. They have been favored by financial, political, and export considerations that have led to increased inequalities within China. Deaton and Drez (2002) report something similar for India, the other giant of the South, where most western and southern states have done better than states in the north and east. Urban areas have done better than rural areas, and IT development constitutes only a very small percentage (2 percent) of the still-largely-agrarian Indian economy.[22] The general point here is that any quantitative improvement on the part of the South needs to be qualified by its spatial concentration, both within certain countries such as China and throughout the South in terms of increasing urban–rural and other types of inequalities.

Conclusions

If the experience of the last century and a third is any indication, the Northern and Southern income per capita might never come anywhere near converging without a concerted Northern effort to narrow the gap. Such an effort could take the form of a carefully engineered Northern economic slowdown accompanied by a once-and-for-all large wealth transfer from North to South, aimed at building social and economic infrastructures and institutions in the South. This massive undertaking would dwarf any economic reconstruction programs ever attempted previously. There would be little comparison in terms of scale with the Marshall Plan or the post-Cold War aid to the Russian economy. Yet, a global reconstruction effort of the South on this scale seems most improbable any time soon in a world system that has experienced serious difficulties coordinating efforts on issues such as AIDs or global warming.

While we suspect that Singer and Wildavsky (1993) exaggerate the homogeneity and perhaps the instability of the "zones of turmoil," we see little prospect for any automatic system-wide leveling processes that would reduce global inequality or expand the zones of peace. The immediate systemic prospect seems to be working in the opposite direction. Production profits in high-tech goods in the North, and income levels, tend to become more concentrated during the upsurge of a new technological wave, in contrast to the gradual lessening of inequality anticipated by liberal philosophy and its neoclassical economics offspring. We pursue the dynamics of this process more closely in the next chapter.

4   Geo-economic limits on technological diffusion

International relations are characterized by a number of dualities. One that seems to have emerged more recently, beginning or becoming more apparent at least by the early nineteenth century, pits a relatively small group of affluent states, the global North, against the rest of the world, the global South. Economic inequalities are hardly a novelty in the history of international relations. In some respects, the North–South divide resembles the imperial center–periphery structures that have been around as long as there have been empires, imperial centers, and hinterlands. Yet, the North is not a centralized empire; nor is the South an undifferentiated hinterland. Instead, we have some 190+ sovereign states – some of which are relatively rich while others are vastly poorer.

While the North might prefer to ignore the many problems of the South, the South tends to hold the North responsible for its disadvantaged plight. A South characterized by variable mixtures of failed states, terrorism, genocide, internal warfare, human rights violations, nuclear proliferation, major power interventions, high population growth, migration pressures, debt crises, respiratory and viral disease incubation, energy source insecurities, humanitarian crises, environmental degradation, and the miseries of poverty and malnutrition, in any event, is not so easy to ignore. The happy solution is to have the South become more like the North as soon as possible. Were that to occur, the central tenor of contemporary international relations would be altered fundamentally and reduced perhaps to squabbles over fishing rights, tourism misadventures, and minor World Trade Organization violations. International relations would become more like what intra-European international relations have become since 1945.

Liberal arguments foresee just such a global future outcome with the gradual diffusion of economic growth to the South. Liberal economic theory sees accelerated growth in the South eventually converging on slowing growth in the North, thereby diminishing appreciatively the North–South gap in income levels. Economic growth in the South would then lead to major gains in democratization and reduced conflict within the South and between the South and the North. However, is this forecast probable?

We think not, as it overlooks or misconstrues what we see as the inherent nature of long-term economic growth.

In our view, long-term economic growth is predicated on intermittent surges of radical technological innovation originating in a system leader situated in the North. The intermittent surges of innovation have far-reaching implications on the innovator's economy, but they diffuse unevenly to the rest of the world economy, absorbed in the North but much less so in the South. Rather than forecasting convergence, an appreciation for uneven technological diffusion suggests the probability of further North–South divergence as the North becomes increasingly more technologically complex in ways that the South cannot hope to emulate.

We evaluate the possibility of this pessimistic prediction by examining the effects of system leader technological innovation on Northern and Southern economic growth. We anticipate that most of the beneficial effects are monopolized by the North with little going to the South. Indeed, as system leaders and Northern economies become technologically more complex and the South does not, the effects of technological innovation should be expected to impact negatively on the South. Empirically, this is precisely what we find on examining North–South growth dynamics over the past 130 years.

The remainder of this chapter proceeds along the following lines. The next section elaborates the technological diffusion problem further in the specific context of the North–South gap. The last section reports our empirical results on the apparent Northern limits to the spread of system leader technological innovations and discusses some of their broad implications.

The technological diffusion problem

Bairoch's (1982) data on the geographical distribution of manufacturing provide a useful starting point for this section, capturing what we think is the crux of the North–South gap. Manufacturing, as one index of the location and innovation of higher technology, became increasingly concentrated in the global North (Western Europe, North America, and, eventually, Japan). Table 4.1 focuses on the chief technology pioneers of the nineteenth and twentieth centuries, Britain and the United States, and two Bairoch aggregations, the Developed Countries (DCs) and the Third World (China, India, and a few Latin American states). We view these two aggregations as rough approximations of the global North and South, respectively.

Table 4.1 shows world manufacturing residing largely in the South through the first third of the nineteenth century but moving increasingly to the North by mid-century.[1] The two individual leaders in this shift are first Britain peaking around 1880 (with 22.9 percent) and second the United States peaking in the early 1950s (44.7 percent). For much of the twentieth century (until the 1990s), Bairoch's data suggest that most of the world outside the most affluent zone produced from 7 to 13 percent of world's

Table 4.1 Proportion of world manufacturing production

	Britain	United States	Developed World	Third World
1750	1.9	0.1	27	73
1800	4.3	0.8	32.2	67.8
1830	9.5	2.4	39.5	60.5
1860	19.9	7.2	63.4	36.6
1880	22.9	14.7	79.1	20.9
1900	18.5	23.6	89	11
1913	13.6	32	92.5	7.5
1928	9.9	39.3	92.8	7.2
1938	10.7	31.4	92.8	7.2
1953	8.4	44.7	87	13
1963	6.4	35.1	91.3	8.7
1973	4.9	33	90.1	9.9
1980	4	31.5	88	12
1991	4.5	23.5	84.2	15.8
1995	4	23.5	81.6	18.4
2000	3.9	26.6	78.8	21.2
2005	3.6	22.3	72.3	27.7

Sources: The 1750–1980 data are based on numbers reported in Bairoch (1982). The 1991–2005 figures are based on calculations performed on World Development Indicators (WDI Online) value-added manufacturing substituting "high income" aggregations for Bairoch's "developed world."

manufacturing output. After 1980, the global South continued to make solid gains but the global North continues to monopolize manufacturing. In 2005, the developed world's roughly 3:1 ratio is exactly the reverse of its 1:3 ratio in 1750.[2]

But why focus so much on manufacturing? Agriculture, not just manufacturing, is influenced by technological innovation. Others argue that the most modern economic development is the movement away from manufacturing to services in finance, communication, and software development. What these observations mean is that technological innovation is manifested in a number of activities. Yet, manufacturing retains the claim to constituting the primary vehicle of economic transformation in the past few centuries. It brought about the possibility of continuous and sustained economic development by transforming worker attitudes and skills as well as structures and institutions of production and socio-political regulation. Lall and Kraemer-Mbula (2005: 5–7) enumerate ten ways (Table 4.2) in which manufacturing impacts economic development processes. The processes of technological diffusion are accelerated by manufacturing compared to agriculture and more widespread in effect in terms of the people, production processes, and institutions that come into contact with the innovations. Manufacturing is also an important avenue for integrating

Table 4.2 The importance of manufacturing to economic development

	Contributions to economic development
1	Manufacturing is the main vehicle for the application of technological progress to production.
2	Manufacturing is itself the major source of innovation.
3	Manufacturing is the hub for diffusing innovation to other activities, providing capital goods and transmitting new technical and organizational knowledge.
4	Manufacturing is a vital source of new skills and attitudes, including industrial work ethics, entrepreneurial capabilities, in-house training, closer interaction between educational institutions and industry, and inflows of foreign skills.
5	Manufacturing led the development of modern institutions and legal structures that modern economies require.
6	Manufacturing innovation and skill creation have large beneficial externalities for other activities.
7	Manufacturing provides the direct demand for the growth of many modern services.
8	Manufacturing is the main source of dynamic comparative advantage in the shift to more advanced manufactured exports.
9	Manufacturing transnational firms have been responsible for the internationalization and integration of a number of national economies.
10	Manufacturing brings exposure to foreign markets, enterprises, skills, and practices that can be the catalyst for modernization of national industrial enterprises.

Source: Based on Lall and Kraemer-Mbula (2005: 5–7).

local production to the world economy and vice versa. Not surprisingly, Lall and Kraemer-Mbula (2005: 4) conclude that manufacturing "has been, and remains, the main engine of structural transformation."

Table 4.3, also relying on Bairoch data, suggests another important dimension of this process. The innovators specialize in new or the latest technology that gradually diffuses to other DCs but much less so to the less developed countries (LDCs). In 1830–1913, Britain controlled some 9.5–22.9 percent of the world's manufacturing output (Table 4.1). Yet, much of this output, especially in 1860–1913, focused heavily on new technology. Other DCs gradually closed the gap. In 1830, the ratio of new technology foci in Britain compared to other DCs was on the order of about 5 to 1 (32–40 percent in Britain versus 6–10 percent in other DCs). By 1913, the ratio was about 1.27 to 1. In marked contrast, new technology was very slow to emerge in the Third World, and by 1913, the new technology specialization ratio remained heavily biased toward Britain (5:1) and other DCs (4:1). Clearly, new technology diffuses highly unevenly.

The South complains that LDCs cannot be expected to make much economic improvement in a world economy already heavily biased in favor

Table 4.3 Estimated shares of new technology in manufacturing output

	1830	1860	1880	1900	1913
Britain	32–40	60–70	62–74	68–78	72–80
Other Developed	6–10	18–24	30–38	49–57	55–65
Third World	0–1	0–1	1–3	4–9	10–19

Source: Kozul-Wright (2006: 118).

of the North. The Northern response tends to rely on the liberal prediction that the poor will eventually become more affluent if they emulate the states that have already become rich. Other things being equal, the fast growth of the rich should slow and the slow growth of the poor should accelerate as it takes advantage of the technology already created by the rich. Ultimately, the playing field should level as the growth rates and development levels of the rich and poor converge. Yet, other things are rarely equal. The global North gained its development lead in an earlier time and that context is not likely to be duplicated exactly in the twenty-first century.[3] One might well ask, for that matter, whether we should want the South to repeat the intense conflicts of the late nineteenth and the first half of the twentieth centuries that the North endured. But such a question would be somewhat rhetorical because Southern states lack the technological infrastructure and development that provided both an economic foundation and substantial motivation for the World Wars of 1914–18 and 1939–45.

In terms of motivation, what we mean is that world wars are fought in part because of ascent and decline patterns in relative technological gains, with late developers challenging early developers. By development, moreover, we do not simply mean production gains. Long-term modern economic growth is propelled by cumulative waves of technological expansion and production frontier discontinuities, including successive waves of early industrialization in iron and textile production, steam engines, chemistry, steel, electrification, gasoline engines, and, today, information technology. Each wave is led by a pioneer economy that develops the new technology and reaps the benefits of pioneering activity. Other economies adapt these technologies as best they can. Some improve on the initial innovations; others simply copy. However, there is no guarantee that all economies will be able to adapt to the newly established production frontiers. On the contrary, those economies that have been most successful at adapting remain restricted to a small set of advanced economies, the North. The rest of the world belongs to the South. Movement out of the South into the North is not impossible, but so far has been accomplished by a few Southern states such as late nineteenth-century Japan or post-1970s South Korea and Taiwan.

Why might that be the case? The two most prominent types of arguments – herein labeled "Liberal optimism" and "Northern vampirism" – do not appear to be as helpful as they might be. Neither one is totally invalid, but neither fully explains the central gap phenomenon – that is, that the gap appears to be widening. The liberal optimism approach predicts that the gap should narrow. The Northern vampirism view predicts that no Southern states should be able to bridge the gap. Instead, the gap widens even though a few LDCs have moved into the North and a few others may follow.

The case for liberal optimism is predicated on the notion that economic growth is a generic activity in which everyone can participate but that, in some cases, various obstacles prevent full participation (for instance, Barro, 1997; Lucas, 2003; Singer and Wildavsky, 1993). If poor countries can rid themselves of such obstacles as government intervention, corruption, land inequalities, low literacy, and excessive population growth – or, in other words, become more like the affluent societies (Dowrick and DeLong, 2003: 204–205) – they too can enjoy faster growth rates. Eventually, the faster growth rates of the later developers should catch up or converge with the de-accelerating growth rates of the early developers, and income levels will converge. As one economics Nobelist puts it:

> Sooner or later everyone will join the industrial revolution ... all economies will grow at the rate common to the wealthiest economies ... percentage differences in income levels will disappear ... Ideas can be imitated and resources can and do flow to places where they earn the highest return (Lucas, 2000: 166).

To be sure, there is empirical evidence for this convergence process but it is almost exclusively restricted to the Northern group. Later developers within the North have been able to absorb or adapt the technological innovations generated by the British (primarily nineteenth century) and American (primarily twentieth century) pioneers. Their income per capita levels, as a consequence, have tended to converge on those of the Northern leaders. The same statement applies only to a few Southern states, and even here the convergence is often far from including the majority of the population.

The "Northern vampirism" arguments emphasize that the North has exploited the South for hundreds of years, and that the wealth of the North is only possible because of this exploitation. The North reserves for itself high-profit manufacturing, which can be purchased by the South, while restricting the South to providing food and raw materials to the North. Since the North is highly unlikely to abandon its own path to success voluntarily, it is up to the South to break its structural dependency on the North somehow and proceed to develop its own industry as autonomously as possible (e.g., Frank, 1978; Wallerstein 1974, 1980, 1989).

Even though we are hard-pressed to deny the evidence for exploitation, there are several problems with this view. One notable problem, already mentioned, is that some southern states have beaten the odds and moved up the technological gradient. Presumably, they should not have been able to do this unless they are either simply anomalies or there are significant weak points in the nature of Northern dominance and exploitation. Either way, upward mobility is not ruled out, and therefore must be explained.

A second problem is that it is not at all clear that Northern prosperity has consistently depended on access to Southern goods or markets. Northern trade, investment, and prosperity are largely Northern-centric. If we are right in according technology a strong driving force, developments in technology have reduced the dependence on Southern raw materials – not intensified them. In many respects, the greater Southern problem these days is how to claim more attention from the North rather than less. Thus, if exploitation was once blatant and prominent, neglect seems more problematic these days.

As noted, we do not rule out the possibilities of liberal catch up or Northern exploitation. Catch up and exploitation clearly do exist. What is missing from these interpretations, however, is the vital role that technology plays in driving economic development. Building in part on Kondratieff (1984) and Freeman and Louca (2001), we argue that technological progress is the main carrier of long-term growth. In our view, progress comes in successive waves that at least partially supplant earlier waves via Schumpeter's (1939) creative destruction, emanates primarily from a single source, and then diffuses unevenly to other economies. If we are correct, the Southern problem is more one of avoiding falling further behind than it is of catching up or evading exploitation. If the South is generally unable to adopt or adapt to successive technological breakthroughs, it will likely fall farther behind a frontier that is intermittently advanced in the North. Some Southern catch up may be feasible in terms of earlier technological waves, but it is likely to remain too many waves behind to make much progress vis-à-vis convergence.[4]

This argument seems eminently testable. We have demonstrated that US technological change has driven US aggregate economic growth and that both US technological change and aggregate economic growth have driven world economic growth (Reuveny and Thompson, 2004a). We can reframe this question in terms of the North–South divide. Does system leader technological change and aggregate growth contribute equally to Northern and Southern economic growth? Or, is it more likely, as we argue here, that these forces primarily diffuse to the North and much less so to the South? We think our theoretical perspective is a useful tool in approaching these questions.

By now, our perspective should be reasonably evident but it does not hurt to re-summarize. The principles that frame our analysis include the following:

– Long-term economic growth (which is not the same as more familiar, short-term economic growth) is highly dependent on waves of new and often radical technological pioneered by a lead economy. In addition to new commercial routes, expanded trade, and new industries, the innovations also modify how information and commodities are exchanged. Profits from these new technologies facilitate the emergence of the lead economy as the world economy's principal source of technological innovation and investment and finance.

– New products and industries, as well as novel ways of communicating information and transporting commodities, as a consequence, emerge discontinuously, reshape technological frontiers, and, often, reduce transaction costs.

– Technological growth and predominance in leading sectors of commerce and industry provide ample incentive and sufficient funding for the lead economy/system leader to develop specialized capabilities of global reach in order to provide protection and security for trade routes. Naval and maritime capabilities have thus been favored historically. Concentration in global reach capabilities tends to follow concentration in technological innovation. De-concentration in technological innovation should lead ultimately to de-concentration in global reach capabilities.

– To a considerable extent, order and governance in the global political economy is dependent on systemic leadership and the concentration of technological innovation and global reach capabilities.

– Radical innovations in the lead economy stimulate economic growth at home and abroad. One important stimulus avenue is technological diffusion by which the capability to produce new products and utilize the new communication/transportation infrastructures is spread selectively to economies that are in a position to adapt and adopt the new economic ways of doing things.

– One incentive for lowering barriers to trade is gaining access to the lead economy's new products. Another is a byproduct of technological diffusion which enables some economies to compete in the production of the new commodities. Systemic openness, therefore, is also dependent to some degree on systemic leadership.

– The long-term economic growth of the world economy is contingent on intermittent technological change, selected technological diffusion, lowered transaction costs, greater openness, and expanded investment. The combination of concentration and uneven diffusion leads to unequal growth impacts that are compounded by differences in resource endowment, climate and location.

To the extent that these principles are accurate, it is not difficult to account for the favoring of Western Europe, North America, Australia/New Zealand in nineteenth- and twentieth-century investment, migration, trade, and technological diffusion. What about the rest of the world? Should we expect further diffusion to even out historical patterns of privilege?

Lall (2003) provides one good handle, summarized selectively in Table 4.4, on the imperfections of the spread of technology. His main point is that economic theory makes assumptions about this process that are not manifested empirically. In theory, technology is freely available to whoever needs it. It can be pulled off the shelf and applied wherever its development seems efficient and appropriate. However, in reality, there are a number of reasons why technology is unlikely to spread widely and easily. Actors may

Table 4.4 Theory and reality in technology development

Theoretical assumptions in economics	Reality
All actors have full knowledge of existing technology, which can be readily transferred. Actor production functions are universal even if national endowments may vary.	Information on technology is difficult to locate and evaluate. Knowledge about technology is imperfect and hazy.
Once technology is perceived to be appropriate, its acquisition and application is immediate in all circumstances.	The successful transfer of technology is a prolonged process and one that is dependent on local learning.
All actors use technology with the same efficiency. If there is any learning involved, it is uniform, predictable, and costless.	Each actor has a unique learning path, depending on initial situation and subsequent efforts. Learning is more costly, riskier, and more uncertain at lower levels of development.
Actors maximize well-defined objectives that are easily switched as appropriate.	Actors satisfy and develop organizational routines that are adapted over time based on experience and imitation. The cumulative nature of learning and path dependence make it difficult to change technological trajectories.
Learning how to use technology is a generic process. Technology is technology.	Learning process is technology-specific. Different technologies involve different learning costs, risks, skills, and linkages. Some are much more difficult than others.
Technology transfer is an autonomous process.	Different technologies have different degrees of interaction with, and dependence on, outside sources of knowledge, resources, and access to markets.
Technological development is a generic process. All technology acquired is beneficial to economic development.	Technology development takes place at different depths. It is possible to use imported technology without being able to adapt or reproduce it, leaving the developer dependent on external actors.

Continued

Table 4.4 Cont'd

Theoretical assumptions in economics	Reality
Appropriately skilled labor, as well as research and development capabilities, will be available for any technological development.	Advanced technologies, as well as research and development capabilities, increasingly require higher levels of knowledge, numeracy, and industrial skills that may be absent or in short supply due to illiteracy, restricted educational infrastructure, and lack of previous industrial experience.
Foreign direct investment (FDI) is readily available as a way to acquire technology.	FDI is highly concentrated. In 1998, 10 states received 76% of total FDI to developing world.
Corporate enterprises can be created as appropriate and potentially anywhere in order to engage in economic competition.	Large firms in industrial countries dominate the world corporate scene, their respective industries, trade, and innovation.

Source: Based on the discussion in Lall (2003: 282–286).

be less aware of what technology might be available than is often assumed. Path dependencies shape trajectories that are often difficult to alter. While technological backwardness can lead to rapid growth as late developers close the gap with pioneers, underdevelopment often means that acquiring technology and learning how to use it is all the more difficult. Critical skills are likely to be lacking. So, too, are supportive linkages to external information and resources. Some technologies are difficult to learn. Moreover, simply learning how an existing technology works may not be sufficient if the capability for innovating new technology remains out of reach.

Yet, even if these adaptation problems are somehow overcome, innovation and technological information has been increasingly controlled by transnational corporations. Economies of scale and vertical and horizontal organizational networks encourage the concentration of production sites. Some states may benefit, but many more will be marginalized.

From Lall's vantage point, the diffusion of Northern technology to the South is therefore a highly uneven process in which only a few states have overcome the structural problems in successfully acquiring technology. The outcome is summarized by Table 4.5's array of the distribution of manufacturing in the developing world toward the end of the twentieth century. Three observations seem most pertinent. Different parts of the global South have done better than other parts. East Asia has done best, followed distantly by Latin America and the Middle East. The positions of the non-Asian regions have deteriorated in 1985–98. Only East Asia has

Table 4.5 Regional shares of developing countries' manufactured exports

Sector	Year	East Asia	South Asia	Middle East	Latin America	Sub-Saharan Africa
All	1985	56.9	4.5	12.9	16.9	2.6
Manufactures	1998	69	3.8	6	8.9	0.8
High	1985	81	1.1	1.8	6.6	1.3
Technology	1998	85.5	0.6	0.7	2.1	0

Note: The numbers in the cells represent percentages of developing countries' total manu-factured exports. The Middle East includes North Africa. Latin America excludes Mexico. Sub-Saharan Africa excludes South Africa.

Source: Based on Lall (2003: 281).

had much success in producing high technology, which we take to be an indicator of what Lall referred to as technology learning of greater depth than is manifested elsewhere.[7]

Table 4.6 offers a quick look at the additional contention that transnational corporations are overwhelmingly Northern. In 1995, 6 of the 500 (1.2 percent) largest corporations in the world (based on revenues) were Southern (see Chapter 3 or Table 4.8 in the next section, which classifies countries as Southern or Northern). By 2005, the proportion had expanded to 34 of 500 (6.8 percent). Table 4.6, however, suggests two qualifications to this growth. Sixteen of the 34 in 2005 are Chinese, and China, presumably, is on course to leaving the South at some point in the twenty-first century. The other 18 are headquartered in Venezuela, Mexico, Thailand, Brazil, Malaysia, Saudi Arabia, Turkey, and India. The exceptions to the predominance of Northern firms then, are highly concentrated. They also tend to focus on national monopolies dealing with petroleum and telecommunications in large countries, owing their size to something other than global competition and technological innovation. Even the Chinese exceptions have so far not represented the Chinese economy as a whole, large parts of which still remain highly underdeveloped.

Putting it all together, the North–South arena is not necessarily static, but there seem to be limitations in diffusing technology. The international political economic structure seems stacked against a substantial or near-future diminishment of the North–South gap. We argue that the system's lead economy periodically extends the technological frontier by introducing radical innovations. Pioneering revolutionary industries help to bestow a substantial production edge on the entire economy that takes the lead.[8] Some other economies are able to absorb the innovations and growth emanating from the leading economy relatively quickly; others do not have the demand, infrastructure, access to investment, or required know-how.

Table 4.6 Southern firms in the Fortune Global 500 largest corporations

1995	2000	2005
Pemex (Mexico)	PDVSA (Venezuela)	Sinopec (China)
Bank of China	Sinopec (China)	State Grid (China)
Indian Oil	State Power (China)	PDVSA (Venezuela)
Cofco (China)	Pemex (Mexico)	China National Petroleum
Itausa-Investimentos (Brazil)	China National Petroleum	Pemex (Mexico)
Telebras (Brazil)	Indian Oil	Petrobras (Brazil)
	Industrial and Commercial Bank of China	Petronas (Malaysia)
	China Telecommunications	China Mobile Communications
	Bank of China	China Life Insurance
	Petronas (Malaysia)	Bank of China
	Sinochem (China)	Hutchison Whampoa (China)
	China Mobile Communications	PTT (Thailand)
	Carso Global Telecommunications (Mexico)	China Southern Power Grid
		Bancow Bradesco (Brazil)
	Banco do Brazil	China Telecommunications
	Agricultural Bank of China	Baosted Group (China)
		Sinochem (China)
		Sabic (Saudi Arabia)
		Reliance (India)
		Koc Holding (Turkey)
		Bharat Petroleum (India)
		Hindustan Petroleum (India)
		America Telecommunications (Mexico)
		Oil and Natural Gas (India)
		Itausa-Investimentos (Brazil)
		China Railway Engineering
		Carso Global Telecommunications (Mexico)
		Cemex (Mexico)
		Cofco (China)
		China First Automotive Works
		Shanghai Automotive (China)
		China Railway Construction
		China State Construction
		State Bank of India

Note: The national identity of the firm is stated in parentheses unless the national identity is found in the firm's name.

Source: The information has been extracted from Fortune (1996, 2001, and 2006).

As a result, other things being equal, the gap between the system leader and the North vis-à-vis the South does not close.

The process is not solely economic. Political factors play a role in the diffusion of technology. Lall (1992, 1996, 2003, 2004a), for example, argues that successful adoption of technological diffusion and buildup of industrial capability require government policies that provide institutional, infrastructural, financial, educational, and coordinative support to the private sector; ameliorate market failures; and promote saving and investments. The East Asian miracle, he argues, demonstrates the importance of an activist approach to industrial and technological development.

While these national policies can have some impact, they do not operate in a political economic vacuum. As Lall (2004b) himself generally wrote, changes in the global economic environment and international "rules of the game" can constrain governments. In our perspective, systemic leadership provides the required international orders for the world economy, including public goods such as institutions that promote freer trade, global financial institutions, stable currency markets, lending of last resort, and political pressures and outright interventions to stabilize crucial regions. While these international orders may not profit everyone equally, they are expected to be beneficial for both North and South, as long as the system leader is in a reasonably strong position to provide them.

So far, we have presented our models, data, and measures. What precisely do we expect to see? An increase in leading sector growth in the lead economy is expected to promote both Northern and Southern growth, but more so in the North, the main beneficiary of technological diffusion. An increase in the system leader's leading sector share is expected to reduce Northern and Southern growth, but more so in the South, which is more likely to fall behind when the leader monopolizes leading goods. An increase in the systemic leader's global reach capability (as a proxy for its order management resources) is expected to promote Northern and Southern growth, since the leader provides international public goods that are good for commerce. An increase in the leader's economic growth rate will promote both Northern and Southern growth, but more so in the North.

For the controls, increases in Northern growth inertia and Southern growth inertia are expected to increase Northern and Southern growth rates, respectively, reflecting greater path dependence. In general, this force may be larger when series are measured in terms of levels, as opposed to growth rates. Since our series are growth rates, which may be erratic over time, their inertia may not be that strong. The inertia may also be stronger in the North than in the South since the Southern economy, by virtue of being dependent on agriculture and resources, may fluctuate more over time. Finally, we do not have strong expectations regarding the respective effects of rises in Northern economic growth in the Southern model, Southern economic growth in the Northern model, and a 1914 dummy in both models. Our primary concern is to control for their possible effects.[9]

Empirical results

This section presents our results. Beginning with plots, the Northern, Southern, and leader growth series are multiplied by 10 for better visualization. Figure 4.1 presents decade averages of Northern and Southern economic growth and systemic leadership. We discern waves in systemic leadership – first the decline of the British, then the absence of prominent peaks between the wars, and then the US peak in the 1950s. These outcomes are anticipated by the leadership long cycle perspective. Examining a longer period than in Figure 4.1, Thompson (1988) and Modelski and Thompson (1996) find that the main peak in British systemic leadership occurred shortly after the Napoleonic Wars, similar in timing to the US case after World War II. Thanks to the victory in war, the exhaustion of opponents, a war-induced military edge, and the platform provided by the leading economy, systemic leadership is strongest shortly after the global war that essentially installs leaders in a trial by combat.

"Long waves" are discernible in the Northern economic growth series. Their length is about 40–50 years. The first wave could be said to peak in the 1890s, and the second, really an extension of the first (they are separated by the World War I interruption) and a post-war spurt, peaks in the late 1920s. Another wave begins in the 1940s, and peaks in the 1960s. The Southern economic growth waves, in contrast, are relatively less pronounced. The first wave peaked in the 1900s and the second in the 1950s, after which the series hovers without much change. The timing of the waves of the Northern series generally correspond to the long

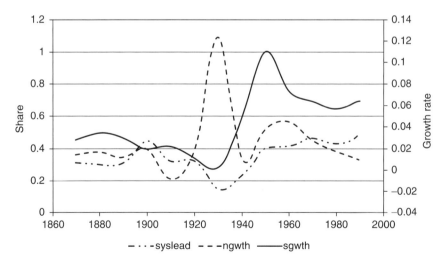

Figure 4.1 Decade-averaged North and South economic growth and systemic leadership.

wave-chronology discussed in the leadership long cycle studies, while the Southern wave is shown here for the first time. The Northern and Southern average economic growth rates are relatively lower before World War II than after 1945; but during most of the years shown, the Southern average economic growth rate is lower than the Northern average growth rate.

The systemic leadership series declines through the 1870s–1930s and since the 1960s, and rises modestly after the collapse of the Soviet Union in the early 1990s. The Northern economic growth series corresponds relatively well with the leadership series since the 1940s, and before the 1920s. After World War II, the series rises, reflecting a small rise in leadership in the 1910s, with some lag. The Southern economic growth series most closely resembles the naval series before the 1890s and after around 1910. Both series seem positively associated with systemic leadership, as expected theoretically.

Figure 4.2 presents the Northern and Southern growth rates together with the share of leading sector production held by the leader. The share series, arguably, suggests one evident peak. As shown in Thompson (1988) and Modelski and Thompson (1996), an earlier peak in the 1840s–50s, which is not included in Figure 4.2, led to the decline shown in Figure 4.2 through the first decade of the 1900s. The buildup to the peak in the 1950s is checked temporarily by the depression of the 1930s. Oscillations in Northern growth correspond roughly to the shape of the US leading sector share monopoly if we factor in the World War II interruption. Periods with

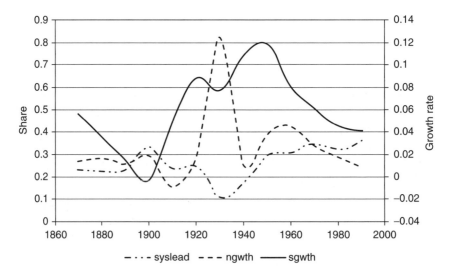

Figure 4.2 Decade-averaged North and South economic growth and leading sector share.

a high leading sector share seem associated with low or declining Southern growth rates, suggesting a negative association between the two series.

Figure 4.3 shows the two growth series with the leader's leading sector growth. The late-nineteenth-century decline in leading sector growth is somewhat arrested toward 1900. There is moderate improvement in technological growth prior to the onset of world depression in the 1930s, while the leading sector growth peak of the 1950s is hard to miss. The series also tracks up in the 1990s. In all, this behavior is in line with leadership long cycle argument for a "twin peaks" phenomenon in which system leaders enjoy spurts of technological growth before and after global wars. Figure 4.3 also suggests that the Northern growth is roughly in synch with the leading sector growth series, subject to a lag. That is, the leading sector growth peaks first and then is followed by a rise in Northern growth. The Southern growth series seems less in synch with these dynamics, although one could argue that the Southern improvement since about 1960 is linked to the spike in system leader innovation of the 1950s. The early-twentieth-century and post-mid-1960s economic growth in the South is much less supportive of this linkage.

Finally, Figure 4.4 shows the leader's aggregated economic growth rate together with the Northern and Southern economic growth series. The leader's growth series is very much like the Northern growth series, with the Northern behavior lagging the leader fluctuations with regularity. This regularity and visual pattern is considerably less evident in the Southern series.

Figures 4.1–4.4 support our theoretical interpretation, which expects different Northern and Southern growth dynamics, and North–South relationships to the system leader. However, figures based on decade

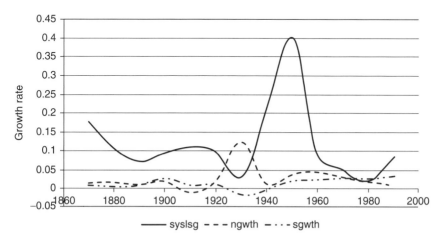

Figure 4.3 Decade-averaged North and South economic growth and leading sector growth.

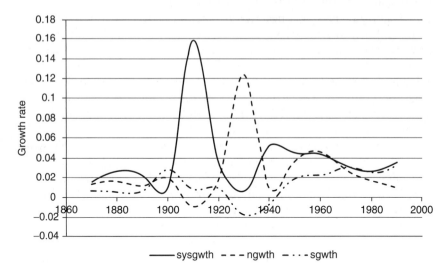

Figure 4.4 Decade-averaged North and South economic growth and leader's growth.

averages cannot be the last word on how or whether our variables relate to each other. To examine these effects, we turn to linear regressions conducted using the raw, non-averaged data.

Table 4.7 presents the results. Column 2 presents results for the Northern economic growth model, and Column 3 presents results for the Southern economic growth model. The goodness of fit in the Northern model, as measured by R squared, is 0.5, but only 0.26 in the Southern model. This suggests that, in general, the leadership platform is less able to explain the Southern economic growth over time than the Northern economic growth, as expected theoretically.

Beginning with the variables of primary interest, the coefficient of leading sector growth in the Northern model is positive and statistically significant. An increase in the growth rate of the system leader's leading sector increases Northern economic growth, as anticipated. The coefficient of this variable in the Southern economic growth model is also positive, but it is not statistically significant, suggesting that an increase in the growth rate of the leader's leading sector has little or no effect on Southern economic growth.

The coefficient obtained for leading sector share is negative in both the Northern and Southern economic growth models, but is statistically significant only for the South, as anticipated. Hence, as expected theoretically, when the leader's global monopoly edge in the leading sector production rises, the South falls behind more than the North. Put differently, as the leader's global edge in producing the leading sector expands, the North and the South are affected negatively, but the North is relatively less affected

Table 4.7 Estimation results: Northern versus Southern economic growth models

Variable	Northern economic growth model	Southern economic growth model
Constant	0.009	0.006
	(0.0072)	(0.0080)
Northern growth inertia	0.080	
	(0.0723)	
Southern growth inertia		0.085
		(0.0897)
Leading sector growth	0.019*	0.006
	(0.0120)	(0.0134)
Leading sector share	−0.016	−0.047**
	(0.0208)	(0.0220)
Leader growth rate	0.078*	0.098
	(0.0525)	(0.0799)
Systemic leadership	0.052***	0.079***
	(0.0176)	(0.0234)
Southern economic growth	−0.201	
	(0.1985)	
Northern economic growth		−0.187
		(0.2293)
1914 Dummy	−0.394***	−0.179
	(0.0611)	(0.1431)
R squared	0.50	0.26
Sample size	131	131

Note: Robust standard errors in parentheses. * denotes significance at the 10% level; ** denotes significance at the 5% level; *** denotes significant at the 1% level. One-tailed tests are used for all the variables, except for Southern economic growth, Northern economic growth, and 1914 Dummy.

than the South, as it is relatively better positioned and more able to absorb the new waves of radical innovations, compared with the South.

The coefficients obtained for leader growth rate are positive in both the Northern and the Southern growth models. However, this coefficient is statistically significant only in the Northern model. The *p* value obtained for the coefficient of leader growth rate in the Southern model is 0.110, suggesting a weaker effect than in the North. Thus, an increase in the overall or aggregate economic growth rate of the leading economy promotes economic growth in the North, and less so in the South, as expected theoretically.

The coefficient of systemic leadership is positive and statistically significant in both models. As expected, a world system with stronger leadership is by and large more politically stable and economically orderly, as the leaders, at least in the previous two centuries, provided political and economic public goods that benefited the economy (mainly, of course, because they benefited their own economies and global connections). With declining systemic leadership, one should expect a decline in trade openness and financial stability, and ultimately, once every 100 years or so, a slide into political chaos that, historically, involved global war from which a new system leader has emerged.

Moving to the controls, the effects of rises in Northern growth inertia and Southern growth inertia on the Northern and Southern economic growth, respectively, are positive, but insignificant, reflecting the variability in the growth series. However, the p value for the Northern inertia is 0.134, while that for the Southern inertia is larger, suggesting a greater role for inertia in the North than in the South, as expected. The effect of a change from 0 to 1 in the 1914 dummy, indicating a new system leader, is statistically significant only for the North. In the Southern model, the p value is 0.105. Thus, the leadership change affects the Northern economy more than the Southern economy. This is intuitive, recalling the relatively tighter links between the leading and the Northern economies. The effects of increases in Northern economic growth and Southern economic growth on each other are statistically insignificant, suggesting that the two blocs generally operate as separate units. This is also suggested by Figures 4.1–4.4, where many Northern fluctuations have no Southern parallels.

We hypothesized that the Northern economies are the primary beneficiaries of the radical innovation emanating from the system's lead economy, while much less trickles down to the South. We tested this argument of uneven technological diffusion with time series dating back to 1870. Our results support a view emphasizing the leader's stronger economic ties with the North vis-à-vis the South. The diffusion of ideas, technologies, and know-how associated with the leading economy are likely to fare better in the North than in the South. System leader demand for Northern products is also likely to be important. Stylized observations suggest that, unlike the North, the leader's growth affects the South by way of stimulating labor-intensive, resource-oriented, or low-level manufacturing production. This type of stimulation is likely to have a smaller effect on growth than the Northern absorption of sectors more associated with the leader's radical innovations. The effects of systemic leadership (as proxied by global reach capabilities) are essentially identical and positive in both the North and the South, indicating that, while the technological and economic dimensions of leadership are restricted primarily to the North, the ordering benefits are enjoyed by both the North and the South. Given the marked persistence of the South's membership, we can only infer that the economic benefits of world order are not as enriching as the diffusion of new technology and system leader economic growth.

An optimistic amendment?

But, where does that leave us vis-à-vis the future of Southern development? The absence of much movement in the North–South gap sets up highly pessimistic scenarios for the future. However, a somewhat more optimistic perspective is advanced by Alice Amsden (2001). Amsden's basic position, similar to ours, is that technology transfer is a necessary condition for development. She also thinks that it is occurring and has occurred widely, albeit with variable success. The core argument is that the "more backward the learner," the less easy is the technology transfer. Backwardness here refers primarily to previous experience with industrial manufacturing.

This starting point leads her to distinguish three groups among contemporary states: the North Atlantic + Japan leaders in technological innovation and expanding the world technological frontier, the "rest," and the "remainder." The "rest" include China, India, Indonesia, South Korea, Malaysia, Taiwan, Thailand, Argentina, Brazil, Chile, Mexico, and Turkey. These are states with economies that had pre-World War II experience in some type of manufacturing (for instance, the production of silk, cotton textiles, and foodstuffs) that was either indigenous or introduced by emigres and/or colonial powers. The "remainder," a rather large number of states, lack much in the way of historical manufacturing experience and have tended to fall farther and farther behind with each extension of the technological frontier.

According to Amsden, simply having some experience with manufacturing guaranteed nothing, but it did establish a foundation with which to work. Even so, the pre-World War II manufacturing experiences were failures in the sense that they never became sufficiently competitive to survive in world markets. Nor were their governments successful in protecting them from outside production. Given their non-competitive nature, potential investors were not attracted. Given the lack of investment, the available capital was too limited to develop large-scale plants, best-practice equipment, strong management teams, and external distribution networks.

After World War II, Amsden sees much more success in industrial development. One indicator is that, as late as 1965, Amsden's "rest" group accounted for 5 percent of world manufacturing output. However, by 1995, their share had increased to 20 percent. The strategies employed to achieve this improved share of technologically derived output is not unfamiliar to the annals of North–South political economy. It involved various combinations of developmental states recapturing domestic markets from foreign exporters (import substitution) and the recapture of domestic business (nationalization). The outcome, aided by investments in education, was a new elite of technical managers and professionals who could build on historical experience and opportunities in the post-war environment to manufacture and market commodities involving increasing production complexity and scale. In the process of doing so, two basic strategies gradually emerged. One stresses independence and involves "making" one's own technology through the creation of national infrastructure and firms. The other emphasizes integration and focuses on "buying" technology by developing strong relationships with foreign firms.

The main predictors on this fork in the development road appear to be the equality of income distribution within the country and the extent of discontinuities in direct foreign investment before and after World War II. The more equal the income distribution and the more discontinuous the investment pattern, the greater is the probability that a "rest" country opted for the independence approach. By and large, the independents appear to be faring better in terms of industrial development than the integrationists, even though both types encountered variable problems with overexpansion in the waning decades of the twentieth century.

Much of this development story is not novel, but Amsden does provide a very useful and comprehensive packaging of the material, along with the interesting innovation of stressing previous manufacturing experience as a partial predictor of success. The optimism is welcome too as long as it is geared to a theoretical interpretation. The question is whether the optimism is warranted. Table 4.8 summarizes a very limited test of Amsden's thesis. Our question is whether the states in our Southern sample that have

Table 4.8 Testing the Amsden thesis

Southern state	GDP/C 1985–2003	Percentage change	Manufacturing % of GDP 1985–2003	Percentage change
Argentina	9788–11436	16.8	29.6–23.9	−5.7
Bangladesh	1111–1672	50.5	14.1–15.8	1.7
Brazil	6594–7360	11.6	33.7–11.4	−22.3
Bulgaria	6073–7304	20.3	nd–18.8	NA
Chile	4924–9706	97.1	16.2–15.8	−0.4
China	1181–4726	300	34.9–39.3	4.4
Colombia	5121–6331	23.6	22–14.1	−7.9
Congo (Zaire)	1874–658	−64.9	9.9–4	−5.9
Egypt	2883–3731	29.4	13.5–18.9	5.4
Ethiopia	569–671	17.9	7.3–nd	NA
India	1385–2731	97.2	16.4–15.8	−0.6
Indonesia	1769–3175	79.5	16–24.7	8.7
Ivory Coast	1947–1395	−28.4	14.6–10.7	−3.9
Kenya	999–980	−1.9	11.7–13.6	1.9
Mexico	7772–8661	11.4	24–18	−6.0
Morocco	3050–3783	24.0	18.6–16.6	−2.0
Nigeria	739–992	34.2	8.7–4	−4.7
Pakistan	1295–1981	53.0	15.9–16.4	0.5
Peru	4884–4968	1.7	36.2–16.2	−20.0
Philippines	3547–4082	15.1	25.2–22.9	−2.3
Romania	6581*–6875	4.5	33.8–30	−3.8
Tanzania	528*–587	11.1	9.3–7.2	−2.1
Thailand	2988–7174	140.1	21.9–35.2	13.3
Turkey	4501–6398	42.1	17.7–13.3	−4.4
Venezuela	5732–4647	−18.9	18.9–9.1	−9.8

* 1990 start dates

improved their income levels between 1985 and 2003, have also expanded the proportion of GDP linked to manufacturing enterprise. Changes in GDP per capita are listed along with changes in the manufacturing proportion of GDP. The outcome is quite mixed.

The overall pattern is made more clear in Table 4.9. Support for Amsden's thesis should lie primarily along the left-to-right diagonal (both variables increasing or decreasing). Less than half of the samples are found on this diagonal. Equally interesting, the largest bloc of states is located in the upper-right-hand corner (increasing GDP per capita but decreasing manufacturing proportion). Small decreases in manufacturing proportion are less problematic since it is possible that manufacturing might expand only as fast or slightly slower than the expansion of GDP. Examples are Chile and India with very small decreases (less than 1 percent). If we remove the "noise" caused by very small changes in the GDP manufacturing proportion, operationalized arbitrarily at 2 percent change, we are left with four states in the upper-left-hand corner and nine states in the upper-right-hand corner of the table. Most critically, three of the four states in the upper-left corner are "rest" states, as are four of the nine in the upper-right corner.

Since Amsden does not predict that all of her "rest" states will adapt higher technology successfully, the outcomes in Tables 4.8 and 4.9 should not be viewed as limited tests of whether she or her interpretation is right or wrong. Rather, Tables 4.8 and 4.9 suggest that Amsden's "rest" are not categorically experiencing success in moving up the world economy's technological gradient by expanding their manufacturing base. Some are. Some are not. Hence, the greatest utility of Amsden's approach may be providing some more specific clues about how industrial technology diffuses (or does not diffuse very well), once innovated, over the past century. It does not appear that the "rest" states are uniformly poised to move into the North. Two of her "rest" states (Taiwan and South Korea) have already made the transition by our standards. A few more may do so in coming decades. But, to the extent that previous manufacturing experience is a prerequisite for

Table 4.9 Changes in GDP/C and manufacturing as % of GDP

	Increase in manufacturing as % of GDP	*Decrease in manufacturing as % of GDP*
Increase in GDP/C	Bangladesh, China, Egypt, Indonesia, Pakistan, Thailand	Argentina, Brazil, Chile, Colombia, India, Mexico, Morocco, Nigeria, Peru, Philippines, Romania, Tanzania, Turkey
Decrease in GDP/C	Kenya	Congo, Ivory Coast, Venezuela

Source: Based on the information reported in Table 4.8.

technological development, the outlook for the "remainder," some three-fourths of the rest of the world system's states, is bleak indeed.

If few prospects for escaping the South are evident for many of these states due to the unevenness of technological diffusion, there are still other processes that constrain the likelihood of economic development. One of these is the propensity for recurring debt crises to act as intermittent external shocks and new hurdles to be mastered. The debt crisis topic is fairly familiar. Less familiar is the systemic foundation that links Northern growth problems to Southern debt crises – a topic to which we turn in Chapter 6. Still another process is the tendency for globalization to proceed as unevenly as technological diffusion – and for many of the same reasons. Chapter 5 takes on this problem.

5 Limits on globalization processes

Hard on the heels of putting the Cold War bogeyman to rest, economic globalization has loomed, at least for some, as either the world system's next crisis carrier or savior. Globalization creates winners and losers and tramples on the distinctiveness of local cultures and sovereignties. For others, though, globalization compels closer economic interactions throughout the globe, carrying technological progress and economic integration to all parts of the planet and accelerating economic growth. Let the market do its job, and the poor will catch up to the rich via trade-driven growth. Global North and South – developed and less developed countries, respectively – cleavages will disintegrate, and the world will be a better and Pareto-optimal, happier place.

While we certainly accept the strong existence of globalization processes, our question in this chapter is whether globalization is truly a "global" process. In other words, is it experienced in the same intensity by the global North, or industrialized countries, and the global South, or the developing countries? There are a number of cleavages that have characterized the global North and South in the past and present. They appear to be growing more acute – rather than less so. Economic globalization especially should be expected to be less than universal if the pulsations and effects of global economic growth are less than universal across the global North and global South. Indeed, to the extent that economic growth and integration are monopolized by the North, the North–South cleavages are likely to be only accentuated – not attenuated – by economic globalization.

In this chapter, we comment first on globalization processes involving the movement of people and health improvements. Migration and demographic changes have had variable impacts on the North–South gap. Nineteenth-century migration contributed to convergence, while twentieth-century migration accentuated divergent tendencies. Divergent tendencies have also been fed by the spread of medicine and sanitation improvements that help people live longer in the global South.

Turning to economic globalization, we anticipate that, in the long run, economic globalization will be significantly more discernible in the global North than in the global South. By long run, we mean time periods encompassing more than 100 years. We remain consistent in our expectation that systemic leadership and long waves of economic growth are drivers of systemic phenomena such as economic globalization. However, we now develop a stronger historical case for the expectation that the impacts of economic growth stimuli should be felt unevenly due to stratified, path dependencies that are entrenched in the modern history of economic growth. Systemic leadership, long waves of economic growth, and economic globalization are expected to be mainly focused in the global North and much less so in the global South, thereby further accentuating the cleavages between North and South and intensifying global inequalities. We test this theory empirically, using statistical analysis.

Economic globalization is a multidimensional concept, involving international movements of goods and services (trade), physical capital (foreign direct investments), financial capital (portfolio investments), and, less so, labor (migration). We focus on trade since annual data on investment, especially in terms of specific Southern investments, are not available for the long time periods that we need to examine. But, how should one best measure trade globalization? We utilize series on exports measured in constant prices, since data on imports are also not available for our long period. Export globalization is defined conventionally by the ratio of export value to gross domestic product (GDP). In addition, the nature of our problem demands data that are highly comparable across time and space. The bulk of these data, therefore, again comes from Angus Maddison (1995).

The empirical analysis consists of two parts: visual and statistical. Visual analysis suggests that export openness in the global system is almost a monopoly of the North. Southern export openness over time does not resemble a completely flat line but, compared to the results for the North, there is considerably little variance demonstrated since 1870. We then utilize our theory in developing a statistical model for Northern export openness. The independent variables are world economic growth rate and level of systemic leadership. Control variables are Northern export openness inertia, level of Northern democracy, and level of Northern conflict (militarized disputes involving a Northern state at least on one side of a dyad, and civil wars that take place inside the North). The Southern model is specified similarly. Southern export openness is regressed on systemic leadership, world economic growth, Southern trade openness inertia, Southern democracy, Southern conflict, and a measure of Southern debt crisis.

In the empirical test, our variables capture much of the variance in Northern export openness. The effects of system leadership, world economic growth, Northern inertia, and Northern democracy on Northern export openness are found to be positive and statistically significant. The effect of Northern conflict on Northern openness is mixed. We then turn to the South. We find that world economic growth, and the levels of Southern democracy and Southern conflict, are not statistically significant determinants of Southern export openness. Systemic leadership has a weak positive effect on Southern export openness. Southern export openness is primarily determined by inertia (its value in the previous period) and Southern debt crises. The effect of Southern export inertia on Southern export openness is positive. The effect of debt crises on Southern export openness is negative in the short run, and positive in the longer run.

In sum, the trade export dimension of globalization is proceeding very unevenly across the planet. The implications for Southern development are not attractive. It is frequently argued that economic globalization, particularly international trade, is the engine of economic growth. While a small number of countries in Asia may have capitalized on the economic growth-promoting influence of focusing their national production on exports, the global South, as a whole, does not appear to be following this path. Thus, contrary to the market optimists, we should not expect that economic globalization will reduce the contemporary growing income gap between the rich global North and the much poorer global South. It seems more likely that economic globalization will expand the gap. How that will affect the argument that globalization will eliminate all national differences and local traditions is less clear. But, if globalization is less than global, one would think that the juggernaut interpretation of globalization as a destroyer of all local traditions and culture is also likely to be exaggerated.

Basic facts about migration and demographic tendencies

In Chapter 1, we suggested that there were 1.5 exceptions to our emphasis on the limits to technology diffusion. The 0.5 exception has already been noted in Chapter 1, but it is worth recapitulating in this section on comparative demographics. All nineteenth-century migration was not confined to movements from Europe to less populated areas in the Americas and Oceania, but the most significant movement for economic growth patterns definitely was centered on this distinctive flow captured in Table 5.1.[1]

This migration contributed to economic growth in two ways. The states in the left-hand column underwent a transition from agrarian to

Table 5.1 European transoceanic migration, 1846–1932

From:	To:
Great Britain/Ireland (18)	United States (34.2)
Italy (11.1)	Argentina/Uruguay (7.1)
Spain/Portugal (6.5)	Canada (5.2)
Austria-Hungary (5.2)	Brazil (4.4)
Germany (4.9)	Australia/New Zealand (3.5)
Poland/Russia (2.9)	Cuba (0.9)
Sweden/Norway (2.1)	

Source: Based on the discussion in Livi-Bacci (2007: 117). Numbers of migrants in millions in parentheses.

industrial economies, thereby creating a surplus labor problem (excess agrarian workers that could not be absorbed quickly by the ongoing industrialization) that could be exported to places that needed agrarian and industrial workers. The states in the right-hand column were the major beneficiaries, with the United States being the principal target of this labor/population transfer. In this respect, the migration globalization which took place predominately in the nineteenth century worked toward improving the connections of the states in the right-hand column to the world economy as well as expanding their labor and skill-set populations. While this transoceanic transfer phenomenon was restricted in focus, it did work toward economic convergence.

If the nineteenth century had a significant North to selected South orientation, the pattern had reversed itself in the twentieth century in which flows from the Old World to the New World were supplanted by flows from poor to rich areas. Table 5.2 describes the distribution of people associated with migration processes – a number that increased by nearly 100 million between 1960 and 2000. Of this 100 million migrant increase, about a fifth can be traced to people either moving to or within the less developed world. Roughly a fourth of the increase can be attributed to movement within the former Soviet Union – much of which involves Central Asians working in Russia. Half of the 1960–2000 migrant stock increase went to North America, Europe, and Oceania. One might say that, with the exception of the movement into Europe, this flow represents more of the same flow observed in the nineteenth century. But what has changed is that North America and Oceania are no longer underdeveloped, and most of their migrants have become increasingly non-European.

Table 5.3 does not indicate where the migrants are originating but demonstrates even more graphically how asymmetrical, and increasingly so, the contemporary migration process is. The more developed regions (North America, Europe, and Oceania), the North, are increasing their

Table 5.2 Estimated migrant stock (thousands)

Area	1960	1980	2000
World	75901	99783	174934
More developed regions	32085 (42.7)	47727 (47.8)	110291 (63)
Less developed regions	43816 (57.7)	52056 (52.2)	64643 (37)
North America	12513 (16.4)	18087 (18.1)	40844 (23.3)
Europe	14015 (18.5)	22163 (22.2)	32803 (18.8)
Oceania	2134 (2.8)	3755 (3.8)	5835 (3.3)
Former USSR	2942 (3.9)	3251 (3.3)	29469 (16.8)

Note: Percentages in parentheses.

Source: The stock data are taken from Livi-Bacci (2007: 192).

Table 5.3 Migrant stock per 100 population

Area	1960	1980	2000
World	2.5	2.3	2.9
More Developed Regions	3.4	4.2	8.7
Less Developed Regions	2.1	1.6	1.3
North America	6.1	7.1	12.9
Europe	3.3	4.6	6.4
Oceania	13.4	16.4	18.8
Former USSR	1.4	1.2	10.2
Africa	3.2	3	2
Asia	1.8	1.3	1.2
Latin America/Caribbean	2.8	1.7	1.1

Source: Based on Livi-Bacci (2007: 192).

migrant stock. The less developed regions (Africa, Asia, and Latin America/Caribbean), the South, are decreasing the proportion of migrants in their population. The two exceptions to this generalization are Asia, which encompasses both Northern and Southern states, and the former Soviet Union, which has been in and out of the Northern category but still attracts a large number of Central Asian laborers.

The more general development, however, is why we count migration globalization as a 0.5 exception. In the nineteenth century, migration globalization worked toward selected convergence. In the twentieth and presumably continuing into the twenty-first century, we have returned to a divergent effect, with more affluent areas benefiting from an inflow of skilled talent and labor from less affluent areas. Southern areas tend to lose some proportion of their best-trained population – the "brain drain" to the North. Less skilled migration to the North is often resisted but is not enough to substantially relieve overpopulation pressures – as occurred in the North a century before.

The full or almost full exception involves public health technology which has diffused fairly widely although there are still constraints on which diseases are the focus of the most research and who can afford medicine manufactured by drug multinationals. Even so, the outcome of the diffusion of public health technology has been a remarkable transformation in the prospects for surviving birth and extended lives in the South. At the same time, Northern affluence has led to a considerable reduction in fertility rates that is also reflected to a lesser extent in Southern fertility rates. So, while the technological diffusion dimension represents an exception, the implications contribute to higher GDP per capita in the North and lower relative incomes in the South.

Table 5.4 summarizes some of the fundamental information needed to assess these partially technological impacts. The most interesting aspect of

Table 5.4 Selected demographic indicators

	Death rate/1000		Fertility rate		Life expectancy at birth	
Area	1950–55	2000–05	1950–55	2000–05	1950–55	2000–05
More developed countries	19.7	8.9	4.99	2.65	46.5	64.7
Less developed countries	24.2	8.6	6.16	2.9	40.9	62.8

Source: United Nations World Population Prospects. The 2004 Revision (2005).

the numbers in the table is the implication of clear North–South convergence in terms of demographic indicators. In the last half of the twentieth century, the death rate per 1000 people was reduced by some 55 percent in the North and 64 percent in the South. On average, the gap between life expectancy in the North and South has been reduced to about 2 years. Fertility rates have been reduced tremendously in both the North and the South.

The averages in Table 5.4, however, suggest somewhat more (and more rapid) convergence than is actually the case because they focus on gains made in the second half of the twentieth century. Most especially, even though fertility rates have declined in the South, they have declined unevenly and have not declined fast enough to avoid some anticipated and considerable population increases in the twenty-first century. Table 5.5 outlines the unevenness for the immediate future. In this century, Northern population is expected to decline by a factor of about 6 percent while Southern population will increase some 81 percent. These projections are based on assumptions about migration, fertility, mortality, and momentum shown in the right-hand side of Table 5.5. The North benefits from positive migration, low mortality, and below-replacement fertility rates. The Southern population growth is predicated largely on above-replacement-level fertility, lower mortality rates, and momentum. Thus, despite technological diffusion on public health and birth control practices, Southern population growth, while slowing, will continue to pose major problems for economic growth throughout the twenty-first century.

The lower two-thirds of Table 5.5 break these numbers down by region, and there is a very striking relationship between economic growth and projected population. The wealthiest regions, by and large, are expected to experience the least growth. The poorest regions are expected to have the most population growth. We may anticipate, therefore, that tendencies toward divergence will be strongest in those areas that are already most divergent. Population growth and the factors that drive it can be expected as a consequence to continue to reinforce the North–South gap through at least 2100.

Table 5.5 2100 Projected population (billions) and factor multipliers

	Population		Multiplier					
	2000	2100	Migration	Fertility	Mortality	Momentum	Product
World	6.07	9.96	1	1.09	1.15	1.31	1.64
North	1.18	1.11	1.02	0.84	1.10	1	0.94
South	4.89	8.86	1	1.13	1.15	1.39	1.81
Europe	0.73	0.61	1.01	0.78	1.12	0.96	0.84
North America	0.31	0.37	1.03	0.99	1.08	1.11	1.22
East Asia	2.04	2.70	1	0.94	1.14	1.25	1.32
Latin America/Caribbean	0.52	0.88	0.99	1.04	1.14	1.45	1.70
South Asia	1.48	2.69	1	1.10	1.15	1.44	1.82
Middle East/North Africa	0.33	0.73	1	1.28	1.14	1.50	2.20
Sub-Saharan Africa	0.67	1.98	1	1.64	1.21	1.50	2.97

Source: Based on Bongaarts and Bulatao (2000).

While more recent migration and demographic trends have contributed, for the most part, to North–South divergence, it still leaves open-ended the question of economic globalization as manifested in trade. That is, it is not inconceivable that migration and demography might work one way and trade another. On the other hand, the migration data are suggestive. In the nineteenth century, European migration to North America and Australia/New Zealand led to increased European trade with these "new" worlds. Southern migration to Europe and North America in the twentieth century is a rather strong hint of economic growth asymmetries that are apt to be reflected in trade patterns as well. While we have good reasons to anticipate structural inequality to be manifested in trade, arguably the most central manifestation of globalization, it remains an open empirical question that deserves closer scrutiny.

Basic expectations about export globalization

In this section, we combine leadership long cycle principles with some selected observations made by economic historians about what might be called the nineteenth- and twentieth-century channels of world economic growth and trade. We retain the assertion of the leadership long cycle perspective that systemic leadership and the long waves of discontinuous economic growth, for which system leaders are primarily responsible, drive long-term fluctuations in world economic activity. Economic innovation in the lead economy of the system leader creates technological spurts that drive long waves of economic growth and fund systemic leadership foundations and capabilities. Yet, economic growth and trade never operate on a level playing field. Some parts of the world economy are always favored over other parts, and we need to build this fact of life into our models of growth and trade.

If we continue with the assertions that technological innovation is critical to modern economic growth, discontinuous in time, and initially concentrated in space, we find, according to leadership long cycle theory, that Britain in the nineteenth century and the United States in the twentieth century have been the most favored locations in the world economy and the lead economies of the past two centuries. But, what about the rest of the world? Is it reasonable to argue that all other parts of the world economy had equal chances to either produce their own leader or to catch up to the technological leaders? We think not.

Economic globalization is an old process of increased interaction and integration between and among populations located initially within Afro-Eurasia and, much later, incorporating the Americas and Australia. Interaction and integration do not proceed inexorably or continuously. Instead, interaction and integration, along with technological innovation and economic growth, pulsate or come in accelerated spurts. However, if the world economy is composed of zones with much different prospects for generating economic growth and trade, it is reasonable to expect that (a) contemporary globalization will proceed unevenly and that (b) Northern participation in contemporary globalization processes should outpace Southern participation. Technological development, led by the world system's lead economy, with implications for the emergence of new products, new ways of production, and faster, less expensive transportation modes, should be more intensely registered within the North than within the South. Northern economies are better prepared to accommodate successive changes in best practices. They are also more inclined to both create products for export that reflect their advanced technology and to trade with other similar advanced economies that can afford and absorb their exports. The contemporary globalization of trade should thus proceed with a marked intra-Northern bias, driven by waves of economic growth and leadership generated by the system leader.

We think the intra-Northern bias is likely to be quite strong. Contemporary trade globalization should be characterized by two zones – one of strong participation and another of weak participation. Still, this bizonal structure is very much an empirical question. Does the available evidence support our expectations? In addition, we also need to assess empirically the extent to which lead economies, global reach capabilities, and long waves of economic growth stimulate waves of globalization.

Empirical results

We first inspect plots of our variables. To improve our ability to visually read the noisy raw data, we average the data over decades. Figure 5.1 presents a decadal look at Northern and Southern openness.[2] From 1870 to the early 1920s, the two series did not change much. Since then, Northern openness declined up to the 1940s, and has risen since then. In the same period, the Southern series continued to hover around openness ratios of about 4–5 percent. As in earlier chapters, it is also possible to discern long waves in the series. The first wave in Northern openness peaks in the 1880s, and the second, or an extension of the first, in the 1920s. A third wave rides a rising trend, beginning in the mid-1940s and peaking in the 1960s. The Southern openness waves are considerably less pronounced than the Northern openness waves. The first wave peaks in the 1910s, the second in the 1940s, and the third in the 1970s. The timing of the openness waves, particularly the Northern series, generally correspond to the long wave-chronology discussed in the leadership long cycle studies, as shown in Figure 5.2.

Figure 5.2 presents the decade averages for systemic leadership and world economic growth. Forty-fifty-year "long waves" are observable for world economic growth. World economic growth peaks are evident in the 1880s, 1920s, and 1960s.[3] Systemic leadership peaks are evident in the 1880s and in the 1950s. The 1950s peak is expected by the leadership long cycle perspective. The 1880s peak for the British leadership is not the

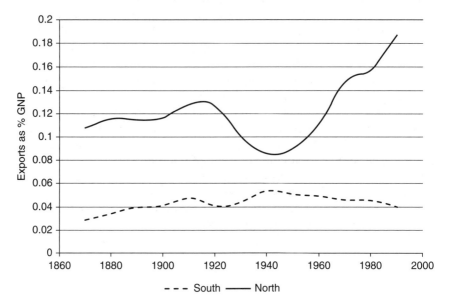

Figure 5.1 Decade-averaged trade openness.

largest one in the nineteenth century. A larger peak in the British leadership data occurred shortly after the Napoleonic Wars (Thompson, 1988), with a similar timing to the US case after World War II. Thanks to the victory in war, exhaustion of opponents, war-induced military edge, and the economic platform provided by the system's leading economy, systemic leadership is strongest immediately after the conclusion of the global war that essentially installs leaders in a trial by combat.

Figures 5.1 and 5.2 suggest that, on average, Northern openness increases when world economic growth and systemic leadership are high, and vice versa. On the other hand, the correspondence between the rise and fall in Southern openness and the two systemic variables is much less evident. In general, it seems that the ups and downs in leadership and world economic growth do not have much effect on Southern openness, which continues to hover around 4–5 percent throughout the sample. These observations generally support our theoretical interpretation, which expects two globalization dynamics, and still another North–South cleavage. Yet, these figures do not pinpoint how our variables relate to each other statistically. To discern these effects, we turn to the regression analyses. These analyses are conducted using the raw, original data (not the averaged data presented in Figures 5.1 and 5.2).

The grid search looking for the lag lengths that fit the data best suggests using the first and second lags for world economic growth, the current value for systemic leadership, and the first lag for Northern democracy

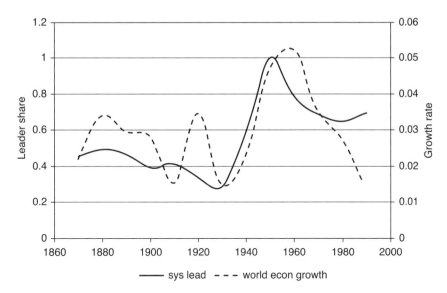

Figure 5.2 Decade-averaged systemic leadership and world economic growth.

and Northern conflict. Table 5.6 presents the estimation results for the North.[4] Columns 1 and 2 present results for the full, 1870–1992 sample. The model's goodness of fit, based on the R-square measure, is 0.96, which is high. The effect of each of the five right-hand-side variables, except Northern conflict, on the level of Northern openness is statistically significant. This result is consistent with the interpretation according to which intense conflict in the North, as witnessed in two World Wars, tends to be offset by increased, war-related production by Maddison's "Western offshoots" that were distant from the combat zones. The effect of Northern openness inertia on Northern openness is positive, the effect of Northern democracy is positive, the effect of world economic growth is positive, and the effect of systemic leadership on Northern openness is also positive. All of these results, including the one for Northern conflict, conform to our theoretical expectations.

In Columns 3–6 of Table 5.6, we present estimation results from the 1870–1945 and 1919–92 periods, as called for in our research design. The R-square in the 1870–1945 period is 0.92, and in the 1919–92 period it is 0.96, both of which continue to be high. The signs and significance of all the five variables in the two additional samples conform with the results in the full sample. The statistical results presented from the full sample then are robust.

Table 5.7 presents the estimation results for the South. Columns 1–2 again present results for the full, 1870–1992 sample. The model's goodness

Table 5.6 Estimation results for the North

Variables	Coefficients 1870–1992	Sums of coefficients 1870–1992	Coefficients 1870–1945	Sums of coefficients 1870–1945	Coefficients 1919–92	Sums of coefficients 1919–92
Northern openness$_{t-1}$	1.0081***		0.5089***		1.0164***	
Northern democracy$_{t-1}$	0.0005*		0.0031***		0.0006**	
Northern conflict$_{t-1}$	0.0095		0.0271**		0.0447	
World Economic Growth$_{t-1}$	0.0071	0.0355***	0.0005	0.0302*	-0.0069	0.0314**
World economic growth$_{t-2}$	0.0284**		0.0297*		0.0383**	
Systemic leadership$_t$	0.0050***		0.0199***		0.0059**	

Note: *** denotes statistical significance at 1 percent level; ** at 5 percent; and * at 10 percent.

of fit, based on the R-square measure, is 0.82, which is also fairly high. The effects of Southern openness inertia and Southern debt defaults are statistically significant. The sign of the effect of Southern openness inertia on Southern openness is positive, as expected. The effect of Southern debt default on Southern openness is negative in the short run, and positive in the longer run – also as expected. None of the effects of the other variables in the model are statistically significant. In particular, Southern openness does not appear to be responding to changes in world economic growth and systemic leadership.

In Columns 3–6 of Table 5.7, we report results for the 1870–1945 and 1919–92 periods. The R-square in the 1870–1945 period is 0.84, and in the 1919–92 period, it is 0.7, both of which are strong, albeit weaker than the corresponding results for the North. The signs and significance levels in the 1870–1945 sample are almost identical to those reported for the full sample. Unlike the full sample, however, the effect of world economic growth is significant, as in the North, suggesting that large changes in growth (see Figure 5.2) do affect Southern trade openness. The effect of debt default on Southern openness resembles the one in the full period, but it is not significant at conventional levels.[5]

The results in the 1919–92 period resemble the results from the full sample, except that now the positive effect of systemic leadership is statistically significant, as in the North. This result suggests that large changes in leadership, which characterize this period, are able to affect Southern economic openness. In sum, as in the North, the results presented from the full sample for the South are robust. Yet, we come away from the Southern analysis with the strong impression that systemic influences are less easy to generalize about than in the North.

Finally, another possible threat to the validity of our analysis is our design decision to focus on series that end in 1992. Is it possible that we are missing a Southern trade globalization explosion that is discernible empirically only after 1992? To check this possibility, we constructed shorter Southern and Northern aggregated exports/GDP series for the 1983–2003 period.[6] The outcome is shown in Figure 5.3. The Southern exports/GDP ratio is 0.058 in 1983 and remains more or less at the same level a decade later in 1992 (0.059). By 2003, however, the trade openness ratio had increased to 0.094 – something on the order of a 62 percent increase between 1983 and 2003. Thus, it may seem that ending an analysis in 1992 biases the outcome somewhat by missing some significant post-1992 activity.[7]

Lest we be too hasty to criticize our own research design, however, the Southern outcome needs to be compared to the Northern outcome. In 1983, the Northern aggregated ratio stood at 0.162. By 2002, the Northern exports/GDP ratio had expanded to 0.267. Thus, in terms of percentage increases, the Southern and Northern series increase roughly on the same order: 62 percent for the South and 65 percent for the North.

Table 5.7 Estimation results for the South

Variables	Coefficients 1870–1992	Sums of coefficients 1870–1992	Coefficients 1870–1945	Sums of coefficients 1870–1945	Coefficients 1919–92	Sums of coefficients 1919–92
Southern openness$_{t-1}$	0.8397***		0.8239***		0.6729***	
Southern democracy$_{t-1}$	0.00002		0.00002		-0.0004	
Southern conflict$_{t-1}$	0.02936		0.0223		0.0443	
World economic growth$_{t-1}$	-0.0069	-0.0107	0.0143*	0.0253**	-0.0057	-0.0099
World economic growth$_{t-2}$	-0.0038		0.0011		-0.0042	
Systemic leadership$_t$	0.0004		-0.0064		0.0052*	
Debt default$_{t-1}$	-0.0057**	-0.0013	-0.0057	-0.0012	-0.0290**	0.0032
Debt default$_{t-2}$	0.0044**		0.0045		0.0322**	

Note: *** denotes statistical significance at 1 percent level; ** at 5 percent; and * at 10 percent.

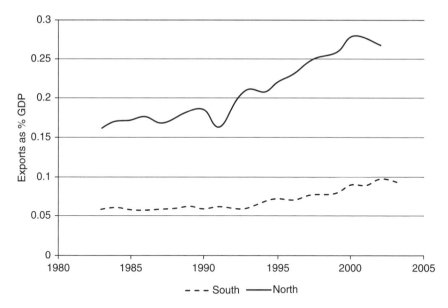

Figure 5.3 Updating the openness gap.

However, the gap between the Southern and Northern positions in 1983 is 0.104. By 2003, this gap had expanded to 0.173 – a roughly 66 percent increase in the size of the North–South trade globalization gap. So, it turns out that stopping our data analysis in 1992 is not as much of a threat to the validity of the analysis as it might otherwise appear. If our data series extended from 1870 into the early 2000s, as opposed to 1992, we probably would have found even stronger evidence for a widening North–South trade globalization gap.

Conclusions

This chapter looks at the extent of economic globalization, measured in terms of trade openness, in the global North and South over a long period of time. Our theoretical perspective expects that world economic growth and systemic leadership will promote Northern economic openness but will have a much smaller effect on the Southern export openness. Our empirical analysis and statistical modeling supports our theory. The results are found to be robust across sub-periods over the past century and a third.

Economic globalization is an old process of increasing pre-existing levels of integration between different units and zones of economic activity. Simply because we refer to it as *global*ization does not make it so.

Or, alternatively, if we make globalization synonymous with increasing economic integration and interaction somewhere, we cannot assume that all actors are equally affected. We are not the first authors to suggest that contemporary globalization is an uneven process.[8] We may be the first to identify, theoretically and empirically, globalization drivers that appear to work more strongly in the North than they do in the South.

Because trade globalization works more strongly in the North than it does in the South, we should expect it to make the gap between North and South worse rather than better. A global North that is more integrated to the world economy should experience higher levels of economic development over time than a global South that is less integrated to the world economy. The gap between North and South standard of living, then, is expected to grow. North–South economic convergence, which is predicted by neoclassical economic growth theory, is not expected to occur from our theoretical perspective any time soon, nor do our empirical results suggest that it occurs in the real world.

While there will always be a few national exceptions to these generalizations, it follows that one cannot rely exclusively on market processes to even out the economic growth playing field. That field is already highly stratified into zones in which the chances for growth and trade have been and continue to be, with some major exceptions, grossly unequal. Economic globalization does not appear to be breaking down these historical stratifications. Rather, it is economic globalization that tends to be channeled by these past grooves of strong and weak growth. The national units that are already integrated to the world economy become more integrated to the world economy; the less well-connected often stay that way. So far, only a very small number of states have managed to break out of the low-growth ruts of the world system. The implications of this grim outcome for world political stability are stark. To the extent that poverty and underdevelopment promote interstate and intrastate violence and terrorism, we may expect to see more of these phenomena in the future, not less.[9]

One of the reasons few states break out of the South is due to the intermittent nature of debt crises. It is not particularly controversial to note that these debt crises have occurred before, or that they handicap the economies in which they take place. Less accepted is the idea that the crises occur fairly regularly and are a structural characteristic of a South that is dependent on the North for capital and demand for its products. Put most simply, Southern debt crises are a function of a variety of factors which include, most prominently, Northern growth slow downs. We turn to this topic in the next chapter.

6 Southern debt crises

Paul Krugman (1995) writes that one of our contemporary conceits is that we think globalization is something novel and unique to our present time. A good case in point is the question of intermittent debt crises that usually are most evident in lesser developed countries (LDCs), or the South. Southern debt crises – situations where Southern countries default on their interest and/or principle payments to Northern lenders, are conventionally understood as isolated policy problems that occur on occasion.[1] At the same time, these crises have recurred periodically since the early nineteenth century and before (Aggarwal, 1996; Eichengreen and Fishlow, 1998; Fishlow, 1989; Marx, Echague, and Sanleris, 2006; Suter, 1992; Tomz, 2007). Aggarwal (1996), for example, captures the periodicity in debt episodes summarized in Table 6.1, and the identity of the states experiencing debt problems clearly underlines their Southern tendencies. Studies often attribute these Southern debt problems to Northern excessive lending zeal and Southern corruption and mismanagement. We do not dispute that these factors play a role in Southern debt crises, but we believe that they are not the root of the problem.

We extend the leadership long cycle approach to argue that Southern debt problems are associated with long waves of economic growth and innovation. In a nutshell, radical innovation in the North periodically facilitates Northern prosperity. This prosperity increases the demand for Southern resources and exports. To meet this demand, Southern countries borrow from the North, which, thanks to the prosperity, has more capital available for investment than is usually the case. As a consequence, Northern bankers are looking for investment projects, and a number of Southern activities appear promising. Eventually, Northern prosperity and the demand for Southern products decline, Southerners become less able to meet payments on their debts. Historically, the North has abandoned the South in terms of new loans until the next growth upswing. From a globalization perspective, debt crises mean that the South cycles in and out of greater integration with the North, depending on Northern prosperity.

Major Northern countries and particularly the system's leader have become more proactive in attempting to ameliorate major Southern

Table 6.1 Aggarwal's debt epoch characteristics

Epoch	Time	Characteristics
1	1820s–60s	1820s – newly independent Latin American states seeking assistance with independence war costs 1830s – American states, Spain, Portugal, Greece, Russia, Turkey Primarily bond flotations in London and Paris financial markets with defaults beginning after 1825, with no uniform pattern in rescheduling
2	1865–1914	Latin America, Egypt, Turkey with states borrowing especially for infrastructural development (i.e., railroads) Predominantly London bond market with defaults beginning in 1872–73, lending increasing in mid-1880s with second round of defaults in early 1890s with no uniform pattern in rescheduling
3	1920s–60s	Europe, Latin America with lending expanding rapidly in 1920s Primarily US bond market with defaults occurring in the 1930s, with no uniform pattern in rescheduling
4	1970s–90s	Developing countries in general Primarily bank loans, often from US banks, with defaults beginning in early 1980s after two oil price shocks, with fairly uniform pattern in rescheduling involving write-downs, extended payment periods, and new loans

Source: Extracted from Aggarwal (1996: 19–41).

debt crises. Yet, systematic leadership is hardly exogenous. Many studies demonstrate that long waves of economic growth and innovation are associated with the level of leadership. Historically, radical innovations have occurred in temporal spurts, centered at first in one country and then diffusing to others.

We argue that systemic leadership also affects Southern debt crises. Turning to a third factor, the North has been the main market for Southern exports and the main source of Southern capital. Northern conflict interferes with Northern market demand and the availability of capital. Thus, it is expected to affect Southern debt problems, but the sign of this effect is driven by competing considerations discussed later. We also contend that the combined operation of world economic growth, systemic leadership, and Northern conflict has influenced the share of Southern countries in the international system experiencing debt problems. Variations on this argument have been made in the literature, but have yet to be fully tested statistically. We test this thesis using yearly data from 1870 to 1989 and find in favor of our approach; the extent of Southern debt problems declines with systemic leadership and world economic growth, and increases with Northern conflict.

More conventional views of debt shocks

Scholars note that when global debt crises occur, the following behaviors tend to emerge: (1) the crisis onset is preceded by optimism about Southern growth prospects; (2) the lending of Northern capital to the South expands; (3) an ensemble of unexpected economic shocks co-occur; (4) Southern terms of trade deteriorate; (5) Southern inflationary pressures increase; (6) interest rates and protectionism rise; (7) the supply of Northern capital to the South abruptly ends; (8) debt settlement negotiations drag on without solving the problem; and (9) debt settlement considerations fade away as the North returns to a period of prosperity (for instance, Aggarwal, 1989; Cardoso and Dornbusch, 1989; Eichengreen and Lindert, 1989; Lindert, 1989).

Less clear is why these crises recur. Four answers are provided. The first three reflect mainstream interpretations and emphasize lending booms and lender excesses (Aggarwal, 1989; Darity and Horn, 1988; Devlin, 1989; Stalling, 1987), idiosyncratic shocks in the world economy (Cardoso and Dornbusch, 1989; Jorgensen and Sachs, 1989; Little, Cooper, Corden and Rajapatirana, 1993; Vos, 1994), and Southern mismanagement (Balassa, Kuczynski and Simonsen, 1986; Dornbusch, 1993). These three arguments are not necessarily mutually exclusive. Analysts tend to combine them with variable emphases on which factor is most responsible. A fourth argument asserts that Southern debt crises are one of the systematic consequences of Northern economic depression and disorder, as opposed to a problem triggered by random shocks and occasional loan frenzies (Suter, 1992). Thus, the analytical question can be reduced to whether the typically observed triggers of Southern debt crises are secondary manifestations of deeper structural processes at work.

Debtor corruption and mismanagement can hardly account for the tendency for major debt crises to cluster across time. Southern debtor policies can certainly aggravate the situation, but if extensive debt problems typically do not emerge in isolation or in prosperous times, there are limitations on the extent to which one can place the blame on the misdeeds of the borrowers. The recurrence of debt crises suggests some common agency emanating from the external environment. Eichengreen and Lindert (1989) support this idea when they observe that each past lending wave combined with some political–economic shock to create a debt crisis.

Implicit to this idea is the argument that debt crises are the outcome of Northern lending booms that turn sour when the economy deteriorates. It is not so much that the South borrows too much, although that is part of the puzzle. The point is that, in lending booms, Northern banks promote lending to the South and display little concern about past debt problems (Eichengreen and Lindert, 1989). Northern optimism turns to pessimism when the Northern and Southern growth prospects no longer seem attractive. Southern exports then decline because Northern demand for Southern commodities declines. A reduction in Southern exports translates into an increased inability to service their loans. Financial alarm bells go off when Northern stock values plummet and/or when perceptions of Southern debt problems leading to Northern bank collapses emerge (Marichal, 1989). The lending boom rapidly turns to bust as lenders lose confidence. A number of Southern states then either default on their loans or seek loan rescheduling. Negotiations between lenders and borrowers ensue, often complicated by lender-induced pressure from creditor governments (e.g., economic intervention, gunboat diplomacy, invasion). The net outcome has been a protracted period of Southern economic decline.

There is a consensus on this outline. But why do lending booms occur in the first place? Two clues in the literature provide a starting point for our answer. Eichengreen (2003: 14–15) argues that the improving growth prospects are conducive settings for loan booms. Are the "random" shocks that turn booms to busts any less nonrandom? A systemic interpretation suggests that both the origins of the lending optimism and lending pessimism require explanation, and that the seemingly random shocks are linked to structural rhythms. Another clue is that the bulk of international lending since the 1800s has come from Britain in the nineteenth century, and the United States in the twentieth century (Lipson, 1989). These countries also are often identified as the system leaders or hegemons, in their respective periods. The economic growth and systemic leadership clues link, albeit differently, to Southern debt crises.

Factors such as oil shocks (as in the 1970s and early 1980s), interest rate increases, terms of trade shifts, and local recessions can be viewed as idiosyncratic and exogenous. But, they also can be seen as manifestations of structural changes in the world political economy. For instance, the oil shocks of the 1970s and early 1980s and the ensuing debt crisis overlap with a period of decline in the extent of political–economic systemic leadership (on the part of the United States). The timing of world economic depressions are also related to leadership decline and major debt crises – as in the 1870/1880s, the 1930s, and the 1970s/1980s. Several analysts, for instance, have observed that Northern loan booms are more likely in periods of world economic expansion and that Southern debt problems emerge in periods of contraction (for instance, Kowalewski, 1989; Marichal, 1989; Pettis, 2001; Suter, 1992). Other systemic factors that discourage world prosperity also can be expected to affect Southern access to Northern capital. One such factor is intensive major power/Northern conflict. Under some circumstances, this conflict may increase Northern expansion into the South as part of intra-Northern competitions over control of Southern raw materials. The absence of leadership that may be able to suppress Northern conflict and expansion into the South and Southern actions challenging the existing global income distribution, as well as stimulate world economic growth, is another such factor.[2]

The systemic argument takes the mainstream understanding of debt crises one step further. Rather than beginning with the advent of loan booms, it portrays loan booms as a product of economic expansion. Rather than focusing on "random" shocks, it sees the shocks as symptomatic of a world economy shifting from an expansionary phase to a contracting one, or vice versa. While mainstream versions may note some apparent relationship between debt crises and Northern decline, this dimension is stressed by systemic interpretations as the prime mover for causing major debt problems. Southern debt crises are not simply intermittent policy problems; they accompany troughs in world economic growth.

Two recent arguments are particularly close to ours. Pettis (2001) argues that, historically, exogenous shocks expand Northern financial liquidity. Liquidity expansion increases Northern investment in new technologies and increased Northern lending to the South. Eventually, the excess liquidity is reversed due to shocks, money flows to the South decline, the Southern economies decline, and debt defaults rise. Pettis observes two types of defaults. One type involves a severe Northern liquidity contraction leading to global crises (1820s, 1870s, 1930s, 1980s). A second type involves localized crises. Pettis, however, does not link global debt crises to long waves of growth, long cycles of leadership, and Northern conflict, all of which are stressed here. Suter (1992) argues that a technological product cycle begins with the introduction of Northern innovations. As the innovations mature, the North expands trade with the South. When production in the South becomes profitable, capital flows there. Northern economy stagnation then leads to South decline, and Southern default increases. Suter notes that systemic leadership can ameliorate debt defaults but does not integrate it into his model.

While we are sympathetic to the systemic interpretation, and think it is compatible with the mainstream depiction, systemic analysts have yet to demonstrate fully the empirical power of the argument. Nor do we know whether Northern conflict or systemic leadership make any significant difference. Empirical analysis, in turn, needs to be couched within a theory that brings together the interdependencies among Northern conflict, world economic growth, and systemic leadership.

One main feature of this process is its discontinuous nature. Economic growth and radical innovations are manifested as long waves that decay when the innovational novelties lose their ability to accelerate growth. Reuveny and Thompson (1999) show that the waves of radical innovation drive systemic leadership, and Reuveny and Thompson (2001) show that they drive world economic growth. We push this interpretation one step further by arguing that Southern debt crises are affected by the level of political–economic systemic leadership, world economic growth, the level of conflict in the North, and also are subject to inertia.

Systemic leadership: According to the leadership long cycle approach, radical technological innovations are temporally and spatially concentrated in a lead economy. The profits from monopolizing the innovation become the platform for this country attaining political–economic systemic leadership. A strong system leader sets the rules of the global political–economic game, and serves as the lender of last resort to Southern countries and their primary source of loans. Strong systemic leadership also promotes world economic growth by being the source of technological innovation and by promoting international order (Chase-Dunn, 1989; Gilpin, 1987; Maddison, 1995; Reuveny and Thompson, 2001). The good times promote a rise in Northern demand for Southern exports, raising Southern revenues and, again, reducing the extent of Southern debt problems. Based on both arguments, we expect that the effect of systematic leadership on Southern debt problems will be negative.

World economic growth: Southern debt is often owed in foreign currency. The South obtains foreign currency by exports, particularly to the North (whose economies represent the lion's share of the world economy). In times of prosperity, demand for Southern exports expands. To serve the increasing demand, the South borrows money from the North. World economic stagnation reduces demand for Southern exports. As Southern exports fall, Southern foreign revenues fall, and the South becomes less able to serve its debt. Hence, the effect of world economic growth on Southern debt problems is expected to be negative.

Northern conflict: Northern conflict is expected to affect Southern debt problems because the North is the chief market for Southern goods and the main source of its capital. However, the effect of Northern conflict on Southern debt problems exhibits competing effects. On one hand, Northern conflict may encourage a Northern preoccupation with its own problems, thereby reducing contact with the South. If Southern exports to the North decline, Southern foreign revenue would decline and Southern debt problems would rise. Second, Northern conflict may promote Northern military intervention in the South, creating further economic problems in the South. Northern countries also may curb links with Southern countries aligned with Northern rivals, reducing overall Southern exports. Third, Northern conflict could reduce world economic growth, increasing further Southern debt problems. On the other hand, greater conflict in the North may imply that the North requires more raw material, resources, and goods from the South. Southern exports then would increase and Southern foreign revenues would rise. Since Northern rivals may seek Southern allies, the South also may be able to manipulate Northern conflict to its own advantage by obtaining more attention and aid than might otherwise have been the case.

Debt problems inertia: One of the continuities in Southern debt problems has been the lack of success in developing quick remedies. Debt problems are more prevalent among LDCs, where a dual economy is more pronounced, the economy is more dependent on natural resources, and the size of foreign reserves is small. Southern corruption and mismanagement can also aggravate debt problems. And once foreign sources of capital are cut, economic development and future debt servicing becomes even more problematic. All this means that Southern debt problems exhibit inertia over time.

Empirical results

To improve our ability to visually read our times series, Figure 6.1 presents the data for systemic leadership, world economic growth and Northern conflict averaged over decades.[3] In addition to the long waves for world economic growth and systemic leadership observed in the previous chapter, Northern/major power conflict peaks are noticeable in the 1910s and 1940s and smaller peaks also are noticeable in the 1880s and 1960s.

Figure 6.2 presents the level of Southern debt problems, averaged over 5-year periods. Long waves with a length of approximately 40 years or so also are discernible in Figure 6.2. Southern debt problem peaks can be detected in the 1880s, the 1910s, the 1940s, and in the 1980s.

Figures 6.1 and 6.2 suggest that Southern debt problems increase when world economic growth and systemic leadership decline. The effect of world

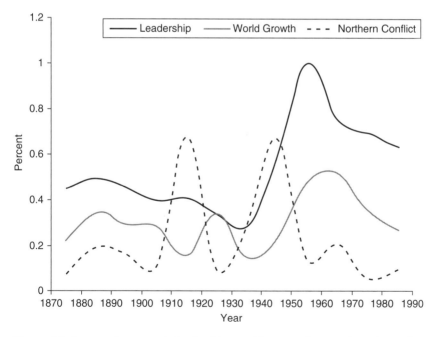

Figure 6.1 Averaged systematic leadership, world economic growth, and Northern conflict.

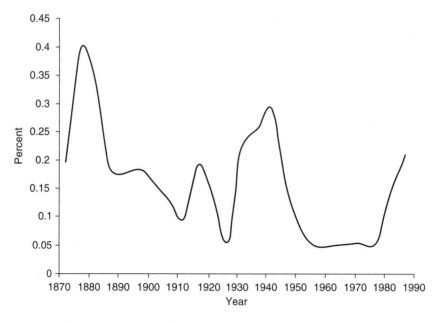

Figure 6.2 Five-year-averaged Southern debt problems.

economic growth on Southern debt default seems a bit less pronounced after 1945, particularly in the 1950s–70s period. The effect of Northern conflict is less clear from these plots. These visual readings of the data generally support our theoretical interpretation. However, Figures 6.1 and 6.2, while illuminating, cannot pinpoint how our variables relate to each other statistically in a multivariate setting. To discern particular effects, we turn to the regression analyses of the raw, non-averaged data.

Table 6.2 presents the estimation results from the 1870–1989 period.[4] The model's goodness of fit, based on R-squares, is 0.92. The effect of each of the four variables on the level of Southern debt problems is found to be statistically significant, and the accompanying signs conform to our theoretical expectations, although in the case of Northern conflict, the expectations were decidedly mixed. Previous Southern debt problems and Northern/major power conflict significantly encourage current Southern debt problems. Systemic leadership and world economic growth discourage Southern debt problems. In all, these results illustrate that periodic Southern debt problems, thus, are genuinely systemic phenomena.

Table 6.3 provides the results from the sub-sample sensitivity analysis. In all the three periods, the model's goodness of fit based on R-squares is high: 0.89 in the 1870–1945 period, 0.92 in the 1946–89 period, and 0.94 in the 1960–89 period. Further, in all the three periods, the effect of lagged Southern debt on current Southern debt is statistically significant

Table 6.2 Debt estimation results for 1870–1989

Variable	Coefficient	Sums of lags
Southern debt$_{t-1}$	0.302***	
Systemic leadership$_{t-1}$	–0.109***	
Northern conflict$_t$	0.295**	
World economic growth$_{t-1}$	–0.257***	–0.874**
World economic growth$_{t-2}$	–0.277***	
World economic growth$_{t-3}$	–0.144**	
World economic growth$_{t-4}$	–0.197***	

Note: *** denotes statistical significance at 1 percent level; ** at 5 percent; and * at 10 percent.

and positive. The effect of systemic leadership is consistently negative. The effect is statistically insignificant in periods of weaker leadership (1870–1945 and 1960–89), as could be expected (as these are periods with relatively weaker systemic leadership).

The negative signs associated with the effects of world economic growth on Southern debt problems also are consistently observed as anticipated. In the 1946–89 period, the signs are correctly anticipated, but the effects are not significant. This outcome may be explained as follows. When we begin the phase in 1946, the debt cycle is swinging down from a peak in the 1930s. In the 1950s–70s, the level of Southern debt problems is low and does not change much. Economic growth improves after 1946. The period also is one of relatively strong systemic leadership. Both of these effects help to explain the relatively low level of debt problems. In contrast, the negative effect of economic growth in the 1960–89 period is found to be significant because it is capturing a period in which economic growth slows, and Southern debt problems climb. The effect of systemic leadership in this period, while negative, is weaker, as leadership in this period is generally declining relative to its level in the 1950s.

The effect of Northern/major power conflict on the level of Southern debt problems is shown by Table 6.3 to be largely confined to the pre-1945 era. After 1945, the absence of intensive conflict along the lines of global warfare appears to drive the non-significant effect of Northern/major powers discord on the level of Southern debt problems.

Finally, we conduct an additional sensitivity analysis to evaluate whether the results are robust in the presence of four new variables, which are not part of our theory, but are called for by our research design: Southern conflict, North–South conflict, a dummy variable set to 1 in 1956 and 0 otherwise, and a dummy variable set to 1 in 1986 and 0 otherwise. The results from this sensitivity analysis are presented in Table 6.4. The results in Table 6.4 are highly consistent with the primary results presented in Table 6.2, in terms of signs, sizes, and levels of significance of effects.

Table 6.3 Debt estimation results for 1870–1945, 1946–89, and 1960–89

Variable	1870–1945		1946–89		1960–89	
	Coefficient	Sums	Coefficient	Sums	Coefficient	Sums
Southern debt$_{t-1}$	0.240**		0.908***		0.941***	
Systemic leadership$_{t-1}$	−0.062		−0.057***		−0.019	
Northern conflict$_{t-1}$	0.317***		0.195		0.227	
World economic growth$_{t-1}$	−0.307***	−1.272***	−0.018	−0.121	−0.506**	−0.846**
World economic growth$_{t-2}$	−0.411***		−0.008		−0.039	
World economic growth$_{t-3}$	−0.277**		−0.018		−0.353*	
World economic growth$_{t-4}$	−0.276**		−0.076		0.053	

Note: *** denotes statistical significance at 1 percent level; ** at 5 percent; and * at 10 percent.

Table 6.4 Debt estimation results for 1870–1989, with Southern conflict, North–South conflict, and 1956 and 1986 dummy variables

Variable	Coefficient	Sums of lags
Southern debt$_{t-1}$	0.262***	
Systemic leadership$_{t-1}$	−0.111***	
Northern conflict$_t$	0.257**	
World economic growth$_{t-1}$	−0.263***	−0.863***
World economic growth$_{t-2}$	−0.304***	
World economic growth$_{t-3}$	−0.141	
World economic growth$_{t-4}$	−0.156**	
Southern conflict$_t$	0.303	
North–South conflict$_t$	0.480	
1956 Dummy variable	0.007	
1986 Dummy variable	0.023	

Note: *** denotes statistical significance at 1 percent level; ** at 5 percent; and * at 10 percent.

The effects of the four new variables are not statistically significant at the level of 10 percent, supporting our theoretical perspective and our not including them in the primary statistical model. All things considered, the results presented here (and in an appendix) are consistent with our theory.

Conclusions

This chapter demonstrates that Southern debt problems are linked systematically to fluctuations in world economic growth, systemic leadership, and Northern conflict. The statistical model that drives this result is found to be robust in a number of sensitivity analyses. We can conclude, therefore, that Southern debt problems are yet another systemic manifestation of discontinuous economic growth across time and space. Put another way, there is a strong external component to the intermittent failures of the South to maintain steady economic growth. The North does not necessarily create the debt crises in the South by design. But, the economic processes of the North (read the world economy) are responsible for creating situations in which Southern debt problems are more likely to become widespread. In this respect, Southern debt crises are mislabeled. They are registered most painfully in the South, but they are crises in which both North and South share culpability. Weaker economies in the world system become especially vulnerable to problems of capital access and debt servicing when the world economy falters and when global conditions are most conducive to political–economic breakdowns.

Whether or not the South actually defaults or resettles under the threat of default is secondary to our approach. The important issue for us is the Southern tendency to face periodically the possibility of default. The various resettlement arrangements are triggered by periodic Southern economic deterioration that leads to the possibility of default. This tendency is a structural manifestation of the current global distribution of wealth. From our perspective, the debate on whether a new era of global economic transformations has recently emerged (e.g., Held, McGrew, Goldblat, and Perraton, 1999; Suter, 1992) is to a large extent tangential. Our findings suggest that nothing fundamental has changed. But then, our analyses stop in 1989. Yet, as of this writing (late 2008), we note that debt crisis management options continue in the discussion mode, as opposed to the implementation mode.

In some circles, there are strong expectations that the twenty-first century international political economy will operate on vastly different principles than have been experienced to date. That may prove to be the case. However, in the interim, we note that the basic dynamic at stake here is quite simple. Northern prosperity encourages Southern economic expansion. When Northern prosperity falters, the Southern position is quite vulnerable. An inability to pay interest on Northern loans is one of the probable outcomes. Unless patterns of economic growth in the world economy suddenly assume new configurations, we see no reason to anticipate that the long-term debt cycle will be broken any time soon. The hardships associated with debt crises may be ameliorated by new approaches to debt rescheduling and forgiveness. Yet, easing the economic effects in one debt crisis is unlikely to break the cyclical tendency as long as Northern economic growth remains intermittent and the gap between North and South development levels persist.

Our systemic perspective may seem obvious for some observers. Perhaps it should be. Nonetheless, our interpretation does not seem to have become a basic starting point for analysts and decision-makers attempting to understand intermittent Southern debt crises. We believe that one of the consequences of this resistance to a systemic perspective is a greater probability of recurrence of debt crises.

A second consequence of the resistance to systemic perspective is a greater probability of maintaining North–South inequalities. In earlier debt crises, the South was abandoned by Northern investors until the world economy improved. Such abandonment translated into something of a decoupling of the South from the North – quite the opposite of the increased integration associated with economic globalization. In the latest debt crisis, greater attention has been paid to Southern problems. The greater attention may be partially attributable to a change in the nature of the periodic lending booms. Previously, the Northern risks of Southern debt problems had been smaller. In the latest debt iteration, a few large Northern banks owned a considerable portion of the debt obligations, and the size of the debt was much larger than before. The potential failure of these Northern banks could have severely disrupted Northern economic processes (Nafziger, 1993). Northern governmental intervention, including strong doses of IMF conditionality, attempted to ameliorate the inherent dangers associated with ignoring the Southern debt problem. In the process, the Northern banks that were most at risk survived. Some Southern states with severe debt problems were allowed to reschedule their loan payments. Some debts were written off, and more of that may yet occur. But the basic problem remains unchanged.

As was vividly demonstrated in the mid- and late-1990s in Mexico and Asia, even after the peak of the 1980s debt crisis, Southern economies remain highly vulnerable to fluctuations in Northern capital flows and Northern prosperity. This excessive vulnerability adversely affects the Southern prospects for sustained economic growth and mobility up the technological gradient of the world economy. Jochnick and Preston (2006: 4), moreover, note that one of the legacies of the latest debt iteration were the average rates of debt to GDP in Africa, the Middle East, and Latin America that remain too high to encourage economic growth. In general, socio-economic crises can be opportunities for experimenting with different strategies. Yet, there is no guarantee that the novel (or traditional) strategies that are tried will alter the fundamental sources of the problem. Negotiating new debt payment schedules or even forgiving debt altogether will not address the basic structural problems at work. If we fail to appreciate the fundamental, recurring, North–South structural identity of the problem, we should expect new debt crises to occur somewhere down the road. We should also expect phases of indebtedness to contribute to continued North–South divergence and inequalities.

7 Growth and conflict

We have good reasons to think that internal and external conflict are not conducive to Southern economic growth (see for instance Table 2.10). But, what brings about conflict in the South? There are to be sure a number of local factors that come into play. Ethnic antagonisms, regional grievances, government repression, and resource scarcities deserve scrutiny and certainly have been examined by others. The bias throughout this book, however, is to emphasize the effects of external factors and processes on local processes. We pursue this bias not because we believe only external factors and processes matter. They do not. But, external factors and processes matter a great deal, and they have been given less attention than they deserve.

Our main questions in this chapter are whether long-term economic growth, primarily a Northern/system leader-generated process, influences conflict universally, or if its impact wanes as one moves away from the center of the world economy. Assuming that Northern conflict is likely to respond to Northern economic growth fluctuations, should we expect Southern and North–South conflict to do so as well? After all, we have seen plenty of evidence for North–South dichotomies, with technological diffusion, economic growth, and export globalization concentrated in the North while debt crises are concentrated in the South. Should we expect conflict to be influenced by universal patterns?

Another question is what drives North–South conflict? Conflicts between rich and poor have a long-established tradition as a central theme in the social sciences. While there is no disagreement about the existence of rich and poor in the global political economy, we still know relatively little about the patterns of North–South conflict. There is, for instance, a debate among previous analysts who have looked at this question from theoretical perspectives. We think we can at least help resolve ongoing disagreements about the respective roles of world economic growth, systemic leadership, and major power conflict in fostering North–South conflict.

In this chapter, we first examine the longitudinal track of various kinds of conflict to see whether they appear to march to the same drummer. We then assess whether the technological growth of the system leader, our basic source of long-term economic growth, impacts all types of conflict equally, and in what way. Here, we are focusing on the reach of the impact of growth at the center of the world economy. Is it linked systematically to different patterns of conflict? If so, does its reach extend beyond a North that tends to monopolize technology, long-term growth, and globalization effects – as demonstrated in earlier chapters? Once we have some general answers to these questions, we move on to more specific questions. We review selectively some arguments that have been made about economic growth and North–South conflict. Advancing our own theoretical interpretation as an alternative foundation, we test anew the relationships between North–South conflict and economic growth.

Longitudinal patterns of economic growth and conflict

Nikolai Kondratieff (1984) is well known in some circles for the early discovery of a number of distinctive economic long wave relationships. One example is the finding that war and revolutions were more likely to occur on the long wave upswing than on the downswing. He attributed this behavior to tensions associated with rapid growth. Other analysts have supported this long wave–war relationship, although not always for the same reasons.[1] Another group of analysts, contrarily, have argued for a downswing–war relationship. There is also a third cluster of arguments to be found suggesting that war leads to upswings or downswings. Still others suggest that the relationship between the long wave and conflict is hegemonic phase-dependent, changing over time, intermittent, or nonexistent. Clearly, the relationship between the long wave and conflict has remained controversial and contested throughout the twentieth century. No doubt, it will remain so through the twenty-first century as well.

One reason for the continued contestation is that analysts disagree about how best to measure the long wave, with some advocating a focus on price fluctuations, as did Kondratieff himself, and others putting forth alternative measures of long-term economic growth. Another reason for continued disagreement may be that the relationship is simply more complex than the simple bivariate relationship found by Kondratieff. For instance, we argue in Chapter 1 that long waves are generated by technological innovation within the lead economy of the system's preeminent global actor. Each system leader generates at least two long waves. The first one precedes the ascent to systemic leadership and dis-equilibrates the systemic status quo. It also triggers or brings to culmination a struggle for succession in the global pecking order that leads to a period of global warfare. A coalition that has tended to join the declining incumbent system leader with the state in possession of the newly emergent lead economy (along with others critical for providing land power to supplement systemic leadership's specialization in sea power) defeats an opposing coalition seeking regional hegemony (thereby threatening the global order).

The ultimate winner of these global wars is determined by superior geopolitical resources, including the lead economy's innovation-based technological superiority and related financial resources. A new system leader emerges at the end of the global war with a position of global preeminence. Its economy is then in a strong position to create another round of radical innovation, thereby generating a second long wave of economic growth before technological diffusion facilitates the catch-up efforts of other economic competitors. Early system leaders (Portugal and the Netherlands) were unable to repeat this pattern more than once. More recent system leaders (Britain and presumably the United States) have been able to double, or are still in the process of doubling, the pattern by generating four long waves each.

This perspective suggests that the relationship between conflict and the long wave is more complex than simply positive or negative. An initial spike of technological innovation leads to intensive conflict among the system's major powers. This conflict yields a re-organization of the global political economy that encourages the generation of another spike of technological innovation. So, economic growth leads to conflict, which leads to more economic growth and, in some cases, less conflict. This latter complication depends in part on the nature of the immediate post-global war era. Assuming a reasonably strong system leader and the relative absence of an immediate challenge to the new system leader, as after 1815, less conflict is associated with economic growth. But, if there is an early challenge, as in the Cold War, less conflict is not assured even if it may fall short of a resumption of global war.

The point here is not so much that the system leader suppresses conflict "hegemonically," but, rather, that extensive conflict, at least among the major powers, is discouraged by favorable systemic conditions (economic growth and the concentration of economic and political–military resources in the control of the system leader) and rebuilding efforts following an intensive global war. This post-global war era is not permanent. It gives way to slower economic growth and deconcentration of economic and political–military resources. Systemic conditions, all other things being equal, no longer favor limited conflict.

Thus, the leadership long cycle perspective argues for a specific interpretation of the long wave – conflict relationship, just as it has a very specific take on the source of long waves of economic growth. Long-term pulsations in economic growth lead to intensive conflict that, in turn, lead to more pulsations in economic growth and, in some conditions, less conflict for some finite period of time before reverting to less growth and more conflict. The principal source of the pulsations in long-term economic growth remain throughout the radical innovations introduced into the world economy primarily by the system's lead economy and sometime system leader.

We tackle two questions in this first part of the chapter: (1) Does the empirical evidence support our expectations about a sequencing pattern in economic growth and conflict? Do we find that growth leads to intensive conflict which leads to more growth and sometimes less conflict? (2) How "deep" is the impact of growth on conflict? If growth is primarily a Northern process (focused on the leader of the North), are any significant linkages to conflict found throughout the system, or are they primarily restricted to the North? Other things being equal, one would expect a "ripple-like" process with the strongest impacts of growth being registered in the North (not unlike the diffusion of technological innovation, as observed in Chapter 4) and becoming less discernible as one moves away from the active zone of the world economy.

Annual conflict data are based on dyadic, aggregated, militarized inter-state disputes (MIDs) information.[2] Our assumption is that years with more MIDs represent higher levels of conflict than years with fewer MIDs. The aggregations encompass: Total (conflict between all country dyads in the system), Northern (conflict between two Northern states), North–South (conflict of dyads linking one Northern and one Southern state), and Southern (conflict between two Southern states). For each year, the appropriate MIDs index is normalized by the maximal number of dyads that can be formed. In addition, we also include the number of Southern civil wars and normalize it by the number of Southern countries in each year.

Empirical analysis

Our empirical analysis is conducted first in terms of a visual inspection of decadal averages of the smoothed time series. Space considerations, however, preclude showing the possible combinations of smoothed conflict and leading sector growth in figures here. Keeping in mind that we have spliced British leading sector growth values (prior to 1914) with American values (after 1913), what we observe is an initial decline in growth after the 1870s (a British depression), a medium bump upwards around World War I, a decline into the 1930s depression, and a large climb upwards during and after World War II before marked decline after the late 1950s. Total interstate conflict in the world system (shown in Figure 7.1), on the other hand, is characterized primarily by two World War spikes in early and mid-twentieth century.

The other figures, focusing on different conflict aggregations possess, in most cases, similar although less than identical configurations. Of the five types of conflict, Southern civil wars are the least similar to the other four in smoothed shape. Northern conflict (Figure 7.2) has the two World War spikes, but also smaller bumps in the 1880s, 1960s, and 1980s – the first one captures pre-World War I tensions, while the latter two pick up on Cold War hostilities. North–South conflict (Figure 7.3) is most similar to total conflict in longitudinal pattern except that the two spikes in the North–South pattern have roughly the same height. Southern conflict (Figure 7.4), on the other hand, is characterized by one major spike around

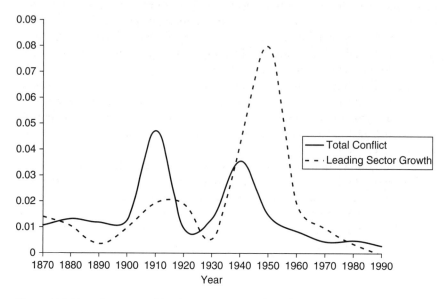

Figure 7.1 Decade-averaged leading sector growth and normalized total conflict.

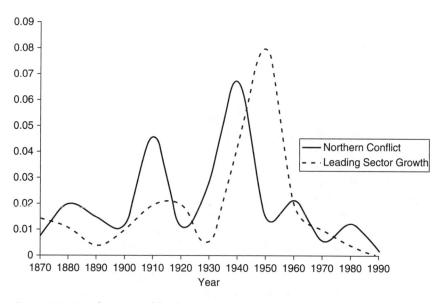

Figure 7.2 Decade-averaged leading sector growth and normalized Northern conflict.

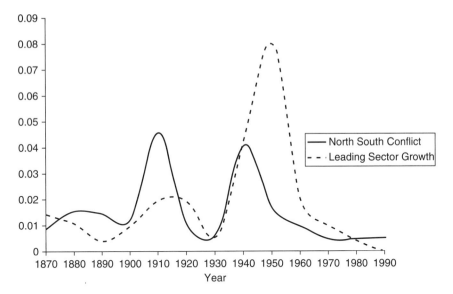

Figure 7.3 Decade-averaged leading sector growth and normalized North–South conflict.

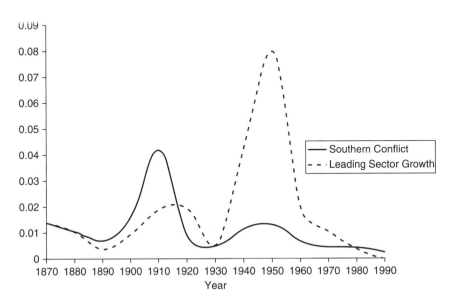

Figure 7.4 Decade-averaged leading sector growth and normalized Southern conflict.

World War I and a markedly smaller bump in the 1940s and 1950s. Southern civil wars (Figure 7.5) were declining into a first trough in the 1880s, then increasing to a peak around the first decade of the twentieth century, declining again into the 1930s, before ramping fairly steadily from the 1930s through the 1980s.

In general, then, our interstate, MIDs-based, conflict series share a bias toward focusing primarily on global warfare. The Northern conflict measure picks up some lesser activity before and after the global wars. Southern conflict is less influenced by World War II, but not much variation in the smoothed data is observed after that war. Southern civil wars are least global war oriented, with peaks slightly before the World War I and well after World War II. The smoothed leading sector growth series captures the post-World War II long wave well, but does less well with the wave that preceded it, because British economic growth basically missed the pre-World War I long wave. All of these considerations tell us that our measurement outcomes were less than perfect and that we need not expect exactly the same outcome in our examinations of the impact of leading sector growth on different types of conflict.

Our next step was to compute cross-correlation coefficients from the raw, annual, leading sector growth and conflict series.[3] In each case, we perform the computations while using various leads and lags of each conflict series relative to the growth series. Table 7.1 reports the results for the highest cross-correlation coefficient that is also statistically significant.

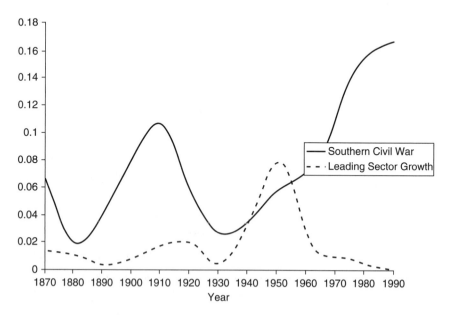

Figure 7.5 Decade-averaged leading sector growth and normalized Southern civil war.

All of the correlations reported in Table 7.1 are similar in behavior. The cross-correlation coefficients between leading sector growth and subsequent conflict (with leads varying from 12 to 21 years) are small and negative. With the exception of the non-significant North–South conflict and Southern civil wars coefficients, positive leading sector growth tends to be associated with a decline in interstate conflict a decade or two later. A decline in leading sector growth leads to a later increase in interstate conflict.

In addition, an increase in interstate conflict is associated uniformly with a subsequent increase in leading sector growth rates (although the lags vary from 4 to 17 years, depending on the type of conflict). Not surprisingly, the highest coefficient (0.45) linking antecedent conflict to leading sector growth is found to be associated with Northern conflict.

Note as well that the interstate results pertaining to leading sector growth leading conflict vary hardly at all in terms of the size of the coefficient. North–South conflict is the least influenced by economic growth, but there is no discernible difference between the outcomes for Northern or Southern interstate conflicts. A diminishing pattern does show up in the coefficients for the conflict to leading sector growth relationships. Northern conflict (0.45), North–South conflict (0.33), and Southern conflict (0.24) coefficients decline as one moves away from the North toward the South.

The outcome for the leading sector growth and Southern civil war correlation is different. Leading sector growth does not lead significantly to more or fewer Southern civil wars. Increasing civil wars in the South, it is suggested, lead to a decline in leading sector growth. This is a curious finding that deserves more scrutiny. It appears to be largely a product of the last third or so of the twentieth century (sharply increasing civil warfare

Table 7.1 Cross-correlations, 1870–1992

Variables	Correlation
Leading sector growth$_{(t)}$ to total conflict$_{(t+12)}$	−0.15*
Total conflict$_{(t-15)}$ to leading sector growth$_{(t)}$	0.28**
Leading sector growth$_{(t)}$ to Northern conflict$_{(t+13)}$	−0.16*
Northern conflict$_{(t-17)}$ to leading sector growth$_{(t)}$	0.45**
Leading sector growth$_{(t)}$ to North–South conflict$_{(t+13)}$	−0.13
North–South conflict$_{(t)}$ to leading sector growth$_{(t)}$	0.33**
Leading sector growth$_{(t)}$ to Southern conflict$_{(t+21)}$	−0.17*
Southern conflict$_{(t-5)}$ to leading sector growth$_{(t)}$	0.24**
Leading sector growth$_{(t)}$ to Southern civil war$_{(t+18)}$	−0.075
Southern civil war$_{(t-15)}$ to leading sector growth$_{(t)}$	−0.20**

* Denotes statistical significance at the level of 5 percent.

** Denotes statistical significance at the level of 10 percent.

and decaying leading sector growth). Prior to World War II, one does not observe any clear pattern linking these two variables. In this case, we would need to push the analysis back further in time (to 1815) before accepting the outcome recorded in Table 7.1 as fully meaningful.

In sum, we find some, but less than complete, support for our expectations. Leading sector growth, our index of the long wave, tends to be related to conflict in a variety of structural settings. Growth leads somewhat weakly to less conflict, not more – contrary to Kondratieff. Conflict, in turn, leads to growth, as we suspected. The conflict–growth relationship does dissipate as one moves away from the center. The growth–conflict relationship, contrary to what one might have surmised, does not vary across different structural settings. These relationships also tend to be stronger for interstate conflict than for intrastate conflict. Still, these findings remain preliminary. We would need to vary the temporal parameters and introduce other explanatory factors to fully assess what difference a US-based long wave measurement might make before we can be reasonably comfortable with the reliability of our present findings.

This is a task that we relegate to another time and place. For now, the preliminary findings are sufficient to support the idea that long-term economic growth and conflict are universally related but not necessarily at equal strengths throughout the system. Conflict, it seems, does not behave like technological diffusion and globalization which tend to be confined to Northern boundaries. We turn now to the contested drivers of North–South conflict.

Arguments and interpretation of North–South conflict

North–South relations have hardly been ignored in the past, but this structured interaction has not been modeled extensively. Two partial exceptions to this generalization are provided by the world-system and the lateral pressure literatures. A third perspective, developed here, extends our own leadership long cycle approach to deal with North–South conflict.

The world-system and lateral pressure perspectives

The world-system literature has long argued that Northern (core) wealth is based on exploitation of the South (periphery). In this view, Northern production depends on cheap Southern raw materials and labor. States in the North have competed for control over Southern territory in order to guarantee their access to Southern resources. Latin American, African, and Asian colonies linked to various European metropoles were thereby created and fought over. However, these conflicts were not waged constantly. Strong hegemonic leadership could suppress conflict within the core. Hegemons also had incentives to break down old colonial relationships that institutionalized previous distributions of benefits. Hegemonic leadership also is associated with global economic growth because hegemons introduce technological innovation. In periods of prosperity, Northern access to Southern resources was less critical. As global economic prosperity waned, major competitors were stimulated by fears of scarcity to expand direct control over Southern commodities and populations. Northern expansion into the South might increase Northern conflict with Southerners but it also reduced intra-Northern conflict propensities. As open colonial space diminished, increased conflict among Northern powers could therefore be anticipated. Northern rivalry led ultimately to periods of hegemonic warfare which, in turn, distracted the core temporarily from further expansion into the periphery.

The world-system perspective has been characterized by less than complete uniformity within the analytical ranks. There is agreement that strong hegemonic leadership and periods of world economic expansion are periods of low core conflict. But, there is disagreement about whether core conflict inhibited (Boswell, 1989; Boswell and Chase-Dunn, 2000; Boswell and Sweat, 1991; Chase-Dunn and Rubinson, 1979) or encouraged (Bergesen and Schoenberg, 1980; Chase-Dunn, 1989; McGowan, 1985) colonial expansion and peripheral resistance. Chase-Dunn (1989) also emphasizes that strong hegemons facilitate peripheral resistance by encouraging decolonization. Yet, if this hegemonic effort is operative at the same time that hegemons restrain core conflict, the signals for conflict over core colonial expansion and peripheral resistance are mixed, unless peripheral resistance associated with decolonization alternates with peripheral resistance related to further colonization. Core-periphery conflict might then resemble something of a constant, with only the tenor changing from time to time.

Lateral pressure interpretations (Choucri and North, 1975, 1992; Goldstein, 1988, 1991; North, 1990; Pollins, 1996; Pollins and Murrin, 1999) suggest another approach. Powerful states come into conflict with other powerful states in their pursuit of resources needed for economic expansion. In what is sometimes referred to as the "war chest" hypothesis, Goldstein (1988: 263) argues: "During the upswings of the world economy, demands will rise, countries will expand and intersect, and competition and war will increase." In other words, states are more likely to fight wars in periods of global economic prosperity.[4] Colonial expansion is perceived to be desirable by major states to the extent that it can capture resources and markets, and, in this respect, is a corollary of increasing lateral pressure. Eventually, the colonial powers collide with one another sufficiently so as to bring about major power war. The lateral pressure perspective shares the expectation that hegemonic leadership constrains core conflict and colonial expansion. However, it views hegemonic leadership as more irregular in occurrence and less closely paired with world economic expansion than do world-system arguments. One would also think that the linkage between major power conflict and colonial expansion would be positive, as long as world economic expansion has a stronger influence than hegemonic constraints. Pollins and Murrin (1999) complicate the issue by arguing that colonial activity should be greatest when the system leader is weak, the world economy is expanding, and core conflict is low. This position reinforces the conflicting signs postulated by lateral pressure arguments for economic expansion and hegemonic constraints, underscores the anticipated weak linkage between hegemony and economic expansion, but arrives at a negative effect of major power conflict on colonial expansion.

Figure 7.6 summarizes the disagreements between the world system and lateral pressure arguments. The world-system school sees hegemony and world economic expansion as closely linked, while the lateral-pressure perspective does not. Both perspectives agree that strong hegemons constrain core, or major power conflict, but diverge on the relationship between world economic expansion and major power conflict. The world-system position portrays the relationship as negative, while the lateral-pressure position emphasizes a positive relationship. Neither perspective has a unified voice on the relationship between major power conflict and

The World-System Argument

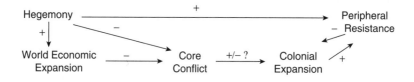

The Lateral Pressure Argument

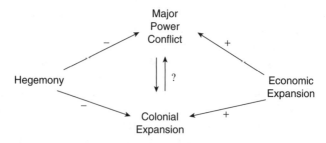

Figure 7.6 Disagreements between world-system and lateral pressure arguments.

colonial expansion. Arguments for either positive or negative linkages can be found in both camps. But, the world-system school argues for a positive if indirect linkage to core-periphery conflict via the hegemon's encouragement of periphery resistance in order to restructure the existing distribution of global benefits in its own favor.

This literature is not directly focused on North–South conflict. However, with some translation, we think it can be harnessed to study North–South conflict. The acquisition of colonies is an old process, dating back perhaps some 5500 years.[5] Like Mueller's (1989) dueling and slavery, however, it is no longer much practiced. We are not suggesting that it is incorrect to examine colonial expansion. On the contrary, the studies we have reviewed are exemplary in their attempts to model long-term, world system dynamics. Moreover, decolonization is a facet of North–South politics that continued throughout the twentieth century. Still, the point remains that (de)colonization is only one facet of North–South relations. North–South conflict continues even as (de)colonization fades away, and it also occurred in the past without reference to colonial expansion.[6] Much of the contemporary verbal conflict between North and South reflects attempts to redress the outcomes of earlier encounters. But, the contemporary North–South conflict is not confined to rhetoric as intermittent wars in Southeast Asia and the Middle East, escalating Southern terrorist attacks on the North, and disputes over oil prices have demonstrated repeatedly. One need not necessarily abandon efforts to model colonial expansion. Rather, what is needed is an expanded focus on North–South conflict. The concepts involved in the colonial expansion literature can be translated, we think, into more generic behavior. Core and major power conflict and peripheral resistance can readily be translated into intra-Northern conflict and North–South conflict, respectively. World economic growth requires no translation, and its effects on colonial expansion can be transformed into effects on North–South conflict. For example, if world economic growth affects Northern expansion into the South, we should find some manifestation in the incidence of North–South conflict. Depressed conditions should also influence Northern and Southern conflict propensities similarly.

One question left open in the literature is whether world economic growth encourages or discourages Northern and/or North–South conflict. This question needs to be answered. But, its reversed form also needs to be answered, namely: What is the effect of conflict on economic growth? There is no reason to assume that the economic growth–conflict nexus is a strictly one-way affair. We also see the need to raise a question about the effects of systemic leadership, the one variable on which world-system and lateral pressure arguments converge as a restraining effect on conflict. To elaborate on these notions, we need to introduce a third perspective.

In the upswing of the catch-up wave, systemic leadership is established and, as argued by the world-system school, the leader encourages decolonization of the South, reorganizing the global economic system to its own benefit. These pressures are welcomed by the South and resisted by existing colonial powers, which generally are Northern/major powers.[7] Colonial powers are especially vulnerable at this juncture due to their exhaustion from engaging in earlier global combat. As a result, North–South conflict can be expected to increase. Northern powers' relationships with their colonial subjects and with independent Southern states become more strained.[8] In the earlier ascent wave, the system leader's attention is focused on the consolidation of its economic edge and the competition with challengers for leadership. As a consequence, the effect of systemic leadership on North–South conflict is expected to be weak.

The predominant leadership long cycle expectation on conflict in a post-global war, upswing phase of the catch-up wave has been one of reduced hostility. This expectation follows from the interpretation of global wars as contests fought to determine systemic leadership. The emergence of a new leader presumes the exhaustion or defeat of challengers and some period of time before new challengers emerge or old ones reemerge.

We have already noted the likelihood of increased North–South conflict in the upswing of the catch-up wave. We think the customary expectation also has played down two other facets of post-global war phenomena. The first is that systemic leadership is an emergent and evolving property. Systemic leadership only began to emerge in the global system of the 1490s. It did not spring forth fully shaped. The Portuguese era of leadership was brief, weak, and primarily restricted to Indian Ocean operations. Its impact on the ongoing Habsburg-Valois feud in Europe was limited. The subsequent Dutch and first British leadership eras in the seventeenth and eighteenth centuries, respectively, also were based on trade dominance. Only after the British industrial revolution does systemic leadership become paired with industrial dominance. As a consequence, the last two system leaders (the United Kingdom and the United States) have been more impressive leaders than the first three were. Hence, the strength of post-global war stability should be expected to emerge only gradually over the past five centuries. Moving to the second facet, the periods of weak British leadership after 1714 (and only a moderate reduction in post-war conflict), and the stronger one after 1815, illustrate reduced conflict in the immediate aftermath of global war. The post-global war and reduced conflict expectation assumes that new system leaders emerge after defeating their principal challenger. However, a new leader may be unable or unwilling to lead. This is what basically happened with the United States in 1918.[9] Alternatively, the challenger may not be defeated sufficiently to prevent a resumption of conflict, as in the Dutch–Spanish case with hostilities resuming in 1621 after a brief truce. It is also possible that a new challenger may emerge almost immediately if the victorious coalition disintegrates at the end of the global war. We suggest that the Soviet–American Cold War exemplifies this possibility.

Summarizing, we depart from previous leadership long cycle arguments, in that we do not necessarily anticipate reduced major power conflict in the immediate aftermath of global wars. Post-global war periods can be characterized by more major power conflict if (1) the timing is early rather than later in the emergence of the system leader phenomenon; (2) the economic foundation for leadership is weak; and/or (3) a primary challenger (old or new) emerges quickly rather than slowly. Turning to a fourth characteristic, we generally expect leadership to be weaker in an ascent wave than in a catch-up wave. Therefore, the constraints on major power conflict should also be less in the former than in the latter. In the absence of one or more of these four characteristics, the post-global war relations among the major powers should be relatively pacific. Our approach also deviates from the unqualified expectations of the world-system and lateral pressure arguments. We do not stipulate an outright negative or positive relationship between world economic expansion and major power/Northern conflict. As noted, it depends on the historical timing, the nature of the economic foundation, the nature of the opposition, and the cycle phase. The post-1945 era generally was a period of strong leadership, global economic prosperity (at least through the early 1970s), and considerable strife among the Northern/major powers, in large part due to the early emergence of a new challenger. We expect that the effect of world economic expansion on major power conflict after 1945 will be positive. Between 1870 and 1945, world economic expansion is more likely to have been negatively related to major power/Northern conflict because systemic leadership was weak and economic growth was predominately limited to the destabilizing early 1900s era leading up to World War I. Hence, we agree with the lateral pressure prediction after World War II and with the world-system prediction before World War II, but in both cases not for the same reasons.

The effect of systemic leadership/world economic expansion on North–South conflict depends on the wave type in progress. The ascent wave is characterized by political instability, some of which is manifested in colonial expansion or Northern movement into the South. Southern resistance to this movement can be anticipated, but it may be weakened by the North's capability advantages and selective Northern expansion.[10] In the catch-up wave, the positive effect of leadership on growth is fully manifested. The system leader moves to break down old colonial relationships. North–South conflict over the pace of the Northern withdrawal from the South should be expected. As this issue recedes as a pressing one, Southern pressure for a new world order with a less-Northern bias will come to the fore, especially as the post-global war leadership and economic expansion-phase begins to wane (Modelski and Thompson, 1987). "System time" intervenes as a mediating third variable. Focusing on the past 130 years, the catch-up wave involves the past 1945 era. We, therefore, expect the effect of growth on North–South conflict in this era to be positive. We expect the effect of economic expansion on North–South conflict to be weakly negative because the North's late-nineteenth-century expansion into the South was more a function of intra-Northern rivalry than it was a matter of resource acquisition in depressed economic conditions.

We expect that major power/Northern conflict and North–South conflict will be positively interrelated. We do not quarrel with the contention that North–South conflict probably has diverted some intra-Northern animosities.[11] It is also possible to find episodes in which intra-Northern conflict has temporarily reduced North–South conflict (or colonial expansion).[12] But major power warfare has become increasingly rare and relatively short in the nineteenth and twentieth centuries. We think that the stronger tendency is for conflict to beget conflict. Major powers seek other Northern and Southern states as allies in their conflicts. Northern and Southern states also seek major power allies for their intra- and inter-mural conflicts. We also endorse the argument that systemic leadership in a catch-up phase presses for the removal of old colonial barriers. If this process takes place when a major power conflict rises due to the early emergence of a primary challenger, as in the post-1945 era, the incentives for conflict begetting conflict should be stronger.

The arguments we have reviewed have focused on the effect of conflict on world economic growth. We also are interested in the effect of conflict on world economic growth. This does not mean to say that the effects of war on the economy have not been studied before. As reviewed by Thompson (1993), the arguments on the effect of war on the economy reflect competing forces. On the negative side, there is the disruption of normal economic activity, destruction of infrastructures and resources, and the diversion of investments to the military (Goldstein, 1991; Mott, 1997). On the positive side, military mobilization can stimulate an economy operating at less than full capacity (Goldstein, 1991; Thompson, 1993), and wars can disrupt the ability of vested interests to extract rents, removing obstacles for growth (Olson, 1982). Losing a war also can stimulate the loser's development of an economic edge over winners (Kugler and Arbetman, 1989), and wartime exigencies can stimulate technological innovation and, by extension, growth (Modelski and Thompson, 1996). The empirical evidence on the effect of war on economic growth is scant and mixed.[13] Other studies investigate the effect of war on economic forces other than growth. Goldstein (1991) finds the effect of war severity (battle deaths) on world industrial production is negative in the short run and positive in the long run. Mansfield (1994) finds that the effect of war severity on trade is negative. A related body of literature finds that the effect of military expenditures on economic growth is insignificant (Chan, 1995). These studies notwithstanding, industrial production and trade are not quite the same as economic growth, and wars and military expenditures, while related phenomena, are not quite the same as conflict. We also are not aware of studies that investigate the effect of major power/Northern conflict and North–South conflict on world economic growth, as we do in this paper.

In our post-1870 period, the damage done by World Wars I and II suggests that the net effect of Northern/major power conflict prior to 1945 will be negative. Less severe conflict in the post-1945 era also should lead to a weaker, albeit negative relationship. At the same time, we recognize that at least one state, the future system leader, benefitted economically from the two World Wars, and that the Cold War encouraged some technological innovation and, therefore, economic growth, on both sides. The effect of North–South conflict on growth is difficult to anticipate. It may be that its potential for severe warfare has only increased as more Southern areas have become independent states after 1945. This may suggest an increasing likelihood of a negative effect of North–South conflict on growth in our period.

Table 7.2 summarizes how our expectations differ from those of the other two perspectives. We agree with the world-system position that growth in the system leader's economy promotes world economic expansion. We diverge from the world-system and lateral pressure arguments about the relationships between leadership and major power/Northern and North–South conflict, and between world economic expansion and the two types of conflict. These two schools tend to make unqualified predictions about the signs of the relationships. Our predictions depend on the presence or absence of a challenger, and/or the timing of the long wave. Where world-system and lateral pressure arguments are divided or missing on the relationships between major power/Northern conflict and North–South conflict, as well as the feedback of conflict on world economic expansion, our predictions are unqualified. One type of conflict should encourage more conflict of the other type, and intense conflict should retard world economic growth.

Empirical findings

This section presents our empirical findings.[14] Figure 7.7 provides a glimpse of the raw data. Periods of high and low or negative world economic growth, and high and low conflict are discernible. The four series do not exhibit a time trend. Hence, they are judged to be stationary.[15]

The raw data presented in Figure 7.7 are not easy to read, but the usual world economic growth peaks are again noticeable in the 1880s, 1920s, and 1960s when the data are averaged in Figure 7.8. The conflict variables generally move together, peaking in the 1880s, 1910s, 1940s, and 1960s. Before 1945, economic prosperity coincides with less conflict. After 1945, economic prosperity coincides with more conflict. These results generally support our expectations.

Table 7. 2 The expectations of three schools

Relationships in question	World-system	Lateral pressure	Leadership long cycle
System leadership–Economic expansion	+	Irregular	+
Systemic leadership–Northern conflict	–	–	Depends on challenger (e.g., + if present; – if absent)
Systemic leadership–North–South conflict	+	–	Depends on long wave phase (e.g., + if in catch-up; – if in ascent)
Economic expansion–Northern conflict	–	+	Depends on long wave phase (e.g., – in catch-up; + if in ascent)
Economic expansion–North–South conflict	Not direct	+	Depends on long wave phase (e.g., + in catch-up; weakly – in ascent)
Northern conflict–North–South conflict	Debated	Unclear*	+
Conflict–Economic expansion	Absent	Absent	–

* By unclear, we mean that the logic of the lateral pressure argument would seem to suggest a different prediction than the one found in the one lateral pressure study that has examined this question (always subject, of course, to our translation of colonial expansion into North–South conflict.

Figures 7.7 and 7.8, while illuminating, cannot pinpoint how our variables relate to each other statistically. To discern particular effects, we conduct a VAR analysis.[16] Focusing on the statistically significant outcomes in Table 7.3, all the effects of variables on themselves are positive, suggesting that past behavior affects present behavior. This finding supports our VAR modeling technique, as it controls for this effect. The effects of North–South conflict on major power conflict and Northern conflict are generally insignificant. This also supports our modeling approach, in the sense that North–South conflict is more influenced by the other two conflict variables than otherwise, and therefore appears last in our variable ordering.

Table 7.3 includes two panels, one for each period. In each panel, there are six cross-variable effects of one conflict variable on another conflict variable. Among the significant effects in Panel A (1870–1945), four of these

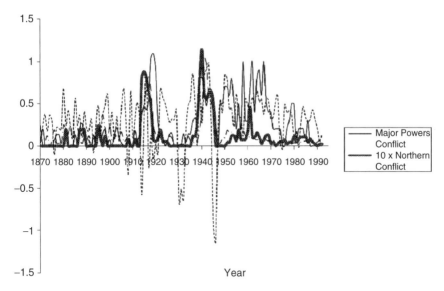

Figure 7.7 World economic growth and conflict per year.

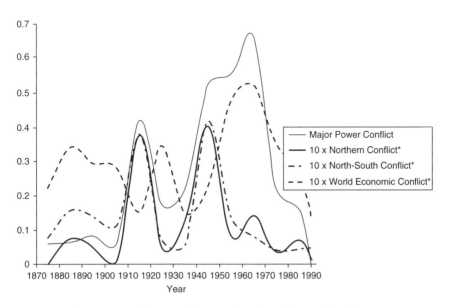

Figure 7.8 Average world economic growth and conflict per decade.

Table 7.3 Empirical effects of variables in the conflict model

Effect of	Effect on			
	World economic growth	Major power conflict	Northern conflict	North–South conflict
Panel A: 1870–1945				
World economic growth	+	–	–	n.s.
Major power conflict	+, –	+	+	+
Northern conflict	–	+	+	+
North–South conflict	+, –	–	n.s.	+
Panel B: 1946–92				
World economic growth	+	+	n.s.	+
Major power conflict	+	+	–	+
Northern conflict	n.s.	+	+	–
North–South conflict	–	n.s.	n.s.	+

Note: Responses are significant at 10 percent or better. The notation n.s. denotes statistical insignificance. The notation +, – indicates that the effect is positive in the short term and negative in the longer term.

effects are positive and one is negative. In Panel B (1946–92), two effects are positive and two are negative. The effect of one conflict variable on another conflict variable then is generally positive, supporting our expectations. Turning to the few negative effects in the results, in 1870–1945, as North–South conflict increases, major power conflict declines. In 1946–92, as Northern conflict rises, North–South conflict declines. While these findings support the idea that North–South conflict can serve as a substitute for core (major power and Northern) conflict, the effect is not strong in our results.[17]

In 1870–1945, the effect of world economic growth on major power conflict and Northern conflict is negative. In 1946–92, the effect of world growth on major power conflict and North–South conflict is positive. The effect of world economic growth on Northern conflict also is positive in this period, but is not significant. The latter is explained by recalling that, after 1945, the incidence of Northern conflict was much lower than major power conflict and North–South conflict. All these results support our expectations.

In 1870–1945, the effect of Northern conflict on world economic growth is negative. The effects of major power and North–South conflict are positive in the short run and negative in the longer term. We believe the negative effects reflect the destructive effect of the two World Wars, while the positive effects reflect the mobilization of resources, before the two World Wars. In 1946–92, the effect of major power conflict on economic growth is positive. This result may reflect the positive effect of the Cold War on technological innovation, and the fact that the Cold War rarely took the form of direct warfare. On the other hand, the effect of North–South conflict on growth in this period is negative, supporting our earlier severity argument. North–South war also was generally unlikely to stimulate technological innovation. The effect of Northern conflict on world economic growth in 1946–92 is not significant, reflecting the relatively weak intensity of Northern conflict in this period.

Conclusions

This chapter has focused on the relationships among world economic growth, major power conflict, Northern conflict, and North–South conflict. Our empirical results generally support our theoretical expectations. In 1870–1945, world economic growth negatively affected major power and Northern conflict, and had little effect on North–South conflict. After 1945, world economic growth positively influenced major power and North–South conflict, while having little impact on Northern conflict. Before 1946, conflict's impact on economic growth is negative. After 1945, the effect of North–South conflict on economic growth is negative, the effect of major power conflict is positive, and the effect of Northern conflict is not significant. The three types of conflict generally affect each other positively.

The world-system and lateral pressure arguments disagree about the relationship between world economic growth and core conflict. World-system analysts see the linkage as negative, while the lateral pressure analysts predict a positive relationship. The two schools are more in agreement on the linkage between what we are calling Northern conflict and North–South conflict, which they see as a positive relationship. Our world growth–Northern/major power conflict results support the world-system argument in the 1870–1945 period, but not in the 1946–92 era. The lateral pressure interpretation of how these variables are linked receives empirical support in the 1946–92 period, but not in the 1870–1945 era. In the more recent period, both the world-system and lateral pressure arguments relating Northern and North–South conflict receive some support, in the sense that the effect of major power conflict on North–South conflict in our results is positive, while the effect of Northern conflict is negative.

Despite the support the lateral pressure/war chest argument receives in our results in 1946–92, it remains unclear why an emphasis on resource acquisition is not supported before 1945. The argument about resource acquisition leading to conflict could well be overstated both before and after 1945, in the sense that technological innovation after 1870 probably led to the need for less, rather than more, Southern resources.

While petroleum is an exception to this generalization, the need for Southern resources seems even further reduced after 1945. If the war chest argument worked at any time, one would think that it should have been most successful before 1946.[18] Instead, we find a non-supportive, negative relationship between economic growth and conflict in the 1870–1945 period, which does not support the war-chest argument.

We think that North–South conflict after World War II was in part a function of a strong system leader pressing for decolonization and the Cold War competition that spilled over into North–South relations. In 1870–1945, in contrast, systemic leadership was either declining (the United Kingdom in the late nineteenth century) or developing (the United States in the 1920s and 1930s), and world economic growth was far more often negative than positive. As such, the effect of world economic growth on North–South conflict was weak, or statistically insignificant.

We have extended leadership long cycle perspective from its past preoccupation with systemic leadership and global war. We have also broadened the scope of the existing inquiries about the effects of imperialism by looking at the growth-retarding and growth-enhancing influences of conflict. We suspect, however, that world economic growth, major power conflict, Northern conflict, and North–South conflict are only four of the variables that can be linked systematically in the study of the dynamics of the global political economy. Other connections remain to be made and linked to these four. There also is no doubt that we are only capturing part of the North–South conflict phenomenon by restricting ourselves to militarized disputes between states.[19] But, even if we are only dealing with a portion of the larger phenomenon, it is clear that North–South conflict is not an isolated or autonomous process. Rather, it is an integral component of macro-systemic processes in the global political economy.

The next chapter returns to the topic of democratization that was linked to the idea of zones of peace and conflict that were discussed in Chapter 1. Singer and Wildavsky (1993) argued that lesser developed states would become richer, more democratic, and more peaceful. In doing so, they would exit the zone of turmoil and enter the zone of peace. We have suggested a fair number of reasons in earlier chapters not to expect too many of these transitions in the future. Rejecting the likelihood of a diminishing "turmoil zone," however, does not preclude expanding democratization. Indeed, some of the same influences that seem to influence conflict also seem to affect democratization. Chapter 8 examines these influences more closely.

8   Southern democracy in the long run

It is a customary reflex to think of democratization processes as national in scope. This instinct is to be expected, given the national scopes of the political systems within which the democratization processes are presumed to be located. The corollary propensities to study the role of national causal factors in democratization are equally natural. This does not mean that systemic factors are never considered in the democracy literature, only that so far they have not received much attention.

While studying the determinants of democracy at the national level of analysis is important, we believe that insights can be gained from employing a systemic perspective in the study of democracy. For example, is the world, viewed as one unit, becoming more democratic or less? What general factors promote world democratization? Is a highly democratic world more peaceful than a world that is substantially less democratic? It should be particularly appealing to study democracy in the aggregate in our age of growing globalization, which implies that the world is increasingly becoming one economic unit, even if, and perhaps especially because, we know that this is not the case. If it is permissible to think in world terms, we should also be allowed to think in terms of meaningful sub-systemic aggregates. One such sub-systemic aggregation follows the global North–South divide that has preoccupied us in earlier chapters. Northern, or developed, states have led the way in democratization, becoming exclusively, or almost exclusively, democratic. Southern, or developing, states have not become exclusively democratic or anything close to it.

This chapter explores the theoretical and empirical implications of a world system increasingly differentiated into Northern and Southern subsystems for the level of democracy in the South, taken as one unit. Our specific question revolves around the effects of systemic leadership and world economic growth on promoting Southern democratization. We find that the effects of increases in the levels of systemic leadership and world economic growth on the Southern democracy are both found to be positive and statistically significant. These findings do not imply that democratization is exclusively a macro-political economic process. But it should be more clear that we cannot rely exclusively on local factors in explaining democratization either. Singer and Wildavsky (1993), moreover, thought that economic convergence would bring about democratization and reduced turmoil. We have found that economic convergence is unlikely but does that mean that democratization is equally implausible? The answer is that it is apparently not. Economic development and democratization need not move hand in hand. However, in the absence of sufficient economic development, Singer and Wildavsky's "zones of turmoil" are less likely to contract all that much. Making the gains in democratization stick, in the absence of a locally supportive environment, may also be more difficult.

Democratization

The literature on democratization is vast, and the list of possible correlates is long.[1] So far, no restricted set of factors has emerged as *the* explanation of democratization. If one adds the further complication that it is possible that older states faced different conditions from those faced by newer states, it is not surprising that we continue to disagree over the determinants of democratization. We do not seek to resolve this debate. Instead, we look for factors applicable across the South, and our bias throughout this book has been for relying on systemic variables. Our ultimate goal in this chapter lies in assessing the effects of systemic leadership and world economic growth on Southern democratization, much like we did in the preceding chapter on conflict. The leadership long cycle approach has long stressed the importance of these factors in systemic and sub-systemic processes. Originally focusing on the rise and decline of major powers, systemic leadership, and global wars, this chapter brings Southern democracy into the story.

Long economic growth waves and Southern democratization

Samuel Huntington (1991) is credited with popularizing the notion that democratization comes in waves. Clusters of political transitions from more authoritarian to more democratic political systems occur with some tendency for reversions back to more authoritarianism leading to a "two steps forward, one step back" pattern, as suggested in Table 8.1. Even so, the net number of democracies continues to expand which, Huntington notes, should lead to expanding zones of peace since democracies tend not to fight each other.

Why these waves should occur is a very complex process according to Huntington. Not only do the hallmarks of democratization vary by wave, so, too, does their causation. In the long nineteenth century, it sufficed for evidence of democratization that 50 percent of adult males be eligible to vote and that a state's chief executive be expected to maintain majority support in an elected legislature or be chosen in intermittent elections. Within this context, the first wave of democratization could be attributed to economic development establishing a minimal economic foundation

Table 8.1 Huntington's three-wave scheme

First wave 1828–1926	Second wave 1943–62	Third wave 1974–
Australia	Botswana	Bulgaria
Canada	Gambia	El Salvador
Finland	Israel	Guatemala
Iceland	Jamaica	Haiti
Ireland	Malaysia	Honduras
New Zealand	Malta	Mongolia
Sweden	Sri Lanka	Namibia
Switzerland	Trinidad and Tobago	Nicaragua
United Kingdom	Venezuela	Panama
United States	Bolivia*	Romania
Chile*	Brazil*	Senegal
Austria*	Ecuador*	Sudan*
Belgium*	India*	Suriname*
Colombia*	South Korea*	
Denmark*	Pakistan*	
France*	Peru*	
West Germany*	Philippines*	
Italy*	Turkey*	
Japan*	Nigeria*	
The Netherlands*	Burma*	
Norway*	Fiji*	
Argentina*	Ghana*	
Czechoslovakia*	Guyana*	
Greece*	Indonesia*	
Hungary*	Lebanon*	
Uruguay*		
East Germany*		
Poland*		
Portugal*		
Spain*		
Estonia*		
Latvia*		
Lithuania*		

Note: Countries are listed in the wave in which they first democratize, but not in chronological order. The asterisk indicates that the state became less democratic in later years, usually during the reverse wave (located between the waves dated in the table).

Source: Based on Huntington (1991: 14–16).

for democratic practices (US$300–500 GNP per capita in 1960 dollars) in Northern Europe, the unusual nature of British settler colonies that combined economic opportunities, income equality, and limited status stratification (see Chapter 2), and the breakup of continental empires in World War I that led to the creation of new states in Central and Southern Europe.

The second wave is largely attributed to World War II. Some states were occupied by the war winners and had democratization imposed on them. Some states took the opportunity to emulate the war winners and became more democratic. Finally, the leading colonial powers had been weakened by the war and chose to respond to increasing nationalistic resistance by both decolonizing and encouraging the new states to adopt the metropole's democratic institutions.

Explaining the first two waves is a relatively straightforward proposition compared to the third cluster. Huntington finds five different patterns at work. Some states were cycling back and forth between variations on autocracy and democracy. Some had experienced a failure of democratic institutions in an earlier iteration but were now prepared to get it right the second time around. A few states had suffered temporary setbacks in the level of democratization and were able to overcome short-term instabilities. Two other groups went from authoritarian systems to more democratic ones relatively abruptly. One of these groups did it more or less voluntarily, and the other had democratic institutions imposed by former colonial powers.

Yet, an emphasis on patterns of change is largely descriptive. They tell us how some groups of states differed from other groups of states without telling the reasons for the differences. Why did these patterns emerge when they did? To answer this question, Huntington offers another five factors. The first two are primarily economic in origin. If poor states are unlikely to democratize and wealthy states tend already to be democratic, the most probable states to experience a political transition are entering some transition zone between poor and wealthy. In general, the 1950s and 1960s were decades of unprecedented economic growth. By the 1960s, a number of developing states had obtained a level of wealth that made democratic practices more feasible (a level of wealth roughly three to four times the GDP per capita required in the first wave). Huntington provides some rather strong evidence on this point. To simplify reading Table 8.2, the column to the far right of the table indicates precisely the anticipated behavior. There is very little change (6 percent) within the poorest interval (<US$250), considerably more in the next interval (27 percent), and the most change (76 percent) in the US$1000–3000 bracket. Most of the states in the analysis above US$3000 GDP per capita were already democratic. Hence, one part of the explanation is that the decades immediately following World War II were unusually prosperous. A number of states benefitted and enhanced their probability of becoming more democratic, albeit subject to a bit of a lag.

The other, at least partially economic dimension is that a variety of shocks, ranging from exogenous ones like the oil shocks of the 1970s and military defeats to more domestic economic problems contributed to undermining the legitimacy of a number of autocracies. In addition, various external actors – the Catholic Church, the European Community, the

Table 8.2 Economic development and third wave democratization

1976 GNP per capita (dollars)	Democratic in 1974	Democratized/ liberalized in 1974–89	Non-democratic	Total	% Countries that democratized/ liberalized
< 250	1	2	31	34	6
250–1000	3	11	27	41	27
1000–3000	5	16	5	26	76
>3000	18	2	3	23	40
Total	27	31	66	124	32

Source: Huntington (1991: 62).

United States – became less supportive of authoritarian regimes.[2] The fifth factor is a type of snowball effect in which early transitions in the third wave encouraged others to take the plunge.

Thus, the multiple explanations tend to reduce to a strong emphasis on preparing the way for democratic practices by expanding a population's access to economic resources (waves 1 and 3), various system shocks that led to decolonization and cue-taking among other things (waves 2 and 3), and an external environment that encouraged democratization (wave 3). All three of these most general factors emphasize external considerations, especially from a Southern point of view: years of prosperity in the world economy, system shocks, and conducive external actors and contexts.

To be sure, not everyone regards years of economic prosperity as an external consideration. But we have argued in earlier chapters that long-term economic growth is stimulated by system leader economic innovation and diffusion that generate long waves of economic growth and contraction. In this respect, domestic economic growth may seem to be an endogenous process but often is not purely endogenous. This observation brings us to an interesting critique of Huntington offered by Fraser (2001). Fraser's basic point is that Huntington provides no dynamic that accounts for how the world system proceeds from one democratization wave to the next. Instead, we are told that each wave is sui generis and needs to be explained in different terms – even though, as we have seen, there are some overlaps in the explanatory framework put forth by Huntington. Focusing on long waves of economic growth and Huntington's own emphasis on economic factors, Fraser contends that it is possible to develop an overarching framework that spans multiple waves, but not without some complications along the way.

One complication is that Fraser thinks the emphasis should be less on the transition from autocracy to democracy and more on democratization per se. If a state significantly expands the number of people who are eligible to vote, for instance, it can be a step toward democratization without the state necessarily exiting the autocracy category. If one looks for these types of advances, as demonstrated in Table 8.3, Fraser finds three democratization waves prior to World War II. Each of Fraser's first three democratization waves appears to be linked to long waves of economic growth in the sense that the democratization clusters (1800–32, 1860–79, and 1901–24) occurred either during or shortly after each economic upswing (1793–1814/25, 1848–73, and 1896–1914/20).[3] The specific changes related to economic upswings are reported in Table 8.4.

So far, Fraser and Huntington are in synch with each other's sense of democratization timing even though Fraser counts more upturns than does Huntington. They diverge in the period during and after World War II. Fraser's next economic upswing is 1948–73, while Huntington's second democratization wave is dated 1943–62 with reversals concentrated in the 1958–75 period. Either the long wave relationship with democratization has changed, was illusory, or other considerations need to be introduced. Fraser opts for the third path by differentiating between endogenous and exogenous transitions. The former are democratization changes predominately executed by domestic political groups while the latter are those in which external actors are primarily responsible for democratization. From a causal perspective, endogenous transitions are most likely to be linked to economic upswings, while exogenous transitions can take place anytime.

Fraser's first two democratization waves (1800–32 and 1860–79) are considered to be endogenous in nature. The third (1901–26) is also described as basically endogenous with strong exogenous encouragement. Huntington's second democratization wave (1943–62), however, is viewed by Fraser as a mixture of endogenous and exogenous transitions,

Table 8.3 Fraser's alternative schema for waves of democratization

Democratization waves		Reverse waves	
Endogenous	*Exogenous*	*Endogenous*	*Exogenous*
First upswing wave 1800–32			
Second upswing wave 1860–79		Failed 1878–90s	
Third upswing wave 1901–24	World War II liberation and decolonization 1944–50s	Third downswing 1922–39	World War II 1940–43 Decolonization 1948–61
Fourth upswing wave 1952–73	Eastern Europe 1989–94		Cold War 1963–76
Elite/crisis transition 1978–90s			

Source: Based on Fraser (2001: 60).

Table 8.4 Fraser's evidence for democratization gains in economic upswings

Waves	Democratic and constitutional reforms, enfranchisement extensions
1800–32	United States (1800–10/1818–21), Belgium (1831), Britain (1832), France (1832)
1860–79	Australia (1860), Greece (1864), Sweden (1965–66), United States (1866–70), Britain (1867), Canada (1867), Prussia/Germany (1860s/1871), Japan (1868), Finland (1869), France (1871/1878), Italy (1871), Spain (1873/1876), Switzerland (1874), and New Zealand (1879)
1901–26	Australia, Canada, Iceland, Ireland, New Zealand, Sweden, United Kingdom, Chile, Austria, Belgium, Colombia, Denmark, Germany, Italy, Japan, The Netherlands, Norway, Argentina, Czechoslovakia, Greece, Hungary, Uruguay, Poland, Portugal, Spain, Estonia, Latvia, and Lithuania
1948–73	Latin America (except Paraguay), France, Mexico, Tunisia, Turkey, United States, Pakistan, Switzerland, Taiwan, Morocco, Portugal (1974), Papua New Guinea (1975), Spain (1975), and Greece (1975)

Source: Extracted from Fraser (2001: 44–45).

but definitely more exogenous than endogenous. The outcome of World War II led to democracy either being imposed or re-introduced in a number of European states in the 1940s and early 1950s. Other states chose to become more democratic because the war winners were democratic. A third type of exogenous transition process involved democratic institutions being imposed on newly independent, former colonies. Fraser, thus, eliminates the potential anomaly of Huntington's second democratization wave by dismissing it as a largely exogenous affair with the more endogenous types of transitions coming later in the 1948–73 period. Reversals coming in Huntington's 1958–75 interval can be explained in exogenous terms pertaining to American opposition to leftist regimes in Latin America or, elsewhere, to former colonies that had been pushed into democratic institutions before they were able to acquire appropriate socioeconomic foundations for democracy.

If long wave prosperity ended in the mid-1970s, how can Fraser explain democratization gains in Latin America in the late 1970s through the early 1990s and in Eastern Europe in the early 1990s? Exogenity is again relied upon. In Latin America, autocracies in control when the world economy slowed down after 1973 took the blame for the economic downturn and were supplanted by more democratic regimes. This process was facilitated by the earlier suppression of leftist movements (thereby making democracy safer) and by declining US support for authoritarian regimes. In Eastern Europe, the determining factor was located outside Eastern Europe – in Soviet decisions to loosen their hold on the smaller states to the west.

Both apparent exceptions to the rule were predominately exogenous in nature and, therefore, not rule exceptions.

Moreover, Fraser adds that upswing democratization appears to be most likely to be associated with bottom–up, mass pressures to liberalize political systems while downswing democratization is most often top–down or elite led often for purposes of gaining or remaining in power. He calls these two types of endogenous transitions but they could also be linked to endogenous (bottom–up) or exogenous (top–down) processes.

Economic downswings are most likely to be linked to reverse waves, but not inevitably since the historical record yields limited reversal in a late-nineteenth-century downswing and democratization gains in Latin America in part of a latter-twentieth-century downswing. The interaction among political parties, economic crisis, and voters may be the intervening consideration. If economic downturns cause voters to focus on economic problems over all else, it may depend on how parties adjust to the perceived need to act to prevent further damage. If mainstream parties are seen as responding appropriately, they are likely to be favored over less mainstream parties with non-democratic objectives in mind. Otherwise, the solutions offered by more radical parties may become most attractive, facilitating the onset of a reverse wave of de-democratization.

These very interesting arguments have led to an enriched macropolitical theory of how democratization may have taken place. We say "may" because neither Huntington or Fraser fully document their arguments. They have shown at best that their arguments are plausible – that is, they seem to fit. Fraser has certainly helped to improve the theoretical parsimony of Huntington's initial observations – even if it is by no means clear that Huntington would welcome Fraser's long wave translation. Yet, Huntington started with a wave interpretation that relied heavily (but hardly exclusively) on economic growth. Fraser took this notion one step farther and linked democratization waves to long waves of economic growth, with some important caveats about exogeneity, endogeneity, and political party activity. The question remains, however, whether democratization is linked systematically and empirically with long waves of economic growth.

One of the reasons why this question is pertinent in the immediate context is that we began our analysis in Chapter 1 with Singer and Wildavsky's argument that economic development and democratization would (a) occur and (b) expand the zones of peace associated with democratic dyads. We are less confident than they are about the economic development part of the equation and have shown that convergence dynamics (Chapter 3) are less compelling than Singer and Wildavsky thought. But, that leaves the status of democratization somewhat open-ended. If Huntington (and many other analysts) is (are) right that one of the major ingredients underlying democratization is a minimal economic foundation for the practice of democratic politics, it is conceivable that there is "enough" economic growth for democratization if not for convergence. Thus, democratization could still move forward without extensive economic development. To the extent that it was geared to long waves of economic development, we should expect to find Huntington's two steps forward – one step backwards, wave pattern. All of this could hold without expecting long-term economic growth to dictate fully what happens with democratization. As both Huntington and Fraser acknowledge, other factors, probably varying over time contribute to promoting democratization. We think, moreover, that there may be some more consistent external influences on democratization, including the activities of systemic leadership and economic growth in general. We now turn to first developing the reasons for this expectation and then empirically assessing its apparent fit to the historical record.

A leadership long cycle interpretation

We argue that the level of Southern democratization is affected by two of the primary emphases of the leadership long cycle perspective: the level of political–economic systemic leadership and the rate of world economic growth.[4] We do not advance this argument as an exclusive two-variable, explanation of democratization. Instead, we seek to contribute to the internal/external debate about democratization drivers (e.g., Schraeder, 2002; Colaresi and Thompson, 2003). Systemic leadership and world economic growth are expected to interact with domestic factors. Given our systemic approach, we will not make most of these factors explicit. Our question is whether systemic leadership and world economic growth deserve special consideration. Believing this to be the case, we now discuss the expected effects of these two systemic drivers in greater detail.

The role of systemic leadership in democratization has received some attention in the literature. Wright (1942/1965) and Huntington (1984) argued that democratization throughout the world was facilitated by first British and later US protection. Historically, these system leaders have led coalitions to suppress authoritarian challengers to their global order. If these coalitions had been defeated in the World Wars of the twentieth century, the systemic context that would have emerged would have most likely been unfavorable to democracy. Once triumphant, the system leader and its allies can choose to change the political regimes of defeated foes or weaker states that need its assistance. After World War II, the system leader also pushed for decolonization, an initial prerequisite for Southern democratization. As a result, many of the new states that emerged in the aftermaths of World War II and the Cold War adopted political institutions resembling those of the older democracies. In doing so, they responded to norms put in place as part of a postwar world order and foreign aid supported by the system leader.

Thus, the anticipated effects of systemic leadership are contextual and direct. Contextually, the values of the successful leader are likely to be emulated by others. Let us assume that the leader possesses a democratic or democratizing political system, as was the case over the last two centuries. Whether the leader chooses to encourage democratization in all cases and times presumably hinges on calculations of short-term costs and benefits. System leaders may accept violations of liberal values in allied and client states in the short run, including authoritarian regimes and human rights abuses, in order to deal collectively with external threats (for instance, Hook, 2002). In the long run, we anticipate that the system leader will push other states to adopt its own political and economic values, a process that would grow stronger following decolonization, itself a process facilitated by system leader pressure.

To be clear, we do not suggest that systemic "hegemons" always force their values on others. Yet, Wilsonian idealism has been at least intermittently a cornerstone of US foreign policy, and the doctrine associated with it argues that the world would be a better place if all of it became more like the United States. As a consequence, the twentieth century system leader had occasionally pushed to expand democratization. In the twentieth century and later, especially after 1945, this contextual norm has privileged democratization as the preferred approach to creating domestic political order even when it has been subordinated to short-term real-politic considerations. Our point is that this norm is not accidental, but rather created by systemic leadership. So, too, organizations such as the United Nations, International Monetary Fund, World Bank, and other global organizations created as part of the leader's approach to world order promote democratization as part of their missions (Hibou, 2002; Joyner, 2002). All of these pressures can be traced back (to a varying extent) to the guiding influence of a predominant system leader.[5]

Having discussed the role of systemic leadership, we turn to world economic growth. In general, economic growth is expected to reduce conflict over inputs of production, outputs, and markets, and make it easier for governments to finance and provide services. People are also more likely to support their political systems in times of prosperity than in times of decline. Similar to several authors including, as discussed earlier, Fraser (2001), we expect that these generalizations should prevail in the global North and South. The question is to what extent world economic growth trickles down to the South.[6] By and large, we expect (and have demonstrated in earlier chapters) that Southern economies will find it hard to absorb, or adapt to, latest innovations and production techniques. However, world economic growth, if nothing else, should increase Northern demand for Southern goods. This should promote Southern economic growth and, therefore, be conducive to democratization.[7]

The alternative is the absence of growth or, worse yet, recessions and depressions. While recessions reflect relatively short-term processes, the leadership long cycle perspective views major depressions (e.g., the 1890s, 1930s, 1980s) as manifestations of extended transitions from one cluster of radical technological change to the next. Other periods should exhibit fewer recessions and depressions.

In general, governments, particularly newer democracies, have poor track records in coping with the political stresses of economic deterioration. Not only are they blamed for the decline, they also find it difficult to mobilize resources in order to do anything about it. As the decline continues, people become less cooperative with governmental goals and increasingly unable to finance them. Sensing the fall in public support, governments may tighten their grip, seeking to replace governance by consent with governance by degree. Thus, we anticipate that a context of global prosperity will encourage Southern democratization, while a context of economic decline will discourage it.

While we view systemic leadership and world economic growth as principal drivers of global democratization processes, we need to control for the effect of other forces suggested by the democratization literature, while focusing on factors that seem most important and can be aggregated across the South. Guided by these considerations, we include measures for economic development, military conflict, and political regime inertia as our controls.

Students of democracy agree that economic development is related to democratization, but disagree on how exactly the relationship works. Some scholars posit development as a prerequisite for democratization. Expanded political participation is dependent on a movement away from subsistence/peasant-based, agrarian economies. Industrialization diffuses control over economic resources, facilitating growing public and interest groups' demand for, and supply of, more political system responsiveness. Economic development and its byproducts, literacy and education, are also likely to promote more liberal attitudes in the population at large.[8] For other scholars, economic development is not a prerequisite for democracy, but rather a force increasing the likelihood that democracies established under whatever circumstances will survive. Democratic regimes, it is argued, are less likely to survive without the reinforcement provided by economic development (Huntington, 1991; Przeworksi, Alvarez, Cheibub and Limongi, 2000). Either way, we expect that an increase in Southern economic development will raise the level of Southern democracy. The relationship may not be necessary, sufficient, or consistent across time and space (for instance, consider the tendency for developing countries to democratize in recent decades), but is expected to be positive and significant for our model.

It also seems reasonable to expect that military conflict will make democratization more difficult. This argument, which can be traced back to de Tocqueville (1835), is not accepted by some scholars who observe that military conflict encouraged the making of domestic bargains of support in exchange for increased political participation in some democratization episodes.[9] That said, authoritarian strategies to cope with external threat may be encouraged even if the political system is already democratic. Then, too, increases in mass political participation can be put off to deal more effectively with external emergencies. Periods of extensive conflict leave particularly little space or financial resources for experimenting with changes in domestic regimes. As a consequence, we anticipate a negative effect of Southern conflict on Southern democratization.[10]

Finally, consider the notion of political regime inertia, the tendency of regime type in the previous period to continue in the current period. Movements toward democratization or authoritarianism are not normally abrupt. Domestic power structures change slowly because elites are reluctant to surrender positions of political privilege. In the absence of major shocks such as defeat in war or occupation, we anticipate that political regime structures will be subject to inertia. They may obviously change, but they and the social contexts they entail (including ethnic and class structures, ownership of means of production, and wealth and income inequality) are not easy to modify. This expectation is all the more applicable in the South since most of the South only gradually attained independence from colonial powers, an initial prerequisite for democratization. Given this colonial past for much of the South, we might also expect inertia to be strongest earlier in our series, becoming weaker later in time.[11]

Empirical results

Our empirical analysis includes three stages: inspecting plots, computing cross correlations, and estimating multivariate regressions. To improve our ability to visually read noisy data, we average them over decades. Figure 8.1 presents the decade average for the level of Southern democracy. It is apparent that Southern democracy is trending up from about –7.5 in the 1870s to close to zero in the early 1990s. Long waves with a length of approximately 40–50 years ride on this trend. Southern democracy peaks in the 1910s, late-1950s/early 1960s, and, more modestly, in the 1880s. The finding of wavelike structures supports our systemic perspective, suggesting that broader, system-wide dynamics are at play, especially if other phenomena share these patterns.

Figure 8.2 presents decade averages for systemic leadership, world economic growth, Southern conflict, and Southern development.[12] Southern development is trending up at a slow rate before the mid-1940s, and at a higher rate thereafter. As we have noted before, world economic growth exhibits 40–50-year "long waves," peaking in the 1880s/1920s, and 1960s, resembling the chronology noted in leadership long cycle studies. Southern conflict peaks in the 1910s and 1940s, and, more modestly, in the 1880s. Systemic leadership peaks in the 1880s and 1950s.[13]

Figures 8.1 and 8.2 hint that Southern democracy rises with world economic growth, systemic leadership, and development, and falls with conflict. These findings support our approach, but "eyeballing" averaged

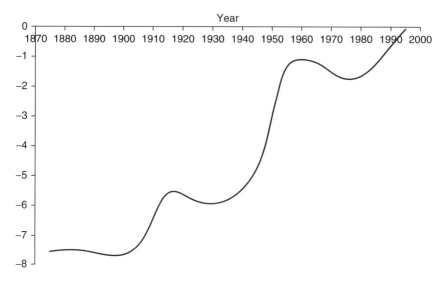

Figure 8.1 Decade-averaged Southern democracy.

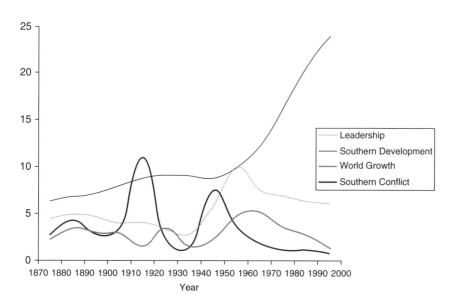

Figure 8.2 Leadership, Southern development, world growth, and Southern conflict.

data plots falls short of a full empirical test. To discern effects more accurately, we turn to the cross-correlation analysis. Our research design calls for using lagged values for the independent variables, except for systemic leadership. Table 8.5 reports cross-correlation results for pair-wise relationships between Southern democracy and, respectively, lagged Southern democracy, lagged world economic growth, lagged Southern conflict, and systemic leadership. The results indicate that Southern democracy is positively associated with its own lag, systemic leadership, Southern development, and world economic growth, and negatively associated with Southern conflict. These results support our approach, but due to their bivariate nature they too fall short of a full test.

Turning to the multivariate regression analysis, a grid search for the best lag length suggests using the first and second lags for Southern conflict, Southern development, and world economic growth, and the current and the first lag for systemic leadership. Table 8.6 presents the results for the 1870–1992 period. The model's R-square is 0.89, which is relatively high.

Table 8.5 Democratization cross-correlation analysis

Variables	Correlation coefficients
Southern democracy–Southern democracy$_{t-1}$	0.923***
Southern democracy–Systemic leadership	0.695***
Southern democracy–Southern conflict$_{t-1}$	−0.228**
Southern democracy–Southern development$_{t-1}$	0.767***
Southern democracy–World economic growth$_{t-1}$	0.172**

Note: *** denotes statistical significance at 1 percent level; ** at 5 percent; and * at 10 percent.

Table 8.6 Democratization estimation results for 1870–1992

Variable	Coefficients	Sums of lagged coefficients
Southern democracy$_{t-1}$	0.576***	
Southern conflict$_{t-1}$	0.812	2.574
Southern conflict$_{t-2}$	1.762	
Systemic leadership$t$	1.795**	2.974***
Systemic leadership$_{t-1}$	1.179*	
Southern development$_{t-1}$	−0.002	0.002***
Southern development$_{t-2}$	0.004**	
World economic growth$_{t-1}$	1.186	6.437**
World economic growth$_{t-2}$	5.251*	

Note: *** denotes statistical significance at 1 percent level; ** at 5 percent; and * at 10 percent.

The results for the individual coefficients are a bit mixed, which is a known feature of distributed lag models, but the signs of the statistically significant coefficients conform to our theoretical expectations. The results for the sums of the lagged coefficients, which give the overall effect of each variable on Southern democracy, also support our approach. We find that increases in previous Southern democracy, systemic leadership, Southern development, and world economic growth promote Southern democracy.

Table 8.7 provides results for the sub-sample analyses. The model's R-square index is 0.60 in the 1870–1913 period, and 0.86 in the 1914–92 period. In the 1946–92 period, the R-square is 0.39, reflecting the larger variability in the data during that period. It should also be noted that, by 1945, the overtime heterogeneity in democratization etiology seems to be a fairly familiar phenomenon. Many of the presumed prerequisites of democratization prior to 1945 seem less applicable after 1945, reflecting in part the top–down adoption of democratic institutions without a corresponding mass political participation. We see this phenomenon as a response to contemporary systemic norms promoted by the system leader and other influential actors, including international organizations.

Turning to the results in 1870–1913, inertia is the only significant determinant of Southern democracy. The system leader of that time, Britain, did not tend to export democratic ideology to a South that was largely subordinated to colonial control, and, in any event, the strength of its leadership was declining (Figure 8.2). Since Southern democracy was generally stagnant in that period, statistical analysis fails to explain it (as it requires change). The results for 1914–92 replicate the full sample results, except that now the negative effect of Southern conflict on Southern democracy is statistically significant. Thus, the effects on Southern democracy of increases in inertia, leadership, development, and world economic growth are positive, and the effect of a rise in conflict is negative, all of which support our approach. The results for 1946–92 resemble those for 1914–92, except that the effect of Southern conflict is not significant in the shorter period.[14]

Conclusions

Scholars are aware that Southern democratization processes do not take place in an international vacuum. However critical domestic processes may be, the influence of external factors is recognized. Yet, these external influences are often restricted to indices such as the number of democracies in the same region. We think there is more going on in the external realm. The international system in which countries are embedded is shaped by a system leader and conditioned by global growth waves caused, as noted, by radical innovations in the system leader's economy.

The empirical results support our theoretical perspective. In particular, we find significant support for the positive influence of systemic leadership and world economic growth on Southern democratization.

Table 8.7 Democratization estimation results for 1870–1913, 1914–92, 1946–92

Variable	1870–1913		1914–92		1946–92	
	Coefficients	Sums of lagged coefficients	coefficients	Sums of lagged coefficients	Coefficients	Sums of lagged coefficients
Southern democracy$_{t-1}$	0.578***		0.191*		-0.036	
Southern conflict$_{t-1}$	-9.998	-19.123	-6.298	-6.458**	-17.522	16.814
Southern conflict$_{t-2}$	-9.125		-0.158		34.336	
Systemic leadership	-3.426	3.373	2.837***	4.930***	0.153	2.957**
Systemic leadership$_{t-1}$	6.799		2.093***		2.804**	
Southern development$_{t-1}$	0.004	0.005	-0.002	0.002***	-0.002	0.002***
Southern development$_{t-2}$	0.001		0.004**		0.004	
World economic growth$_{t-1}$	-4.859	-0.708	4.824***	12.592***	8.549	24.410***
World economic growth$_{t-2}$	4.151		7.768**		15.861***	

Note: *** denotes statistical significance at 1 percent level; ** at 5 percent; and * at 10 percent.

Ordinarily, these factors are excluded from national-level analyses. We suggest that their omission in the future is not desirable. Among the control variables, the effect of a rise in Southern economic development on Southern democratization is positive. The influence of military conflict depends on the time period examined. A longer examination in the twentieth century gives it a greater role than do examinations restricted to the post-1945 era or pre-1914 era. Finally, the effect of inertia on Southern democratization has decayed as we move forward in time, away from the strong restraints of the colonial era into the pro-democratic norms of the current era.

As the South evolved toward a state of affairs exhibiting fewer colonial constraints imposed by metropoles on the periphery, the influence of systemic leadership and world economic growth on Southern democratization became more important, which is reflected in our analysis by their significant coefficients in the post-World War II era. Our empirical results, then, suggest that systemic leadership and world economic growth essentially establish the long-run context in which national-level democratization processes work in the South.

These results have important implications, suggesting that expectations of continuously expanding democratization around the world are vulnerable on two counts. First, a new leadership competition seems to be in the making between a rising China and relatively declining United States. The real beginning of this competition may be a generation or more in the future. The form it might take and how it might be ultimately resolved remains to be seen, but we cannot overrule the possibility that a non-democratic China might ascend to systemic leadership. Should this happen, our model suggests that there would be a concomitant decline in the level of democracy in the South. A widespread reversion to more autocratic forms of governance in the future, then, is not out of the question.

Second, if the rate of world economic growth should decline in the future, one could expect to see a decline in the level of democracy in the South. The tendency of world economic growth to follow the rise and decline of the long wave hardly precludes the advent of a future world depression. We have already seen more than once the number of democracies decline during depressions. We can also think of at least one relatively novel reason why world economic growth might decline more permanently in the future: climate change. The exact nature and etiology of climate change are still not fully known. However, if climate change is fully materialized in the way it is currently predicted, world economic growth, and particularly Southern economic growth, will decline substantially. In this worst-case scenario, our model suggests that the level of Southern democracy would decline as well. In all, while Southern democratization and the associated democratic peace may continue to expand for some time into the future, radical systemic changes cannot be ruled out at some point in the twenty-first century. Nor can we ignore, based on our findings, their probable negative implications for democratization and, therefore, for local and world political stability.

We began our inquiry with skepticism about an argument that predicted continuing transition from zones of turmoil to zones of peace via transformations in Southern economic development and democratization. The empirical evidence seems to readily buttress our skepticism about the likelihood of widespread economic development. Democratization, on the other hand, appears to be more probable. We wonder, however, whether democratization, assuming systemic leadership and world economic growth – neither of which should be assumed – without economic development is a recipe for peace or more turmoil.[15] To be consistent with our tone throughout this book, we are inclined to opt for the more turmoil alternative.

9 Uneven growth processes and prospects

Optimistic images

We began our analysis with two sets of generalizations. One that we have mentioned repeatedly (Singer and Wildavsky, 1993) talked about a bifurcation of the world into zones of peace and turmoil. The zones of peace were populated by developed and democratic states that no longer fought one another. The zones of turmoil, the rest of the world, were less developed, more autocratic, and prone to internal and external strife. But this structural divide was thought to be transitory. As states in the zones of turmoil developed economically and became more democratic, they would move from the zones of turmoil into the zones of peace. This conceptualization is, of course, a popularization of the liberal proposition that the poor get richer as they emulate their practices while the growth of the rich will eventually slow down.

The second argument/imagery was that the world was becoming more flat as information technology enabled everyone and anyone to become more competitive in the world economy. This conceptualization is really only a variation on the liberal notion that new technology is freely available to all and can be utilized to catch up with early developers. In this case, the poor will get richer as they adopt the new technology pioneered by the rich. At some point, rich and poor skill levels and technology capabilities should converge.

We can now add a third image that captures a newly prevailing optimism about the growth prospects of a majority of the South. Paul Collier (2007: 3) writes that:

> The Third World has shrunk. For forty years, the development challenge has been a richer world of one billion people facing a poor world of five billion people.... By 2015, however, it will be apparent that this way of conceptualizing development has become outdated. Most of the five billion, about 80 percent, live in countries that are indeed developing, often at amazing speed. The real challenge of development is that there is a group of countries at the bottom that are falling behind, and often falling apart.

Collier is not specific about which states populate his bottom billion, but he does buttress his forecast with data on comparative growth rates. Table 9.1 looks at growth rates for Collier's bottom and middle groups (ignoring the top billion). The bottom billion have been marking time and experiencing little in the way of positive growth. Relatively "good" decades of positive growth tend to be followed by decades of negative growth. The economic outcome is as if they are standing still no better off than they were more than a generation ago.

In contrast, Collier's very large middle group, at least half of which must be comprised of China and India, appear to be on an upward growth trajectory that will leave the bottom billion far behind. The explanation for this phenomenon, according to Collier, is that the bottom group is mired in various conflicts, lacking in natural resources, landlocked with bad neighbors, and having bad governance traps, while the middle group has managed to work their way free of such growth constraints.

We have no argument with the observation that the South is heterogeneous and that some states are much worse off than others. Collier's bottom billion categorization is probably similar to our earlier "lower South."[1] The growth prospects of this group, which is very large in terms of the number of states encompassed, do seem dismal. Nor do we contend that there will be no further adjustments in North and South categorizations. We fully expect more Southern states to move into the North in the coming decades, barring major environmental catastrophes. In our 1870–2003 sample, eight states moved from South to North, as did a few states outside of our sample (for example, Israel and Singapore). We can easily envision another 10–12 states making the transition sometime in the twenty-first century. But, even if that were to happen, it would still leave a substantial North–South gap, with many more people living in the South than in the North.

It is also possible that Collier is right about the trend in economic growth rates, with his middle four billion growing economically "at amazing speed." Imagine, if you will, if (a) the North and South remained relatively constant in membership through 2050 and (b) the Northern group experienced average mediocre growth rates of 1.5 percent while the Southern group managed to achieve 5 percent growth rates, despite being held back by the lower South or Collier's bottom billion. Figure 9.1 charts what would

Table 9.1 Comparative economic growth rates

Decade	Middle four billion	Bottom one billion
1970s	2.5	0.5
1980s	4	−0.4
1990s	4	−0.5
Early 2000s	4.5	1.7

Source: Based on the discussion in Collier (2007: 8–9). "Billion" refers to world population.

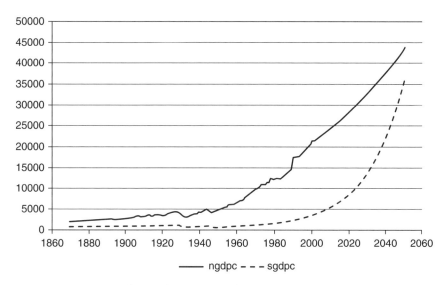

Figure 9.1 One possible North–South gap future.

happen to the North–South gap if this were to come to pass. Sometime in the second half of the twenty-first century, the gap would cease to exist, and a good proportion of the world's population would be fairly well off.

We and most other observers would be absolutely delighted if this future were to come to pass. The problem is that it is based on an exceedingly optimistic forecast. The first assumption, involving little or no change in the memberships of the North and South through 2050, is far more likely to be realized than is the likelihood that the South will enjoy a collective 5 percent growth rate over the next 40+ years. Forty years of mediocre Northern growth also seems unlikely if we are right about how technological innovation is concentrated and diffused. It would imply either the absence of continuing radical innovation, as in the past, or that we are simply wrong about the nature of long-term economic growth. We cannot rule out either of these possibilities completely, of course, but it seems more prudent to assume that life will continue as it has in the past. If it does, and should it turn out that we are not misinterpreting the role of technological change in long-term growth, the North–South gap will be with us for some time to come, even if a few states become more developed in the decades to come.

Thus, we are confronting three images. One describes a world of rich and poor, in which the poor gradually become richer and escape the zone of turmoil. A second argues that the most recent iteration of radical technological change is flattening the world, in the sense that it is now possible to compete in economic production terms around the globe, regardless of history, location, and investment propensities. The third view envisions substantial development progress for a majority of the current pool of poorer states but leaving a sixth of the world's population mired in Singer and Wildavsky's zone of turmoil.

Pessimistic evidence

Our point is that none of the interpretations of world political economy seem all that well supported by the evidence. Yes, some of the poor have become less poor, and a number have become more democratic. The rich, meanwhile, continue to become more rich. Economic development, in terms of highly technological industrialization, remains fairly concentrated. Even information technology, which in many respects might be thought to be quite susceptible to widespread diffusion, continues to be most common in the more affluent zones of the world economy. The outcome is that the gap between the rich (the North) and the poor (the South) is expanding in the twenty-first century, has continued to expand since at least the nineteenth century, and gives few signs of going away in the next 100 years – short of some very peculiar and highly asymmetrical growth rates in the North and the South (as portrayed in Figure 9.1).

If one thinks that economic growth is natural and that it only becomes constrained when bad institutions are created or when corrupt decision-makers rule, it follows that economic growth should become more widespread once the bad institutions and corrupt decision-makers are removed. If one thinks that there is a single path to economic "modernity," that a number of economies/states have shown the way, and that all one has to do is to copy their formulas for success, it follows that the trick is to convince decision-makers in poorer countries to emulate the practices of decision-makers in richer countries. If one thinks that affluence and democratization is all that it takes to reduce conflict, then it follows that the preferred strategy should be to encourage everyone to become more affluent and democratic. Internal and external peace will be an outcome of the interaction between wealth and open institutions.

Unfortunately, there seems to be more to economic development than simply creating the right institutions, eliminating corruption, or emulating the policies of affluent states. Institutions and appropriate policies certainly matter, but location matters as well. History matters too. The highly variable ability to adopt new technology is critical in our opinion. A variety of factors including location, history, and technological adoption problems have interacted to produce a North and a South. If the world economy is flattening, it is doing so very unevenly. While some parts of the world may be flattening, other parts are becoming even more unflat.

We see the world economy as having been structured by intermittent bursts of radical innovations that have, selectively, led to great wealth, complexity, and technological sophistication. The process is not static. States and their economies do not simply become more technologically complex overnight and, once transformed, stay that way forever.

New innovations emerge in extremely concentrated circumstances, diffuse unevenly, and give great advantages to pioneers and early adopters. Later developers find it increasingly more difficult to catch up to a moving target. Each successive wave of new technology pushes the more affluent states further ahead of the less affluent, less technologically sophisticated states and economies. The nature of this process does not preclude catching-up but it makes it more and more difficult to do so. As a consequence, the gap between rich and poor widens, interstate inequalities become greater, and North–South tensions should be anticipated to increase.

Why are we so pessimistic? Theoretically, we have reasons to expect an increasing North–South gap (Chapters 2 and 3). Given the significance of technological change for long-term economic growth, divergence seems more probable than is convergence. Empirically, the evidence, unfortunately, is quite consistent with these theoretical expectations. Populations that have been most receptive to adapting new technology emanating initially from Europe and later from North America, which have enjoyed access to oceanic trade routes, avoided tropical climates, and encouraged large European settlements have done well in contemporary economic history. Other places have done less well in part because their geography, climate, and population densities have been less favorable and because, in many cases, they have suffered (and continue to suffer) regimes that have not been particularly oriented to facilitating technological adaptation.

For a number of reasons discussed in Chapter 4, technology is not available to whoever wants or needs it. Path dependencies, costs, skill deficits, infrastructural lacunae, disinterested multinational corporations and governments, and other tendencies conspire to keep new technology concentrated largely within the North. Similarly, the economic integration implicit to accelerated globalization (Chapter 4) also remains more of a Northern process than one that is likely to bring North and South closer through increased trade. Investment favors the North. So, too, do migration propensities. Northerners no longer emigrate to the South as they did in the nineteenth century. Now, many Southerners head North when they can.

The South has not been completely frozen out of the systemic order. Commodity distribution around the globe has become faster, cheaper, and less subject to barriers to trade than once was the case. Formal colonial regimes have been withdrawn. Aid programs provide some relief. Some conflict has been ameliorated by intervention. Yet, structural prerogatives continue to favor the North over the South in terms of who benefits most from economic growth processes. When radical new technology is introduced by the system's lead economy, it is the North that gets the lion share. When economic growth falters in the North, moreover, it is the South that suffers debt crises (Chapter 6). The debt crises may or may not linger on, but the tendency for Southern growth to be periodically set back persists just as it tends to fall farther behind with each new wave of innovation.

Conflict (Chapter 7), however, is less subject to North–South differentiations. When growth slows, conflict increases in both the North and the South. When conflict increases, growth tends to slow down again in both the North and the South. North–South conflict, alternatively, was once relatively immune to economic growth fluctuations, but the two processes have become more positively inter-related since 1945. Resistance to at least the psychological impacts of accelerated globalization, if not always the more material gains associated with economic integration, is hardly inexplicable.

Finally, systemic leadership and world economic growth have encouraged the expansion of Southern democratization (Chapter 8) even if the local economic foundation for sustaining democracy is not equally affected. Democratization can then proceed without parallel advances in economic development, but it remains to be seen just how viable new political orders can be without a supportive economic context.

Implications

Taking a broader view, the basic nature of contemporary international relations would change if the North–South gap evaporated. Much of present-day turmoil is concentrated in the South. Wars, famine, humanitarian crises, the genesis of new diseases – the traditional four horsemen of the apocalypse – take place, for the most part now, in the South. While many Northerners might like to turn their backs on the problems of the global Southern ghetto, they cannot ignore the impacts. Population growth everywhere puts stress on the global environment and food supply. Many Southerners are drawn to Northern affluence, if they can find ways to penetrate Northern barriers to Southern migration. New diseases emerge in places where people have considerable contact with animals or where once inaccessible jungles are penetrated by the outside world and then tend to spread around the planet. Northern targets are prime and hardly inexplicable foci for Southern terrorism seeking the withdrawal of Northern troops and support for client states in the South. For some, prominent targets of affluence will suffice for motivation. Southern humanitarian crises, involving famine, refugees, genocide, and natural disasters, no longer seem as remote as they once did. All in all, the North cannot really ignore the South.

The world would no doubt be a nicer place if the North–South gap disappeared. But, it appears unlikely to go away anytime soon. The evidence suggests that whatever the case for global trickle down, catching up, and exploitation, there is a structural problem with the imperfections of technological diffusion. The liberal theory assumption that technology is freely available to whoever might need it does not seem to hold. New technology developed by the lead economy diffuses mainly within the North. Northern economies become more technologically sophisticated, while Southern economies benefit much less or stagnate.

Barring basic changes in foreign assistance and development approaches, the inherent duality of contemporary international relations predicated on uneven and unequal development propensities will probably be with us through much of the twenty-first century. The implied Southern focus on the technological paradigms of yesterday suggests three possible futures. The resulting North–South income gap may not vary that much over time, as the South works harder and harder but is only able to grow its income in a rate similar to that obtained by the North. In a second scenario, the income gap grows over time, as the current Northern gains lay the foundations needed to share disproportionally the gains from the next radical technological wave. But, the gap may also fluctuate over time. Things may get better for a while, seemingly vindicating the development policy approach of the day, but the structural Southern problems will eventually and inevitably resurface with the advent of the next wave of radical innovation.

The expected persistence of a North–South income gap in these scenarios does not preclude some Southern states joining the North. A few states have managed to do this. If China eventually moves up the world's technology gradient, the Northern population will expand considerably. India or Brazil might also move up at some point. All of these states, however, are characterized by very high internal income inequality, and it may be more accurate to say that only segments of their populations and economies currently have much potential to move into the North. But, even if these nations somehow beat the structural odds against them, large portions of Asia, the Middle East, sub-Saharan Africa, and Latin America are likely to be left behind.

Does the persistence of the North South gap mean that all of the Southern problems will continue to escalate? The answer is is that it is not necessarily so, and maybe even probably not. The number of civil wars expanded in the post-World War II era in part because there were a number of new states created (Hironaka, 2005). New states are more prone to civil war than old states, but this does not mean that newer states must experience perpetual internal warfare. Ways of dealing with old and new diseases are being developed, and some success has been achieved in coping with problems such as HIV and AIDS. New (and old) approaches to controlling terrorism and migration pressures are being tried, including relying on the most ancient technique in the play book, building walls to keep the "barbarians" out. Democratization has managed to expand to places that one might not expect to be very receptive to such arcane political practices as being able to vote the incumbent rascals out of office. Of course, it also remains to be seen whether these new ways of doing things will stick and/or whether they will ameliorate problems or make them worse.

Our message is neither that the sky is falling or that things will only get worse. Rather, there appear to be good reasons for not expecting Southern problems to go away in the near, and quite possibly the distant, future. Liberal optimism about the future is well and good but it remains just that – more an optimistic attitude than an empirically and theoretically sound forecast of the future of international relations. It seems highly unlikely that Lucas' (2000: 166) forecast that sooner or later all states will join the industrial revolution will be realized in this century. For that matter, it seems unlikely that all states will join the industrial revolution at any point in time.

It follows, then, that we should look for alternative solutions to what are likely to be enduring North–South policy problems. Waiting for economic convergence is a bad bet. Holding out for a massive Marshall Plan for the global South might be desirable but seems equally unlikely to come to pass. Foreign aid and humanitarian relief may ameliorate short-term problems but cannot be expected to resolve fundamental structural problems in planetary economic growth patterns. Acknowledging the existence of a major problem would be a step in the right direction. Only then might we expect the development of new ideas for old policy problems. Only then might we expect to come to terms with the realities of a dualistic globe and its implications for future economic growth, conflict, and living standards.

One example of a possible step in the right direction was suggested by Pritchett (1997). Given the major divergences in economic growth experiences, why should we be searching for a universal theory of economic growth? Moreover, it seems even more dubious to base any such exercise on the early developers. A one-size-fits-all theory is not likely to be all that useful if it fails to explain why there has been so little movement between North and South over the past 137 some years. In the interim, we might do better to develop different theories and policies that apply specifically to economies that already have substantial industry, as opposed to those that are attempting to climb out of poverty traps or are caught somewhere in between.[2] We also need to think more creatively about what should be/can be done with states that are unlikely to move up the technological gradient at any point in the future.

To the extent that the North–South axis becomes the, or at least a, premiere context for international relations in the twenty-first century, we may also need to adjust appropriately our non-economic theorizing. During the Cold War, polarity reigned as one of the most critical variables in our analytical repertoire. In a world increasingly divided between North and South, polarization may become more significant. The widely embraced democratic peace may be expected to remain far less than universal for some time to come. International institutions and norms may also be expected to function on less than universal principles and probably even less well than perhaps they once did. Varieties of asymmetrical warfare (insurgency, terrorism, Northern interventions into perceived Southern problem areas) may not just be a passing fancy of the past few decades but the new norm – in contrast to the classical fixation on more symmetrical, interstate warfare. To mangle an old French saying, the more things remain the same, the more things we study as students of international relations may have to change.

But perhaps not everything is subject to flux. Nye (2004: 119) notes that,

> Roughly speaking, there are three types of countries in the world today: poor, weak, pre-industrial states, which are often the chaotic remnants of collapsed empires; modernizing industrial states like India or China; and the postindustrial societies that prevail in Europe, North America, and Japan.

Is there any reason to assume that we will not be able to say something quite similar in 2050, or perhaps even 2100?

Nostrums that global inequalities are due primarily to the rich exploiting the poor or the poor not being bright enough to emulate the rich do not seem to take us very far. We certainly do not deny ample evidence of Northern exploitation or Southern corruption. Yet, global interstate inequality seems due more to the unevenness and imperfections of technological diffusion. It is also due to path dependencies, climate, demographic processes, and geography. To the extent that we are right about global inequality's main sources, it is unlikely to go away soon. Indeed, it is more likely to continue expanding in this century than it is to diminish. Accelerated globalization may or may not continue but there will be very clear constraints on its ability to operate on a genuinely global basis.

Appendix

Variable operationalizations

Conflict Data are taken from the dyadic Militarized Interstate Disputes (MIDs) data set, covering the years 1816–1992.[1] While it is possible to differentiate MIDs in terms of a verbal threat to use force, limited use of force, and war, it is not clear that a limited use of military force is necessarily more conflictual than a strong verbal threat to use force. Consequently, we count all MIDs in a year, assuming that the years with more MIDs are more conflictual than other years. The MIDs (and civil wars) are aggregated for Northern/major power conflict (conflict between two Northern countries, two major powers, or a Northern country and a major power) and North–South conflict (conflict between a Northern country and a Southern country), and Southern conflict (conflict between two Southern countries). All conflict counts are normalized by the number of dyads that could be formed among the countries in the particular groups in each year. See Goldstein (1988) and Pollins (1996) for justifications for waves of world economic growth impacting all forms of interstate warfare, including specifically MIDs.

Democratization Levels are measured based on Polity III data (Jaggars and Gurr, 1995). This data set offers a 10-point index that measures democratic characteristics of national regimes since the early nineteenth century and a 10-point index that measures autocratic tendencies. Because many governments have both democratic and autocratic characteristics, we measure the level of democracy as the difference between the two indices (see, for instance, Londegran and Poole, 1996; Mansfield and Snyder, 1995; and Oneal and Russett, 1999). This procedure generates a yearly national index ranging between –10 (most autocratic regime) and +10 (most democratic regime). We aggregate these national indices across the North and across the South. Since these indices represent countries with different populations, in aggregating them we use a weighted average, in which yearly weights are given by the ratio of national population to the total Northern or Southern population, respectively.

Lead Economy is identified as Britain or the United Kingdom in 1870–1914 and the United States after 1914.

Leader Growth Rate is based on the real GDP growth rate of Britain prior to 1915 and the United States after 1914.

Leading Sector indicators simplify the complex changes underway in shifting technological trajectories while not attempting to capture all possible facets of the new innovations. For 1870–1945, we develop an index focusing on iron/steel production, sulfuric acid production, and electricity consumption. For 1914–992, we rely on motor vehicle and semiconductor production and, after 1973, selected ISIC production that focus on office/computing machinery, communication equipment, and scientific equipment (see Hall and Preston, 1988). British values are used between 1870 and 1914 and US data thereafter. We view this design assumption as a conservative one. Britain was in relative decline at the end of the nineteenth century and certainly no longer the locus of long-term economic growth. Yet, it is usually considered the leading economic state actor up to World War I. Its principal challengers, the United States and Germany, were more innovative in the second half of the nineteenth century. We might have chosen to focus instead on the long-term growth of the United States that, we know with the advantage of hindsight, triumphed ultimately and initiated another round of growth at the end of the 1914–45 conflicts. But, an exclusive focus on US economic pulsations is the one most likely to support our arguments. We adopt, therefore, the more challenging, spliced approach to looking at long-term growth in the world economy.

Leading Sector Growth measures the yearly growth rate of leading sector production in the system's lead economy.

Leading Sector Share measures the yearly share of the global leading sector production claimed by the system's lead economy.

Major Power status is based on the classifications offered by the Correlates of War listing that ostensibly codify consensus diplomatic historian perceptions (Small and Singer, 1982).

Northern Economic Growth is the growth rate of the aggregated Northern economy, in which the identification of the North excludes the leading economy.

Northern Growth Inertia is the past value of Northern Economic Growth.

Southern Debt data are taken from Suter's (1992) 1826–1989 series. Focus is placed on data that index the number of countries in debt default (do not service their debt in terms of making interest payments or paying the principle due) or undergoing debt rescheduling (postponing payment deadlines and renegotiating terms and amounts). The debt default series ends in 1985, and the rescheduling series begins in 1956 and ends in 1989. Between 1956 and 1985, we average the two series and use this average as our measure. Whether a country defaulted or was allowed to reschedule its debt is not relevant for our immediate purposes since we are focusing on debt problems and not their type. After 1985, we rely solely on rescheduling information. The debt problems of non-Southern states are excluded.

We control for changes in system size by normalizing the number of Southern countries exhibiting debt problems by the Correlates of War's annual count of the number of states in the system.

Southern Economic Growth is the growth rate of the aggregated Southern economy.

Southern Growth Inertia is the past value of Southern Economic Growth.

Systemic Leadership is measured by the leader's share of global reach capabilities, as approximated by naval data as reported in Modelski and Thompson (1988). Capabilities are measured in terms of a formula that, for different periods of time, combines information on naval expenditures, battleships, aircraft carriers, nuclear submarines, and SLBM attributes for Britain, France, Germany, Japan, Russia/USSR, and the United States. Sea power and the ability to act coercively over long distances were largely synonymous in much of the post-1494 era. The more recent global reach capabilities such as air power, satellites, and cruise missiles also often require naval support. With the possible exception of land forces, we suspect and assume that the preponderant profile established by naval leadership reflects leads in most other coercive components. The series is spliced (British values before and US values afterwards) at 1945.[2]

Trade Openness is measured as the ratio of total export value of the North or the South to the world, expressed in constant dollars, to total gross domestic product (GDP) of the North or South, also expressed in constant dollars from the same base year. More specifically, our approach consisted of first calculating, for each country in our sample, the proportion of world trade as reported in Banks (1971), and updated via various volumes of the UN *Statistical Yearbook*. We then aggregated this information into Southern and Northern proportion of world trade. Maddison (1995: 239) reports a series on the value of world exports in constant 1990 dollars for 1870, 1881–1913, 1924–38, and 1950–92. After interpolating straightforwardly for the missing years, we then converted the world export figures into Southern and Northern exports for each year between 1870 and 1992, based on our classification of countries to North and South. These numbers were then divided by the respective GDP aggregations for the South and North to create macro-trade openness indices (exports/GDP). We had also attempted to utilize the economic globalization series developed by Chase-Dunn, Kawano, and Brewer (2000). In trying to decompose it into Northern and Southern components, we found the data to be highly dependent on Northern data well into the twentieth century. Nonetheless, we are indebted to Christopher Chase-Dunn for the opportunity of examining the raw data used to construct the series.

Trade Openness Inertia is measured as the lagged trade openness indicator.

World Economic Growth is based on aggregated, annual real GDP data, expressed in 1990 dollars for 17 major countries (Australia, Austria,

Belgium, Canada, Denmark, Finland, France, Germany, Italy, Japan, the Netherlands, New Zealand, Norway, Sweden, Switzerland, United Kingdom, and the United States, with Japanese data beginning in 1885 and Swiss data commencing in 1899) (Maddison, 1995).

Statistical and research design details for selected chapters

Chapter 5

In Chapter 5, we use the following model for each of our two units of analysis, North and South:

(1) EXPOPEN = f (SYSLEAD, WGROWTH, CONFLICT, DEMOCRACY, INERTIA, DEBTDEF).

In this model, export openness of a region (EXPOPEN) depends on six variables: systemic leadership (SYSLEAD), World economic growth (WGROWTH), level of conflict that involves countries in the region (CONFLICT), level of democracy in the region (DEMOCRACY), export openness inertia (INERTIA) – a lagged value of EXPOPEN, and the level of debt default in the region – failure to service debt on time or pay due principle – (DEBTDEF). Given that debt defaults did not occur often in the North, DEBTDEF is only included in the Southern model.

Given this model, we need to consider several design issues. First, some of the right-hand-side variables could be affected by export openness. A decline in openness could promote a debt crisis as foreign reserves are depleted. A rise in openness could promote democracy, as economic freedom can promote political freedom. To the extent that trade is an engine of growth, world economic growth could be affected. Trade could have a pacifying effect on conflict. On the other hand, leadership is not likely to be directly affected by export openness. In our leadership long cycle perspective, systemic leadership is a function of the performance of the system leader in leading economic sectors.

In general, if a statistical model ignores reciprocal relationships between variables, the results will likely be biased. At the same time, fully accounting for all possible reciprocal effects can obviously turn into a monumental task. In addition, the size of the simultaneity bias in practice may be small. While most empirical studies, in fact, ignore reciprocal effects, some models deal with simultaneity by lagging the independent variables (e.g., Li and Reuveny, 2003; Muller and Seligson, 1994, Oneal and Russett, 1999). The rationale for this method is that the current value of a variable cannot affect the past value of another variable. We will use this method for world economic growth, democracy, conflict, and debt default. For systemic leadership, we do not employ this method because our theoretical perspective does not attribute a causal factor to trade openness in bringing about leadership.

The effects of many social–political–economic forces develop relatively slowly, or adjust dynamically (Greene, 1997). Dynamic adjustment is commonly modeled by employing lags of variables – distributed lags. This approach assumes that the past levels of the explanatory forces can affect the dependent variable. Our method of dealing with simultaneity employs the first lag of explanatory variables (except for leadership). This itself is dynamic adjustment with a lag length of one. In general, the adjustment lag lengths may be longer than one, and may vary across variables.

World economic growth and democracy may take more than one period to influence trade openness. Current values of leadership could affect openness, but current openness may also incorporate previous leadership effects. However, when all is said and done, our argument (similar to most dynamic interpretations in social science) does not specify the number of lags for the empirical analysis. "The appropriate length of lag is rarely, if ever, known, so one must undertake a specification search" (Greene, 1997: 786). As is done in many studies, we chose the lag structure from a systematic search. Our search will provide many results, from which we chose the best specification in terms of goodness of fit, levels of significance, and signs of effects compared with theoretical expectations.[3]

Our primary empirical model will be the one specified for Northern openness. We expect weaker effects of our leadership long cycle variables in the South, and perhaps no effect at all. Therefore, we look for the lag structure found to fit the Northern model, and then employ the same specification as a baseline in testing whether our findings hold for Southern openness.

It is tempting to translate distributed lags into substantive terms. In distributed lag models, however, one looks for lags first as a check on causality – if x influences y, x should antecede y as a matter of data fitting. As noted, our theory does not tell us what sorts of lags to anticipate. Moreover, we rarely have enough observations to examine long lags of, say, generational length. Thus, one should be reticent to attribute considerable significance to the lag length. The question is not so much whether we can isolate lagged effects precisely in terms of time between impact and maximum effect. Rather, do we find significant relationships, and do the signs of the effects agree with the theoretical predictions?

When models include distributed lags, the interpretation of results can be complicated. The signs and significance levels of lags for the same variables may vary. As many studies do, we will report results from both individual coefficients and sums of lag coefficients for each variable (Greene, 1997). These sums have the same interpretation as individual coefficients, but give the overall effect of a shock with a duration of its lag length in a right-hand-side variable on the dependent variable.

In addition to our variables, a number of structural variables that could affect export openness (e.g., structure of contracts, institutional qualities, internal power distribution) are absent. Structural variables typically change slowly, and their effects are manifested by export openness inertia, which, as noted, is typically modeled by including a lagged dependent variable. Hence, in addition to the theoretical notion of openness inertia, the lagged dependent variable captures effects of potentially missing structural variables. As noted by Burkhart and Lewis-Beck (1994) and others, this method makes it more difficult for spurious effects to be reported. It also makes it harder to find significant results (Li and Reuveny, 2003). Hence, our modeling approach can be said to be conservative.

Given the time series nature of our data, we need to consider the possibility of serial correlation. With serial correlation, estimated coefficients are not biased, but their standard errors are biased. The inclusion of the lagged dependent variable on the right-hand side is expected to alleviate problems associated with serial correlation (Beck and Katz, 1995). Nevertheless, we also will estimate robust standard errors, as suggested by Newey and West (1987). In concordance with Morrow et al. (1998) and Oneal and Russett (1999), we use a one-tailed t-test for coefficients whose sign is theoretically expected, and two-tailed t-tests otherwise. Hence, for world economic growth, leadership, inertia, democracy, and debt default, we employ a one-tailed t-test, and for conflict we employ a two-tailed t-test.[4]

After 1945, the leadership data are based on US values; before 1946, they are based on British values. Since our theory is expected to work in the long run, we use the full sample. But, it is desirable to employ samples that combine US and British leadership data, as well as use portions of the sample for robustness checks. It is also clear that a sample that is too short will exhibit only part of the dynamics, leading to spurious results. These considerations suggest using three samples: 1870–1992, 1870–1945, and, 1919–92.

Finally, Equation (1) assumes that trade openness processes can be profitably aggregated into Northern and Southern processes. The reader may recall that our theory predicts different behaviors for North and South. If we are correct, we would expect to see significant effects for the North, and much less so for the South. But, one may argue that changes in Northern national openness are brought about by unique national factors. We think this threat is unlikely to be so serious as to completely undermine our approach for the North. If Northern trade openness has a clear dynamic, different countries in the region are probably reacting to common stimuli. For our purpose, it does not really matter if there are elements associated with some cases and not with others, as long as there are common factors across cases. The possibility that Northern openness is traced primarily to idiosyncratic national factors is relegated to the statistical error term in any case, and should work against us in the test. If this threat is large, our model should not find empirical support.

Southern openness is expected to be less responsive to leadership and world economic growth. Again, it is possible that some Southern countries will be positively affected by growth and leadership, absorb radical inno-vations emanating from the lead economy, break the shackles of underde-velopment, and forge ahead in export openness. This possibility certainly exists but it is not expected to be the general case. If most of the South does not adhere to this assumption, our findings should not support our expectations.

Chapter 6

Historically, there have been both global debt crises and local crises. We focus on the former exclusively, ignoring the latter as relatively idiosyn-cratic problems. Our theory implies the need to test the following model:

$$SD = f\ (WG,\ SL,\ NC,\ SD_{t-1}). \tag{1}$$

The dependent variable SD denotes Southern debt default – the number of Southern countries that cannot service their debt or pay their principle, divided by the number of countries in the international system. WG denotes world economic growth, SL denotes systemic leadership, and NC denotes Northern conflict. The effects of increases in WG and SL on SD are expected to be negative, the effect of NC on SD could be positive or negative, and the impact of SD_{t-1} on SD should be positive.

Socio-economic forces typically change over time, or follow dynamic adjustment (Greene, 1997). Dynamic adjustment is modeled by employing lags of explanatory variables in order to accommodate changes over time. Theories, including our own, typically do not specify the number of lags. As noted by Greene (1997: 786), "the appropriate length of lag is rarely, if ever, known, so one must undertake a specification search" (Greene, 1997: 786).

In choosing the number of lags, some studies employ trial-and-error search from the goodness of fit of models to the data, or the significance levels and signs of effects compared with theoretical expectations. Other studies employ information criteria that minimize a function of the residual sum of squares combined with a penalty designed to limit the number of lags. Several such methods have been developed, where the difference among them is the exact function minimized (e.g., Akaike, 1974; Schwartz, 1978). We will employ both approaches.

We believe that the past values of forces may well affect our current dependent variable. That is, these effects may exhibit dynamic adjustment, and the speed of adjustment (lag length) may vary across variables.[5] The effect of changes in world economic growth may take more than one period to filter through the system and influence Southern debt problems. Past values of systemic leadership also could affect current debt problems, just as current debt arrangements may incorporate previous leadership effects. The effect of Northern conflict on Southern debt problems may be faster, as wars typically affect societies without lags.

We first conducted trial-and-error tests in order to choose the lag structure that fits the data best from the above criteria. Second, we employed the Schwartz criterion. Both the Schwartz and Akaike methods formulate the principle of parsimony in model building. The Schwarz method is more conservative or leads to more parsimonious models (Cavanaugh and Neath, 2001; Doan, 2000). Another problem with the Akaike approach is that it retains a positive probability of model over-fitting even as the sample is very large (Greene, 1997). We therefore rely on the Schwartz criterion.

Next, it is tempting to translate lag structures into substantive terms. In our modeling type, however, one looks for lags first as a check on causality – if x influences y, x should antecede y – and second, as a matter of data fitting. On the other hand, we lack sufficiently specified theory to tell us what sorts of lags to anticipate. Moreover, we rarely have a sufficient number of observations to examine the possibility of longer lags of, say, generational length. As a consequence, one should be reticent to attribute considerable substantive significance to the lags. A 1-year lag is unlikely to be substantively different from a 4-year lag. The question is not so much whether we can isolate a lagged effect precisely in terms of chronological time between impact and maximum effect. Rather, do we find significant relationships?

When models include distributed lags, the interpretation of results from the individual coefficients can be complicated. Many studies analyze the sums of lag coefficients for each variable (Greene, 1997). These sums have the same interpretation as individual coefficients, but give the overall effect of a shock in an independent variable on the dependent variable, with a duration of its lag length. We report results from both the individual coefficients and their sums. As in Morrow, Siverson, and Tabares (1998) and Oneal and Russett (1999), we use a one-tailed t-test for coefficients whose sign is theoretically expected, and two-tailed t-tests otherwise. Hence, for the effect of world economic growth, lagged Southern debt default, and systemic leadership, we employ a one-tailed t-test, and for Northern conflict we employ a two-tailed t-test.

In addition to our variables, there could be structural variables that affect Southern debt default (e.g. civic culture, political regime). Structural variables typically change relatively slowly over time, and their effect is manifested by a tendency of Southern debt problems to exhibit inertia. Inertia generally is modeled by including a lagged dependent variable. Hence, in addition to the theoretical notion of debt inertia, the lagged dependent variable captures the effects of potentially relevant structural variables not included. As noted before by Burkhart and Lewis-Beck (1994), for example, this method makes it more difficult for spurious effects to be reported. The use of the lagged dependent variable as an independent variable also makes it harder to find significant results (Li and Reuveny, 2003). Hence, our approach can be said to be conservative.

Southern debt problems might affect world economic growth. Or, Southern debt problems might affect leadership (less likely). While most studies ignore reciprocal effects, some studies deal with this issue by lagging the independent variables (e.g., Muller and Seligson, 1994; Oneal and Russett, 1999). We use this method for world economic growth and systemic leadership. For Northern conflict, we do not employ this method as we are not aware of compelling reasons why Southern debt problems would be a causal factor in Northern conflict.

Given the time series nature of our data, we need to consider the possibility of serial correlation. With serial correlation, the estimated coefficients are not biased, but their standard errors are not efficient and could be biased. The inclusion of the lagged dependent variable as an independent variable is expected to alleviate problems associated with serial correlation (Beck and Katz, 1995). Nevertheless, we will check for the presence of serial correlation and, if needed, adjust the estimation technique accordingly.

Finally, our data suggest the need for sensitivity analyses. First, from 1870 to 1945, our leadership data are based on British values. From 1946 to 1989, they are based on US values. Some studies also argue that the height of the US leadership was in the 1950s and early 1960s, after which it experienced relative decline (e.g., Goldstein, 1988; Mansfield, 1994; Pollins, 1996). Consequently, we look at four samples: 1870–1945, 1946–89, 1960–89, and 1870–1989. Second, our debt data are constructed from two series that overlap from 1956 to 1985, which are discussed in the 'Variable Operationalization' section. From 1956 to 1985, the full series employs the average of the two series. The dynamics of these components in the overlapping period of the two series are visually similar. However, to make sure that the shift in data does not drive part of our results, we will include dummy variables for the years 1956 and 1986 in the model. Third, while not called for by our theory, we add Southern conflict and North–South conflict variables to the model, to check whether these two variables have an effect on global debt crises, particularly during World War I and World War II.

Our research design is vulnerable to several threats. We assumed that globalized debt crises are comparable across time and space. It could be that localized debt problems are somewhat unique. We also think that we can profitably aggregate all of the states in the South into one group for our purpose. But, each country's debt problems may also be brought about by unique factors. That said, we think these threats are unlikely to be serious obstacles. If global debt problems cluster in time repeatedly, there is a good chance that different countries are reacting to similar external and internal stimuli. For our purposes, it may not matter much if there are elements associated with some clusters and not with others. For instance, the sources and nature of lending were different in the nineteenth century than in the twentieth century (more direct and from large banks in the late twentieth century). So, too, was the search for policy solutions (e.g., absent in the nineteenth and more visible in the late twentieth centuries). The debt problems may be initiated in the private sector and then migrate to the public sector or vice versa. None of these should matter much to questions pertaining to the timing of relationships among the spread of global debt problems (crises) and fluctuations in the world economy and systemic leadership.

Some Southern debt problems also can be traceable to influences that lie outside our modeling efforts. We do not deny that Southern corruption and poor planning have explanatory value. Some countries also may be encouraged to default because they see others doing the same thing. Banking apprehensions may be subject to contagious processes. These perceptual processes may facilitate the spread of a debt crisis once a global one is already in process. We think it unlikely, however, that global debt crises can be traced ultimately to imitation or irrational panic as the root causes. Global crises spread too far, last too long, and tend to repeat historically to be that easily explained.

All these design threats are relegated to the error term and should work against us in finding statistically significant results. If these threats are very large, our global-debt-crisis-focused argument should not find empirical support.

Chapter 7

Our perspective involves dynamic interactions among four endogenous variables. As discussed by Williams (1993) and others, two types of statistical methodologies may be used to study such cases, the VAR model and the simultaneous equation model (SEM). The specification of an SEM requires imposing identifying dynamic restrictions necessary for specifying a structural statistical model. The theories we have reviewed, including the one we have developed, do not specify such restrictions with great certainty, but rather generate predictions on the general changes or movements in the endogenous variables. In such cases, the estimation results from an SEM may be biased, and a VAR model is typically used.[6] The VAR approach is employed here.

The model's equations are as follows:

$$WG_t = WG_0 + \sum_{i=1}^{L} \alpha_{WG_i} WG_{t-i} + \sum_{i=1}^{L} \alpha_{NN_i} NN_{t-i} + \sum_{i=1}^{L} \alpha_{MM_i} MM_{t-i} + \sum_{i=1}^{L} \alpha_{NS_i} NS_{t-i} + \varepsilon_t$$

$$NN_t = NN_0 + \sum_{i=1}^{L} \beta_{WG_i} WG_{t-i} + \sum_{i=1}^{L} \beta_{NN_i} NN_{t-i} + \sum_{i=1}^{L} \beta_{MM_i} MM_{t-i} + \sum_{i=1}^{L} \beta_{NS_i} NS_{t-i} + e_t$$

$$MM_t = MM_0 + \sum_{i=1}^{L} \gamma_{WG_i} WG_{t-i} + \sum_{i=1}^{L} \gamma_{NN_i} NN_{t-i} + \sum_{i=1}^{L} \gamma_{MM_i} MM_{t-i} + \sum_{w=1}^{L} \gamma_{NS_i} NS_{t-i} + v_t$$

$$NS_t = NS_0 + \sum_{i=1}^{L} \delta_{WG_i} WG_{t-i} + \sum_{i=1}^{L} \delta_{NN_i} NN_{t-i} + \sum_{i=1}^{L} \delta_{MM_i} MM_{t-i} + \sum_{i=1}^{N} \delta_{NS_i} NS_{t-i} + u_t$$

Equations 1 through 4 describe a typical VAR model: the same lag length (L) is used for all variables, the same variables appear in each equation, and constant terms (WG_0, MM_0, NN_0, NS_0) are used. WG denotes world economic growth rate, NN denotes North–North conflict, NS denotes North–South conflict, MM denotes major power conflict, the subscripts t and i denote time, the subscripts WG, NN, MM, and NS identify coefficients, the symbols α, β, γ, and δ denote the coefficients to be estimated, and ε_t, e_t, u_t, and v_t are the error terms.

As noted by Freeman, Williams, and Lin (1989) and Greene (1997), some researchers argue that VAR models are atheoretical because they include the lags of all endogenous variables in all equations. To the extent that this criticism holds, the atheoretical nature of VARs can also be viewed as an empirical asset. VARs can be useful precisely because they are flexible and do not impose many restrictions on the relationships between variables. Regardless, as noted and exemplified in Sims (1980), Freeman, Williams, and Lin (1989), Goldstein (1991), Doan (2000), and Greene (1997), VARs are used by many studies in the social sciences.

VAR models are estimated from Ordinary Least Squares (OLS). To our best knowledge, the VAR methodology is only available within an OLS framework, which assumes that the dependent variable is continuous. Our conflict variables are ratios based on counts of MIDs and as such are not strictly continuous. Greene (1997: 931) and Johnston and DiNardo (1997: 414) note that count models are typically estimated from traditional linear regression, and they do not find any fault in this practice. However, Greene also notes that one could improve on the performance of OLS and a linear model in this case with a specification that takes into account the discrete nature of a count as the dependent variable. The Poisson regression model is sometimes used in these cases. That said, the extent of the added improvement from using Poisson regression on OLS is a matter of degree.[7] Since the VAR methodology is the most appropriate for our purpose, we employ it in this chapter.

We chose the lag length for the model using the method suggested by Sims (1980) and Doan (1992). If the lag length is not appropriate, it will most likely be reflected by serial correlation in the error terms of Equations (1)–(4). Accordingly, we estimate the VAR from the chosen lag length, and then inspect the error terms of all equations for the presence of serial correlation from two methods.[8] Even though some researchers doubt the importance of unit roots (Doan, 1992; McCallum, 1993; Sims, 1988), we employed Dickey and Fuller's (1979) and Phillips and Perron's (1988) tests, systematically trying one to eight lags for each series/sample. All series were found to be stationary at a significance level of 5 percent. The test statistics are much smaller than the critical values: –3.2 and –3.3 for 1870–1945 and 1946–92, respectively.

After determining the number of lags to be used from Sims' (1980) test, we inspected the residuals for serial correlation. Since VAR equations include lags of the dependent variable, the Durbin-Watson test may be biased. One alternative is to use the Durbin-h test. But several researchers (for example, Inder, 1984) find this test has low power. In addition, this test assumes that the serial correlation is an auto-regression order one type, which does not have to be the case. We use two methods to test for serial correlation of a general type, which are valid in VARs: Q test (Greene, 1997), and the cumulative periodogram test (Doan, 1992). The latter is based on the Fourier transformation of the residuals. The cumulative periodogram of the residual is compared to that of white noise from a Kolmogorov-Smirnov test. If the two periodograms are statistically similar, the residuals are not serially correlated.

Most of the F test outcomes in Table A1 are statistically significant. The insignificant outcomes are not inexplicable as the F tests do not consider indirect effects that are present in a VAR. The block exogeneity test in Table A2 compare two VARs. The restricted VAR includes some independent variables. The unrestricted VAR adds more variables. The null hypothesis is that a block of variables does not enter another block (Sims, 1980). The test does not involve all of the model's equations and may miss indirect effects. Moreover, when a block of variables is found to not enter certain equations, this does not eliminate the possibility that individual variables from that block enter the equations. We divide the variables into political

Table A1 Joint significance tests

Dependent variable	Independent variable	Panel A 1870–1945	Panel B 1946–92
World economic growth	World economic growth	0.744	0.023***
	Major power conflict	0.166*	0.154*
	Northern conflict	0.031***	0.003***
	North–South conflict	0.036***	0.098**
Major power conflict	World economic growth	0.512	0.179*
	Major power conflict	0***	0.165*
	Northern conflict	0.206	0.672
	North–South conflict	0.766	0.331
Northern conflict	World economic growth	0.362	0.036***
	Major power conflict	0.125*	0.328
	Northern conflict	0.002***	0.022**
	North–South conflict	0.390	0.780
North–South conflict	World economic growth	0.154*	0.064**
	Major power conflict	0***	0.072**
	Northern conflict	0.020***	0.244
	North–South conflict	0.017***	0***

Note: Entries denoted the significance levels from a test rejecting the null hypothesis that a group of lags of a certain independent variable in a given equation are not jointly significant. Three asterisks indicates statistical significance at the 0.05 level or better, two asterisks at the 0.10 level or better, and one asterisk at the 0.20 level or better.

Table A2 Block exogeneity tests

Variables in the restricted model	Variables in the non restricted model	Period	Significance level	Decision
Political	Political + economic	1870–1945	0.088**	Reject restricted
		1946–92	0.100**	Reject restricted
Economic	Economic + political	1870–1945	0.022***	Reject restricted
		1946–92	0.020***	Reject restricted

Note: A low significance indicates that the hypothesis that a block of variables does not enter the equations of another block of variables should be rejected. The political variables include major power conflict, Northern conflict, and North–South conflict, and the economic variables include world economic growth. The restricted model includes a subset of variables as regressors. The non-restricted model includes all the variables as regressors. Three asterisks indicates statistical significance at the 0.05 level or better, two asterisks at the 0.10 level or better, and one asterisk at the 0.20 level or better.

(MM, NN, NS) and economic (WG) blocks. Table A2 illustrates that the two blocks affect each other.

The order of variables can affect the impulse responses since it affects the VAR's orthogonalized form. In VARs, some ordering of the variables must be chosen by the modeler. If the correlations among the variables are low (say, 0.2), using different orders of variables may not matter. Of course, if these correlations are low, one may wonder why these variables are put in the same model. Since our correlations are between 0.2 and 0.8, the ordering of variables may matter. We use the ordering WG, MM, NN, and NS. We also examined the ordering MM, NN, NS, and WG. The spirit of the results from this ordering is mostly similar to the reported results, but the model fits the data less well.

In the Monte Carlo simulations, covariance of the coefficients is first estimated. N impulse responses are then computed. In each case, the coefficients of the VAR are drawn from a multivariate normal distribution with the above covariance, and a mean given by the estimated coefficient. The N responses are then used to compute the standard deviations and confidence intervals.

Second, we tested the joint significance of lag coefficients from F tests and conduct block exogeneity tests. The results are reported below. While providing some guidance, these two tests can tell only a partial story since they are computed separately from each equation (for F tests), or from a partial set of equations (for block exogeneity tests). As argued in Doan (1992), this is a limitation, because these tests ignore the fact that, in a VAR, variables also affect each other through their effect on the lags of other variables. Nevertheless, the F test results suggest that our four variables affect each other, which supports a theory (such as ours) suggesting that we put them together in the same model in the first place. The block exogeneity tests suggest that there are two blocks of variables in the model – political (major power conflict, Northern conflict, North–South conflict) and economic (world economic growth), which again affect each other.

Third, we computed impulse (shock) responses, which give the dynamic reaction of each variable to a positive impulse in each variable, applied one at a time. The order in which the variables are written in the VAR may matter in this analysis. This need not be viewed necessarily as a limitation. We (and others) believe that the order of variables is part of a theory. In line with our interpretation, we ordered the variables as world economic growth, major power conflict, Northern conflict, and North–South conflict.[9]

The impulse responses are computed from the estimated coefficients. Similar to all regression-based analyses, these responses might have changed had we performed the analysis from repeated samples. Obviously, we only have one historical realization of our variables with which to work. To learn about the statistical significance of the effects, we compute confidence intervals from a Monte Carlo simulation.[10] Table 7.3 in Chapter 7 summarizes the effects implied by the impulse responses that were created.

Notes

1. Unreal and unflat worlds

1. We should at least see some linkages among these phenomena. US support for mujahedeen in Afghanistan led to jihadi terrorism and the US movement into Iraq for a second time. We do not insist, of course, that it had to happen this way. Nevertheless, the three types of activity are very much related.
2. We fully expect that North–South relations will vie for global issue-area primacy along with the threat of Chinese ascent as the two main issues related to structural change in world politics.
3. The quoted passages are found in Friedman (2007: 9–10).
4. In 2008, the percentage was inching towards 75 percent.
5. Given its scope, we cannot review fully the leadership long cycle literature. Basically, it is a structural interpretation of world politics that emphasizes the significance and concentration of technological innovation over the past millennium. Beginning with an economic development breakthrough in Sung China in the eleventh and twelfth centuries, subsequent foci of innovation spurts can be associated with Genoese, Venetian, Portuguese, Dutch, British, and US economic activities with increasing importance for limited forms of systemic governance restricted initially to inter-regional commercial transactions. The timing and location of the serial spurts of concentrated technological innovation have generated an evolving framework for world politics. For more detailed expositions (without attention to Northern and Southern globalization), see Modelski and Thompson (1996) and Thompson (2000).
6. See, for example, Modelski (1987, 1996), Modelski, Devezas, and Thompson (2008), Modelski and Thompson (1988, 1996), Rasler and Thompson (1994), Reuveny and Thompson (1999, 2000, 2001, 2004b), Thompson (1988, 2000).
7. Examples of these radical innovations include mechanized textile looms, steam engines, electrification, automobiles, jet engines, and computers.
8. Migration to Southern areas without surplus land and dense populations also took place in the nineteenth century, but the migrants tended to be from the South, were employed as plantation workers, and did not always remain in the places to which they had moved. As a consequence, their impact appears to have been much less substantial.

2. Interpreting economic growth and development

1. Conversely, increasing piracy, not unlike calls for reforming the rules of international finance, are indicators of a decaying world order.

2. In Chapter 5, we will comment on 1.5 exceptions (nineteenth century migration and the diffusion of public health information) to the constraints on technological diffusion.

3. The major exception to the stickiness of the regional hierarchy is the heterogeneous Asian region.

4. Hatton and Williamson (2005: 17) note that while New World emigrants in 1900 were similar to those in 2000, they were very different from 1800 emigrants. Apparently, then, it is difficult to make over-arching generalizations that span "only" a century.

5. Compare this perspective with Diamond's (1997) not entirely contradictory interpretation of Eurasia's long-term advantage in urbanization, food surpluses, and technological innovation based on geography. We certainly do not dismiss the idea of horizontal axes that facilitate the diffusion of people, ideas, and germs versus vertical axes that combine with geographical and climate barriers to restrict diffusion. But, we prefer to focus on more recent sources of diffusion-restricting developments.

6. Since they introduced Eurasian diseases into the unprepared American population that led to considerable loss of life and the need to import laborers from Africa, it is difficult to contest the idea that European settlers were healthier than the native Americans.

7. Acemoglu, Johnson, and Robinson argue, interestingly, that institutions are most likely to matter to industrialization when new technology adoption requires investment from a broad cross-section of the population. We think the emphasis on investment should be expanded to incorporate participation in new technology adoption. Populations have to be inclined to, and prepared to, use new technology in addition to having financial support for its availability.

8. Sachs (2008: 86) notes that institutions have become the panacea for all developmental problems. The problems with this single factor explanation are that (a) income improvements are pegged to Western ideas, and (b) the source of the developmental problem is local and only local agents can fix the problem. We agree with Sachs (2008: 86) that "the barriers to development ... are far more complex than institutional shortcomings" alone.

9. Other analysts would describe the development strategies as import substitution policies.

10. The rationale for these particular thresholds will be discussed at greater length in Chapter 3. For immediate purposes, exactly how one divides the less wealthy/developed from the more wealthy/developed is highly arbitrary. But, if one is interested in over-time comparisons, it is difficult to use a single per capita figure that has the same meaning in earlier time periods as it does in later ones.

11. Note that China remains in the poorest group up to 2000, according to these data. We will return to this question in subsequent chapters.

12. Krieckhaus (2006) attributes these Asian gains largely to defensive modernization efforts by states that evaded direct colonial control, but there are a number of complications. Taiwan and Korea, ironically, benefitted in the long run by being subordinated within the Japanese empire prior to World War II. They were expected to play significant roles in the imperial division of economic labor and, as a consequence, experienced land reform, literacy, and infrastructural development. Hong Kong and Singapore equally benefitted from their entrepot functions within the British Empire. In other words, their colonial histories primed them for later success even if that was not the intent of the colonial governments.

13. Chapter 5 reviews the evidence on the migration dimension of this phenomenon.

14. The major exception, as previously noted, appears to be Japanese colonial regimes which are credited with diminishing agrarian inequality and illiteracy in Korea and Taiwan as part of a plan for Japanese imperial economic growth.

15. There are, of course, exceptions. Japan and Korea, to name but two, profited economically from the Cold War in general and wars in Korea and Vietnam in particular.

16. We return to this subject in Chapter 6's focus on recurring debt problems in the South.

17. There appears to be a pattern of distance making some difference in technology diffusion. Areas in the immediate neighborhood of an intensively innovative center tend to experience some spillover. This pattern first became noticeable in the modern era with the advent of the British industrial revolution in the late eighteenth century and appears to persist into the twenty-first. Of course, one could also trace this type of pattern back to the emergence of the original Mesopotamian cities in the fourth millennium BCE and subsequent hot spots of concentrated economic growth.

18. We are well aware that all Northern states are not located in the Northern hemisphere. We might just as easily call the Northern states "developed" and Southern states as "developing." Yet, that practice has its disadvantages as well. Most, if not all, of the developed states continue to develop. As we will see in subsequent chapters, that is part of the problem. We could also point to the fact that not all developing states are developing very much.

19. Russia in the 1990s is an example of a state that lost its hard-won Northern status, at least temporarily, when the Soviet Union collapsed.

3. Exploring the North–South gap longitudinally

1. Maddison's (2007) data makes the sampling approach less necessary since he has broadened his data set to include many more poor states after 1950. However, the new data only became available as we were completing our analyses. Since many of our analyses had been based on the sample, our basic choice was one of either re-estimating all of our analyses with a larger N or assuming that the addition of more poor countries would only accentuate the plight of Southern states already well manifested in the sample. We opted for the latter approach. As part of our sensitivity analyses later in this chapter, we will demonstrate that our findings are not biased substantially by any of our assumptions. See Kentor (2000) for a much different approach to the problem.

2. For review of these issues, see, for example, Jones (1998).

3. These models make strong assumptions about the production function describing the economy. Other new growth theory models are similar to neoclassical growth theory in that the saving rate does not affect the economic growth rate (see Jones, 1998).

4. For reviews, see, among others, Passe-Smith (1996, 1998) and Temple (1999). We should also note that we are focusing exclusively on between-country analyses. For within-country studies of inequality, see Bornschier (2002), Bourguignon and Morrisson (2002), Firebaugh (2003), and Sala-I-Martin (2002).

5. Not all analysts qualify their arguments about divergence. See, for instance, Milanovic (2005) and Wade (2007).

6. Most of the Southern information made available by Maddison in subsequent expansions of the original sample encompasses African and Middle Eastern states that are among the poorest states in the world system.

7. GDP per capita may not be the best indicator of economic inequality. However, the convergence literature that we are addressing is concerned predominately with this indicator. For contrasting views on the pluses and minuses of Maddison's data, see Hanson (1997), Holz (2006), and Verspagen (1998). Our view is that there are no real alternatives to Maddison's data if one wants consistent, comparable, and long series.

8. In the 1995 dataset, information for 15 states (Australia, Austria, Belgium, Canada, Denmark, Finland, France, Germany, Italy, the Netherlands, New Zealand, Norway, Sweden, Britain, and the United States) are complete from 1870 through 1992. Data for the other 41 states either begin later than 1870, have gaps, or both. We interpolate data for the following countries and years: Japan (1871–84); Switzerland (1871–98); Spain (1871–89, 1891–99); Argentina (1871–89, 1891–99); Brazil (1871–89, 1891–99); Mexico (1871–89, 1891–99); China (1871–89, 1891–99, 1901–12, 1914–28, 1939–49); India (1871–99, 1891–99); Indonesia (1871–89, 1891–99); Ireland (1871–89, 1891–99, 1901–12, 1914–25, 1927–28, 1930, 1932, 1934–35, 1939–46); Portugal (1871–89, 1891–99, 1901–12, 1914–28, 1930–37, 1939–46); Hungary (1871–99, 1901–13, 1914–19, 1921–23, 1943–45); Czechoslovakia (1871–89, 1891–99, 1901–12, 1914–19, 1938–47); Russia/USSR (1871–89, 1891–99, 1901–12, 1914–27, 1941–46); Egypt (1901–12, 1914–49); Ghana (1901–12, 1914–49); Greece (1914–28, 1940–41, 1943–44); Turkey (1914–22); Bulgaria (1914–23, 1946–49); Poland (1939–49); Romania (1939–48, 1949, 1951–54, 1956–59); Yugoslavia (1914–19, 1940–47); Colombia (1901–12, 1914–24); Peru (1901–12); Bangladesh (1901–12, 1914–28, 1930–31, 1933–37, 1939–47); Burma (1902–05, 1907–10, 1912, 1914–15, 1917–20, 1922–25, 1927–30, 1932–35, 1937, 1939–49); Pakistan (1901–12, 1914–28, 1930–31, 1933–37, 1939–47); Philippines (1901–12, 1914–28, 1930–37, 1939–49); South Korea (1901–12); Taiwan (1901–02); Thailand (1871–89, 1891–99, 1901–12, 1914–28, 1930–37, 1939–49); and South Africa (1914–49). Chile and Venezuela have complete series from 1900 on. Ivory Coast, Ethiopia, Kenya, Morocco, Nigeria, Tanzania, and Zaire have complete series from 1950 on.

9. For instance, are the technological development gains associated with Indian computer word processing the equivalent of developing the technology to manufacture computer hardware? Or is it a matter of Northern firms searching for inexpensive labor in the South?

10. Kuznets (1972), e.g., suggests a US$1000 threshold, and Passe-Smith (1998) suggests US$4000.

11. Interestingly, Maddison's data and other PPP estimations have undergone considerable re-evaluation and re-estimation. One of the consequences is that if we had started with the 2007 data, a 25 percent threshold would not have been perceived as satisfactory as a 33 or 40 percent threshold. But, we opted to stay with the 25 percent threshold in this book's analyses and hasten to remind the reader that any threshold is quite arbitrary.

12. The oil producers definitely have capitalized on their ability to provide an important raw material, but are still basically underdeveloped relative to the North.

13. We are aware that all South American states are not equally less developed. However, this wholesale regional censoring does not really influence our results in any significant way. In related work (Rasler and Thompson, 2009), world inequality looks much the same with or without the South American assumption.

14. Spain, Ireland, Australia, and New Zealand may qualify too early. However, they do not represent large economies that can distort the aggregate picture.

There also is the issue of data availability prior to independence. If we were linking North–South identity to foreign policy making, we would eliminate non-independent states from our analysis. In this paper, it seems arbitrary to ignore data prior to independence. We assign states to groups whenever our economic criteria are satisfied.

15. The countries missing from "our" Northern sample are few and small in economic size (Hong Kong, Luxembourg, Iceland, Israel, Singapore, East Germany, and Slovenia).

16. GDP per capita approximates income per capita. We use the terms "GDP per capita" and "income per capita" interchangeably.

17. Illustrating the fact that all categorization schemes have their problems, this regional approach means that Papua New Guinea, Tonga, and Mongolia would be considered Northern. Taiwan, grouped by Goldstein along with Hong Kong and Macau as part of China, is classified as Southern. Restricted to our 56-state sample, this regional approach places the United States, Canada (as North American states), Germany, France, Britain, Italy, Spain, the Netherlands, Belgium, Sweden, Switzerland, Austria, Portugal, Denmark, Norway, Greece, Finland, Ireland (as Western European states), Japan, Australia, New Zealand (as Japan/Pacific states), and Russia, Czech Republic/Slovenia, and Hungary (as Russia and Eastern European states) in the North. The South is represented by China, India, Indonesia, Thailand (the last three are called South Asian states), Argentina, Brazil, and Mexico (as Latin American states).

18. The threshold used in this figure, however, is 33 percent of the system leader's GNP per capita. This series and figure are taken from an independent project on global inequality.

19. Recent oil discoveries are likely to alter the appearance of flatness.

20. The inability to make the transition also could prove inflammatory. The possible disintegration of China or India (or Indonesia), would probably increase the size of the North–South gap.

21. In particular, it applies equally well to India which doubled its GDP per capita between 1985 and 2003.

22. See, as well, Muller and Patel (2004).

4. Geo-economic limits on technological diffusion

1. Keep in mind that eighteenth-century manufacturing was not as complex an enterprise as manufacturing became in the nineteenth and twentieth centuries.

2. In 2005, one state, China, claimed more than a third (36 percent) of the 27.7 percent proportion attributed to the less developed world. In 1991, it had accounted for 16.5 percent of the Third World's 15.8 proportional share.

3. For insight into the domestic nature of the earlier context, see Chang (2002).

4. Prebisch (1950) and Myrdal (1957) offer similar views, but without technological waves pioneered by a single source, assuming that the innovations remain the monopoly of DCs. Neoclassical growth theory (e.g., Solow, 1956) also stresses technological change but does not explain its source. New growth theory (e.g., Romer, 1986) reserves a key place for progress, but focuses on generic knowledge. Both theories assume that technology and human capital are fully mobile, though empirical economists observe that they are not (Baumol, 1986; Abramowitz and David, 1996), attributing failures to adopt innovations to something missing in the receiving side (e.g., savings, good government, education).

5. We do not suggest that the leader's economic growth always reduces all types of transaction costs. Our emphasis here is placed on reducing the costs of globally transporting products and information.

6. Diffusion processes may include knowledge transfer that often accompanies trade or foreign direct investments, relocation of entrepreneurs, government policies that attract foreign business, knowledge transfer from studying in foreign countries, migrant contacts with the home country, and government-to-government transfers. We think these complex processes are better studied separately.

7. A more optimistic interpretation is put forward by World Bank (2008). However, Comin and Hobijn's (2008) work is also interesting on this point. Their modeling of technology diffusion suggests that the respective accelerated developments of Japan and the East Asian Tigers were associated with a significant reduction in the lag time related to technology adoption in comparison to OECD states. They also find unusually long lags associated with sub-Saharan African economies and a slowing down of adoption in Latin America after 1950. Moreover, they are in a position to assert that differences in technology adoption lags account for a quarter of the variance in per capita income differences.

8. For example, Ford's assembly line changed the automobile industry and diffused to other industries.

9. The 1914 dummy is used to control for a shift in systemic leadership from Britain to the United States. All variables used in our empirical tests are defined in the Appendix.

5. Limits on globalization processes

1. Some 50 million, mainly Chinese and Indian, laborers migrated to other parts of the South in the nineteenth century but no one claims that their impact was comparable to the European movements to the "offshoots," in part because a large number returned to their home countries and in part because much of the intra-Southern migration was channeled into plantation work (Hatton and Williamson, 2005).

2. As in other chapters, our variables are defined in the Appendix. Details pertaining to the research design and statistics employed in this chapter may also be found there.

3. We view the 1880s and 1920s as parts of the same long wave that is disrupted by World War I.

4. We used the statistical package Regression Analysis Time of Time Series (RATS) (Doan, 2000). We guard against the possibility of serial correlation by estimating the model from the method of Newey and West (1987), which generates robust standard errors.

5. The difference in the result for debt seems to reflect both the large changes of world economic growth, which leave less of the small variance in Southern openness to be explained by the debt variable, and the smaller sample.

6. The data come from a World Bank source at http://devdata.worldbank.org/dataonline. We used exports of goods and services and GDP enumerated in constant 1995 US dollars. We were able to obtain data for very similar samples to those constructed using Maddison's data. The Southern group encompasses Argentina, Bangladesh, Bolivia, Brazil, Bulgaria, Chile, China, Colombia, Congo/Zaire, Cote d'Ivoire, Egypt, Ethiopia, India, Indonesia, Kenya, Mexico, Morocco, Nigeria, Pakistan, Peru, Romania, Tanzania, Thailand, Turkey, and Venezuela. The Northern group includes Austria, Australia, Belgium, Canada, Czechoslovakia/Czech Republic, Denmark, Finland, France, Germany, Greece, Hungary, Ireland, Italy, Japan, South Korea, the Netherlands, New Zealand, Norway, Poland, Portugal, Russia, Spain, Sweden, Switzerland, the United Kingdom, and the United States.

7. Some of this change definitely can be attributed to China. Removing China from the Southern group reduces the 1983 ratio from 0.058 to 0.055. The 2003 ratio would be reduced from 0.094 to 0.089. Still, the changes are not exactly overwhelming.

8. See, among others, Hirst and Thompson (1999).

9. We are aware that the relationships among poverty, development, and conflict/terrorism continue to be debated.

6. Southern debt crises

1. Roodman (2006: 13) notes that the late-twentieth-century debt problems had two dimensions – one of which took on crisis characteristics while the other did not. Basically, he argues that when middle-level-income countries such as Mexico, Turkey, or Brazil (our upper Southern states) experience problems in debt servicing, the impact is abrupt and policy-makers scurry to resolve the problem in a crisis-like atmosphere. This type of behavior characterized the early 1980s through the early 1990s. The second dimension alludes to the impact on the poorest states in the system (our lower South) that are less likely to develop solutions for their debt problems. Instead, they remain constrained by heavy debts that come to resemble more a "chronic syndrome" blocking development than a short-lived crisis.

2. For variations, see Chase-Dunn and Rubinson (1979), Pollins and Murrin (1999), and Reuveny and Thompson (2003).

3. Economic growth and conflict are multiplied by 10 for visual purposes.

4. The 1989 stopping point is dictated by the length of the debt series developed by Suter. Our dependent variable is continuous and OLS is appropriate in this case. We used the package Regression Analysis Time of Time Series (RATS). Tests reveal possible serial correlation. We estimated the model with a correction for serial correlation. A computerized grid search is used to find the error's auto-regressive coefficient. As in other chapters, the variables examined are defined in the Appendix. Research design and statistical details for this chapter's analyses are also located there.

7. Growth and conflict

1. See Modelski and Thompson (1996) for a review of this extensive literature.

2. Using MIDs data also represents a challenge to an argument that is predicated on global war. The auxiliary question that we are addressing here is whether inter-state (and intra-state) conflict in general is impacted by long-term fluctuations in economic growth. Goldstein (1988) has made a case for the Kondratieff influencing all interstate warfare. Pollins (1996) has made the case for applying long wave arguments to more continuous forms of conflicts, as measured by MIDs activity.

3. The variables examined are defined in the Appendix.

4. It is possible to argue that this argument pertains to severe wars, and not to all wars. For example, Goldstein (1991: 303) writes: "Periods of severe war follow phases of robust economic growth." Regardless, we translate the war chest argument into conflict terms. In this paper, larger wars in up-phases of the world economy mean more conflict in these time periods.

5. For arguments about North–South relationships in the world's first international system around 3500 BC, see Algaze (1993), Lupton (1996), and Stein (1999).

6. Examples include the intervention of European powers to contain Mohammed Ali in the 1830s–40s (not entirely unlike the containment of Saddam Hussein

in the 1990s), and the gunboat diplomacy of the nineteenth and early twentieth centuries as European powers sought to obtain a diminishment of local attacks on their maritime commerce, debt repayments, or access to closed markets (e.g., penetrating China and Japan between the sixteenth and early twentieth centuries).

7. Some former Northern powers have lapsed into Southern status for a time (e.g., Spain, Portugal) or had become colonial/imperial powers before attaining full Northern status (e.g., Russia).

8. A case in point was the Anglo–French collusion with Israel in the 1956 attack on Egypt. The British and French sought to remove Gamal Abdel Nasir as a rallying point for attempts to diminish the Anglo–French presence in the Middle East and North Africa. The US effort to force a British–French retreat in 1956 exemplifies the role that system leaders play in breaking down previous colonial boundaries after a global war.

9. The US case after World War I was actually a combination of both "unable" and "unwilling."

10. By "selective," we mean that, historically, Northern states did not attempt to conquer the entire South at one stroke. Rather, they focused on one area at a time. For instance, the French expansion into Algeria, Tunisia, and Morocco was sequential over nearly 90 years.

11. Examples of such behavior, as in the case of Franco–Italian competition in North Africa from the 1880s to the 1940s, are observed. But, it seems likely that a weak Italy and a more powerful France might never have fought regardless of the availability of Southern territory.

12. For instance, the possession of old colonies has changed hands, but new colonies have been unlikely to emerge in the midst of global war.

13. For instance, Kuznets (1971) finds a short-run negative effect and a long-run positive effect. Organski and Kugler (1980) argue that losers grow faster than winners. Barbera (1973) argues that the effects of World War I and World War II on US growth were insignificant. Rasler and Thompson (1985, 1989) argue the effect of these wars on US growth was positive.

14. See the Appendix for variable definitions and research design/statistical details pertaining to the analyses conducted in this chapter.

15. As reported in the Appendix, statistical unit root tests confirm this conclusion.

16. We use version 4.2 of the statistical software package RATS.

17. For one, the effect of major power conflict on North–South conflict in 1870–1945 is positive. Also, in 1946–92, the effect of North–South conflict on major power conflict is not significant. As for the negative effect of major power conflict on Northern conflict in 1946–92, recalling that after 1945 the North was generally allied facing the USSR, it is conceivable that a rise in major power (United States–USSR) conflict would reduce Northern conflict.

18. At the same time, it is difficult to see the World Wars primarily as fights over resources, although, admittedly, some aspects of World War II offer a better fit to this conceptualization.

19. The problem, of course, is that the MIDs series is long and other possible indicators of conflict are not.

8. Southern democracy in the long run

1. Factors thought to be causally significant include, for example, economic development and performance, economic dependence, constitutional structures, education levels, colonial experiences, civil society, institutions, the availability of information via mass media, literacy, urbanization, homogeneity in terms

of ethnic, religious, racial, linguistic, or sectional cleavages, income inequality, elite compacts, class structure, the strength of the military and their attitudes toward intervention, political culture or supportive values and belief systems, property rights and the rule of law, international organizations, insularity from and/or exposure to conflict, and the presence or absence of foreign/external influence.

2. For some reason, Huntington counts this factor as two separate explanations. The Catholic Church is one factor and everybody else is a second one.
3. Fraser relies on Hobsbawm (1962, 1975, 1989, and 1994) for the dating of economic long waves.
4. Modelski and Perry (1991, 2002) studied democratization from a leadership long cycle perspective, but did not model it. Huntley (1996), Whitehead (2001), and Kegley and Hermann (2002) qualitatively studied external effects on democratization. Kurth (1979) linked Northern democratization to technological growth waves.
5. Our take differs from, but is not necessarily incompatible with, arguments focusing on warfare or the number of democracies as antecedents of democratization (e.g., Mitchell et al., 1999; Pevehouse, 2002; Werner, 1996). We regard these forces as intermediate components of systemic orders.
6. For example, see Bernhard et al. (2001), Feng (2003), Haggard and Kaufman (1995), and Seligson and Muller (1987).
7. At the same time, Southern leaders are told that they can expect better economic performance if they adopt democratic institutions. Whether these expectations hold is another story (Johnson, 2002).
8. Compare, among others, Burkhart and Lewis-Beck (1994), Colaresi and Thompson (2003), Lipset (1994), and Londegran (1996).
9. For arguments, pros and cons, see Colaresi and Thompson (2003), Gates et al. (1996), Gleditsch and Ward (2000), James et al. (1999), Layne (1994), Midlarsky (1995), Mousseau and Shi (1999), Rasler and Thompson (2004, 2005), Reuveny and Li (2003), and Thompson (1996).
10. Obviously, we are working at a general level here. More external conflict should have a stronger effect than less conflict. Issues such as the type of conflict (civil wars versus external wars, for instance) or the intensity of conflict (threat versus war) are better handled in separate analyses at a later date.
11. We remind readers once again that the variables that we analyze are defined in the Appendix.
12. For visual purposes, Southern conflict is multiplied by 250, world economic growth by 100, systemic leadership by 10, and Southern development is divided by 100.
13. As noted before, the 1880s peak for the British leadership is not the largest one in the nineteenth century; a larger peak occurred shortly after the Napoleonic Wars, resembling the timing of the post-World War II US peak.
14. Working at the national level of analysis, Reiter (2001) also fails to find evidence for external conflict influencing democratization in the post-war period.
15. There is also the contrarian observation that the leading Southern leader in economic development, China, appears to be engaged in the opposite type of transformation – economic development without concomitant democratization. This development does not bode well for peace and stability either.

9. Uneven growth processes and prospects

1. In Chapter 3, we divided the South into two by designating states with gross domestic products per capita between 12.5 and 25 percent of the system leader's as upper South and below 12.5 percent as lower South.

2. Something similar is advocated by Sach's (2005) call for clinical economics and differential diagnoses.

Appendix

1. The most recent conflict data can be found at cow2.la.psu.edu/datasets/ htm. However, we used Zeev Maoz's 2.1 version (http://www.spirit.tau. ac.il/~zeevmaoz).
2. For some earlier uses of this indicator, see Boswell and Sweat (1991), McKeown (1991), Modelski and Thompson (1988), Rasler and Thompson (1994), and Thompson (1988).
3. Many studies employ this approach, including Campbell and Mankiw (1987), Geraci and Preow (1982), Rasler and Thompson (1994), Reuveny (2001), and Reuveny and Thompson (2004a, 2004b).
4. Significance levels of 1, 5, and 10 percent are used.
5. We use the formulation in Doan (2000): minimize T(log (RSS)) + 2K for Akaike, and T(log(RSS)+K(log T)) for Schwartz. T is sample size, RSS is sum of squared residuals, and K is number of regressors.
6. For VAR applications in systemic analysis of the war–economy nexus, see Goldstein (1991), Reuveny and Thompson (1999), Williams (1993), and Williams et al. (1994).
7. Taken to the extreme, US GDP also is not a continuous variable, but it appears as the dependent variable in numerous OLS models. Indeed, as noted by Brandt and Williams (2000), several studies in political science treat count data as if they are coming from a normal distribution, and the improvement from using a count distribution is smaller, the larger is the range of the count used. For example, Goldstein (1991), Williams (1993), and Williams et al. (1994) employ OLS to study the interactions of growth and a count of war death. Other examples include Brophy-Baermann and Conybeare (1994), Mansfield (1992), and O'Brien (1996).
8. The lag test compares a VAR with N lags to a VAR with N+1 lags, deciding whether to reject one model in favor of the other. We started with N=1 and increased N by 1 in successive iterations. For 1870–1945, we tested models with up to six lags. For 1946–92, we tested models with up to three lags.
9. Technically, this implies that the growth shock will have lagged and immediate effects on all the variables. The shock in major power conflict will have lagged effects on all the variables, but immediate effects only on itself and the variables that come after it in the ordering, etc. The Appendix further discusses the issue of ordering. As noted there, the result reported here are robust to changes in the ordering of the variables.
10. In the Monte Carlo simulations, we used a significance level of 10 percent. This level is used in many VAR studies (e.g., Kang and Reuveny, 2001; Williams, 1993; Williams et al., 1994). The 10 percent level is a middle-ground position between 5 percent and 20 percent, as some studies suggest using a level of 20 percent in VAR and Granger models (Moore, 1995).

References

Abramowitz, Moses. 1986. "Catching Up, Forging Ahead, and Falling Behind." *Journal of Economic History* 46: 385–406.

Abramowitz, Moses and Paul A. David. 1996. "Convergence and Deferred Catch Up," in Ralph Landau, Timothy Taylor, and Gavin Wright, eds., *The Mosaic of Economic Growth*. Stanford: Stanford University Press.

Acemoglu, Daron, Simon Johnson, and James A. Robinson. 2001. "The Colonial Origins of Comparative Development: An Empirical Investigation." *American Economic Review* 91: 1369–1401.

Acemoglu, Daron, Simon Johnson, and James A. Robinson. 2002. "Reversal of Fortune: Geography and Institutions in the Making of the Modern World Income Distribution." *Quarterly Journal of Economics* 117: 1231–1294.

Aggarwal, Vinod K. 1989. "Interpreting the History of Mexico's External Debt Crises," in Barry Eichengreen and Peter H. Lindert, eds., *The International Debt Crisis in Historical Perspective*. Cambridge, MA: MIT Press.

Aggarwal, Vinod K. 1996. *Debt Games: Strategic Interaction in International Debt Rescheduling*. Cambridge: Cambridge University Press.

Akaike, Hirotsugu. 1974. "A New Look at the Statistical Identification Model." *IEEE Transactions on Automatic Control* 19(3): 716–723.

Algaze, Guillermo. 1993. *The Uruk World-System*. Chicago, IL: University of Chicago Press.

Amsden, Alice H. 2001. *The Rise of "the Rest": Challenges to the West from Late-Industrializing Economies*. Oxford: Oxford University Press.

Bairoch, Paul. 1982. "International Industrialization Levels from 1750 to 1980." *Journal of European Economic History* 11: 269–333.

Bairoch, Paul. 1993. *Economics and World History: Myths and Paradoxes*. Chicago: University of Chicago Press.

Balassa, Bela G., Bueno P. Kuczynski, and Mario Simonsen. 1986. *Toward Renewed Growth in Latin America*. Washington, DC: Institute for International Economics.

Banks, Arthur. 1971. *Cross-Polity Time Series Data*. Cambridge, MA: MIT Press.

Barbera, H. 1973. *Rich Nations and Poor in Peace and War*. Lexington, MA: Lexington

Barro, Robert. 1997. *Determinants of Economic Growth: A Cross-Country Empirical Study*. Cambridge, MA: MIT Press.

Barro, R. J. and X. Sala-I-Martin. 1992. "Convergence." *Journal of Political Economy* 100: 223–251.

Baumol, William. 1986. "Productivity Growth, Convergence and Welfare: What the Long-run Data Show." *American Economic Review* 76: 1072–1085.

Beck, Nathaniel and Jonathan N. Katz. 1995. "What to Do (and Not to Do) With Time-Series Cross-Section Data," *American Political Science Review* 89(3): 634–647.

Bergesen, Albert and Ronald Schoenberg. 1980. "Long Waves of Colonial Expansion and Contraction, 1415–1969," in Albert Bergesen, ed., *Studies of the Modern World-System*. New York: Academic Press.

Bernhard, Michael, Timothy Nordstrom, and Christopher Reenock. 2001. "Economic Performance, International Intermediation, and Democratic Survival." *Journal of Politics* 63(3): 775–803.

Bongaarts, John and Rodolfo A. Bulatao. 2000. *Beyond Six Billion: Forecasting the World's Population*. Washington, DC: National Academy Press.

Bornschier, Volker. 2002. "Changing Income Equality in the Second Half of the 20th Century: Preliminary Findings and Propositions for Explanations." *Journal of World-System Research* 8: 99–127.

Boswell, Terry. 1989. "Colonial Empires and the Capitalist World-Economy: A Time Series Analysis of the Colonization, 1640–1960." *American Sociological Review* 54: 180–196.

Boswell, Terry and Christopher Chase-Dunn. 2000. *The Spiral of Socialism and Capitalism*. Boulder, CO: Lynne Rienner.

Boswell, Terry and Michael Sweat. 1991. "Hegemony, Long Waves, and Major Wars: A Time Series Analysis of System Dynamics, 1496–1967." *International Studies Quarterly* 35(2): 123–149.

Bourguignon, Francois and Christian Morrisson. 2002. "The Size Distribution of Income Among World Citizens, 1820–1990." *American Economic Review* 92: 727–744.

Brandt, Patrick T. and John T. Williams. 2000. "A Linear Poisson Autoregressive Model: The Poisson AR (p) Model." *Political Analysis* 9: 164–184.

Brophy-Baermann, Bryan and John A. C. Conybeare. 1994. "Retaliating Against Terrorism: Rational Expectations and the Optimality of Rule Versus Discretion." *American Journal of Political Science* 38: 196–210.

Burkhart, Ross E. and Michael Lewis-Beck. 1994. "Comparative Democracy: The Economic Development Thesis." *American Political Science Review* 88(4): 903–910.

Campbell, John Y. and Gregory Mankiw. 1987. "Are Output Fluctuations Transitory?" *The Quarterly Journal of Economics* 102(4): 857–880.

Cardoso, Enrique A. and Roudiger, Dornbusch. 1989. "Brazilian Debt Crises: Past and Present," in Barry Eichengreen and Peter H. Lindert, eds., *The International Debt Crisis in Historical Perspective*, Cambridge, MA: MIT Press.

Cashin, Paul and Ratna Sahay. 1996. "Regional Economic Growth and Convergence in India." *Finance and Development* 33: 49–52.

Cavanaugh, Joseph E. and Andrea A. Neath. 2001. "Regression and Time Series Model Selection Using Variants of the Schwartz Information Criterion." *Department of Mathematics and Statistics*, Southern Illinois University, Illinois.

Chan, Steve. 1995. "Grasping the Peace Dividend: Some Propositions on the Conversion of Swords into Plowshares." *Mershon International Studies Review* 39: 53–95.

Chang, Ha-Joon. 2002. *Kicking Away the Ladder: Development Strategy in Historical Perspective*. London: Anthem.

Chase-Dunn, Christopher. 1989. *Global Formation: Structures of the World-Economy*. Cambridge, MA: Basil Blackwell.

Chase-Dunn, Christopher, Yukio Kawano, and Benjamin Brewer. 2000. "Trade Globalization Since 1795: Waves of Integration in the World-System." *American Sociological Review* 65(1): 77–95.

Chase-Dunn, Christopher and Richard Rubinson. 1979. "Toward a Structural Perspective on the World-System." *Politics and Society* 7: 453–476.

Choucri, Nazli and Robert North. 1975. *Nations in Conflict: National Growth and International Violence*. San Francisco: W. H. Freeman.

Choucri, Nazli, Robert North, and Susumu Yamakage. 1992. *The Challenge of Japan Before World War II and After*. London: Routledge.

Colaresi, Michael and William R. Thompson. 2003. "The Economic Development-Democratization Relationship: Does the Outside World Matter?" *Comparative Political Studies* 36: 381–403.

Collier, Paul. 2007. *The Bottom Billion: Why the Poorest Countries Are Failing, and What Can Be Done About It*. Oxford: Oxford University Press.

Comin, Diego A. and Bart Hobijn. 2008. "An Exploration of Technology Diffusion." Cambridge, MA: Harvard Business School Working Paper 08-093.

Cooper, Richard N. 2007. "Introduction: Growth and Poverty in the World Economy, 1950–2000," in Ernest Aryeety and Natalia Dinello, eds., *Testing Global Interdependence: Issues on Trade, Aid, Migration and Development*. Cheltenham, UK: Edward Elgar.

Darity, William A. and Bobbie L. Horn. 1988. *The Loan Pushers: The Role of Commercial Banks in the International Debt Crisis*. Cambridge, MA: Ballinger.

Deaton, Angus and Jean Drez. 2002. "Poverty and Inequality in India: A Reexamination." Working Paper, No. 107, Centre for Development Economics. Http://www.cdedse.org/pdf/work107.pdf.

DeLong, J. Bradford. 1986. "Productivity Growth, Convergence and Welfare: Comment." *American Economic Review* 78: 1138–1153.

Devlin, Robert. 1989. *Debt and Crisis in Latin America: The Supply-side of the Story*. Princeton, NJ: Princeton University Press.

Diamond, Jared. 1997. *Guns, Germs, and Steel: The Fates of Human Societies*. New York: W.W. Norton.

Dickey, David and Wayne A. Fuller. 1979. "Distribution of the Estimators for Time Series Regressions with a Unit Root." *Journal of the American Statistical Association* 74: 427–431.

Doan, Thomas A. 2000. *Regression Analysis Time Series (RATS)*. Evanston, IL: Estima.

Dollar, David. 2007. "Globalization, Poverty and Inequality Since 1980," in David Held and Ayse Kaya, eds., *Global Inequality: Patterns and Explanations*. Cambridge: Polity.

Dornbusch, Roudiger. 1993. *Stabilization, Debt and Reform: Policy Analysis for Developing Countries*. Englewood Cliffs, NJ: Prentice-Hall.

Dowrick, Steve and J. Bradford DeLong. 2003. "Globalization and Convergence." in Michael D. Bordo, Alan M. Taylor, and Jeffrey G. Williamson, eds., *Globalization in Historical Perspective*. Chicago: University of Chicago Press.

Edelstein, Michael. 1982. *Overseas Investment in the Age of High Imperialism: The United Kingdom, 1850–1914*. New York: Columbia University Press.

Eichengreen, Barry and Albert Fishlow. 1998. "Contending with Capital Flows: What is Different About the 1990s?," in Miles Kahler, ed., *Capital Flows and Financial Crises*. Ithaca, NY: Cornell University Press.

Eichengreen, Barry and Peter H. Lindert. 1989. "Overview," in Barry Eichengreen and Peter H. Lindert, eds., *The International Debt Crisis in Historical Perspective*. Cambridge, MA: MIT Press.

Feng, Yi. 2003. *Democracy, Governance, and Economic Performance: Theory, Data Analysis, and Case Studies*. Cambridge, MA: MIT Press.

Firebaugh, Glenn. 2003. *The New Geography of Global Income Inequality*. Cambridge, MA: Harvard University Press.

Fishlow, Albert. 1989. "Conditionality and Willingness to Pay: Some Parallels from the 1890s," in Barry Eichengreen and Peter H. Lindert, eds., *The International Debt Crisis in Historical Perspective*. Cambridge, MA: MIT Press.

Fortune. 1996. "The World's Largest Corporations." *Fortune* 134 (3, August 5): F1–F10.

Fortune. 2001. "The World's Largest Corporations." *Fortune* 144 (2, July 23): F1–F10.

Fortune. 2006. "World's Largest Corporations." *Fortune* 154 (2, July 24): 113–120.

Frank, Andre Gunder. 1978. *World Accumulation, 1492–1789*. New York: Monthly Review Press.

Fraser, Duncan. 2001. "Long Waves in Economics – Waves of Democracy." *Democratization* 8(4): 41–64.

Freeman, Christopher and Francisco Louca. 2001. *As Time Goes By: From the Industrial Revolution to the Information Revolution*. Oxford: Oxford University Press

Freeman, Christopher and Carlota Perez. 1988. "Structural Crises of Adjustment: Business Cycles and Investment Behavior," in Giovannia Dosi, Christopher Freeman, Richard Nelson, Gerald Silverberg, and Luc Soete, eds., *Technical Change and Economic Theory*. London: Pinter.

Freeman, John R., John T. Williams, and Tse-min Lin. 1989. "Vector Auto-regressions and the Study of Politics." *American Journal of Political Science* 33: 842–877.

Friedman, Thomas L. 2007. *The World is Flat: A Brief History of the Twenty-first Century*, further updated and expanded. New York: Picador/Farrar, Strauss and Giroux.

Galbraith, James K., Ludmila Krytynskaia, and Qifei Wang. 2003. "The Experience of Rising Inequality in Russia and China During the Transition." UTIP Working Paper, No. 23. Http://www.utip.gov.utexas.edu/ucb/workingpaper/risinginequality in china and russia3.pdf.

Gates, Scott, Torbjorn L. Knutsen, and Jonathan W. Moses. 1996. "Democracy and Peace: A More Skeptical View." *Journal of Peace Research* 33: 1–10.

Geraci, Vincent J. and Wilfred Preow. 1982. "An Empirical Demand and Supply Model of Bilateral Trade." *The Review of Economics and Statistics* 64(3): 432–661.

Gilpin, Robert. 1975. *U.S. Power and the Multinational Corporation*. New York: Basic Books.

Gilpin, Robert. 1987. *The Political Economy of International Relations*. Princeton, NJ: Princeton University Press.

Gleditsch, Kristian S. and Michael D. Ward. 2000. "War and Peace in Space and Time: The Role of Democratization." *International Studies Quarterly* 44: 1–29.

Goldstein, Joshua S. 1988. *Long Cycles*. New Haven, CT: Yale University Press.

Goldstein, Joshua S. 1991. "A War-Economy Theory of the Long Wave," in Neils Thygesen, Kumaraswamy Velupillai, and Stefano Zambelli, eds., *Business Cycles: Theory, Evidence, and Analysis*. New York: New York University Press.

Goldstein, Joshua S. 2002. *International Relations*, brief edition. New York: Longman.

Greene, William H. 1997. *Econometric Analysis*. Upper Saddle River, N.J.: Prentice Hall.

Haggard, Stephen and Robert R. Kaufman. 1995. *The Political Economy of Democratic Transitions*. Princeton, NJ: Princeton University Press.

Hall, Peter and P. Preston. 1988. *The Carrier Wave: New Information Technology and the Geography of Innovation, 1846–2003*. London: Unwin-Hyman.

Hanson, John R. II. 1980. *Trade in Transition: Exports from the Third World, 1840–1900*. New York: Academic Press.

Hanson, John R. II. 1997. "Review of Angus Maddison's Monitoring the World Economy: 1820–1992." *EH. Net Economic History Services*. Feb 5, 1997. http:eh.net/bookreviews/library/0021.

Hatton, Timothy and Jeffry G. Williamson. 2005. *Global Migration and the World Economy: Two Centuries of Policy and Performance*. Cambridge, MA: MIT Press.

Held, David, Anthony McGrew, David Goldblat and Jonathan Perraton, 1999. *Global Transformations: Politics, Economics and Culture*. Stanford, CA: Stanford University Press.

Heshmati, Almas. 2007. *Global Trends in Income Inequality*. New York: Nova Science Publishers.

Hibou, Beatrice. 2002. "The World Bank: Missing Deeds (and Misdeeds)," in Peter J. Schraeder, ed., *Exporting Democracy: Rhetoric vs. Reality*. Boulder, CO: Lynne Rienner.

Hironaka, Ann. 2005. *Neverending Wars: The International Community, Weak States, and the Perpetuation of Civil War*. Cambridge, MA: Harvard University Press.

Hirst, Paul F. and Grahame F. Thompson. 1999. *Globalization in Question: The International Economy and the Possibilities of Governance*, 2nd ed. Cambridge: Polity.

Hobsbawm, Eric J. 1962. *The Age of Revolution: Europe, 1789–1848*. London: Weidenfeld and Nicolson.

Hobsbawm, Eric J. 1975. *The Age of Capital*. London: Weidenfeld and Nicolson.

Hobsbawm, Eric J. 1989. *The Age of Empire, 1875–1914*. New York: Vintage.

Hobsbawm, Eric J. 1994. *The Age of Extremes: The Short Twentieth Century, 1914–1991*. London: Penguin.

Holz, Carsten A. 2006. "China's Reform Period Economic Growth: How Reliable Are Angus Maddison's Estimates?" *Review of Income and Wealth* 52(1): 85–119.

Hook, Steven W. 2002. "Inconsistent U.S. Efforts to Promote Democracy Abroad," in Peter J. Schraeder, ed., *Exporting Democracy: Rhetoric vs. Reality*. Boulder, CO: Lynne Rienner.

Huntington, Samuel P. 1984. "Will More Countries Become Democratic?" *Political Science Quarterly* 99: 193–218.

Huntington, Samuel P. 1991. *The Third Wave: Democratization in the Late Twentieth Century*. Norman: University of Oklahoma Press.

Huntley, Wade L. 1996. "Kant's Third Image: Systemic Sources of the Liberal Peace." *International Studies Quarterly* 40: 45–76.

Inder, B. A. 1984. "Finite Sample Power of Tests for Autocorrelation in Models Containing Lagged Dependent Variables." *Economic Letters* 14: 179–185.

Jaggers, Keith and Ted Robert Gurr. 1995. "Tracking Democracy's Third Wave With the Polity III Data." *Journal of Peace Research* 32: 469–483.

James, Patrick, Eric Solberg, and Murray Wolfson. 1999. "An Identified System Model of the Democracy-Peace Nexus." *Defense and Peace Economics* 10: 1–37.

Jochnick, Chris and Fraser A. Preston. 2006. "Introduction," in Chris Jochnick and Fraser A. Preston, ed., *Sovereign Debt at the Crossroads: Challenges and Proposals for Resolving the Third World Debt Crisis*. Oxford: Oxford University Press.

Johnson, Juliet. 2002. "In Pursuit of a Prosperous International System," in Peter J. Schraeder, ed., *Exporting Democracy: Rhetoric vs. Reality*. Boulder, CO: Lynne Rienner.

Johnston, J. and J. DiNardo. 1997. *Econometric Methods*. New York: McGraw-Hill.

Jones, C. I. 1998. *Introduction to Economic Growth*. New York: W. W. Norton.

Jorgensen, Erika and Jeffrey Sachs. 1989. "Default and Renegotiation of Latin American Foreign Debts in the Interwar Period," in Barry Eichengreen and Peter H. Lindert, eds., *The International Debt Crisis in Historical Perspective*. Cambridge, MA: MIT Press.

Joyner, Christopher C. 2002. "The United Nations: Strengthening an International Norm," in Peter J. Schraeder, ed., *Exporting Democracy: Rhetoric vs. Reality*. Boulder, CO: Lynne Rienner.

Kang, Heejoon and Rafael Reuveny. 2001. "Exploring Multi-Country Dynamic Relations Between Trade and Conflict." *Defense and Peace Economics* 12: 175–196.

Kegley, Charles W., Jr. and Margaret G. Hermann. 2002. "In Pursuit of a Peaceful International System," in Peter Schraeder, ed., *Exporting Democracy: Rhetoric vs. Reality*. Boulder, CO: Lynne Rienner.

Kentor, Jeffrey. 2000. *Capital and Coercion: The Economic and Military Processes That Have Shaped the World Economy, 1800–1990*. New York: Garland.

Kondratieff, Nikolai. 1984. *The Long Wave Cycle*, translated by Guy Daniels. New York: Richardson and Snyder.

Kowalewski, David. 1989. "Global Debt Crises in Structural-Cyclical Perspective: 1754–1984," in William P. Avery and David P. Rapkin, eds., *Markets, Politics and Change in the Global Political Economy*. Boulder, CO: Lynne Rienner.

Kozul-Wright, Richard. 2006. "Globalization Now and Again," in K.S. Jomo, ed., *Globalization Under Hegemony: The Changing World Economy*. New Delhi: Oxford University Press.

Krieckhaus, Jonathan. 2006. *Dictating Development: How Europe Shaped the Global Periphery*. Pittsburgh, PA: University of Pittsburgh Press.

Krugman, Paul. 1995. "Growing World Trade: Causes and Consequences," *Brookings Papers on Economic Activity* 1(1): 327–362.

Kugler, Jacek and Marina Arbetman. 1989. "Exploring the 'Phoenix Factor' with the Collective Goods Perspective." *Journal of Conflict Resolution* 33: 84–112.

Kurth, James. 1979. "The Political Consequences of the Product Cycle." *International Organization* 33: 1–34.

Kuznets, Simon S. 1971. *Economic Growth of Nations: Total Output and Production Structure*. Cambridge, MA: Harvard University Press.

Kuznets, Simon S. 1972. *Postwar Economic Growth*. Cambridge, MA: Harvard University Press.

Lall, Sanjaya. 1992. "Technological Capabilities and Industrialization." *World Development* 20(2): 165–186.

Lall, Sanjaya. 1996. *Learning from the Asian Tigers*. London: McMillan.

Lall, Sanjaya. 2003. "Technology and Industrial Development in an Era of Globalization." in Ha-Joon Chang, ed., *Rethinking Development Economics*. London: Anthem Press.

Lall, Sanjaya. 2004a. "Reinventing Industrial Policy: The Role of Government Policy in Building Industrial Competitiveness." *G-24 Discussion Paper Series*, Number 28, United Nations Conference on Trade and Development (UNCTAD), Geneva, Switzerland.

Lall, Sanjaya. 2004b. "Selective Trade and Industrial Policies in Developing Countries: Theoretical and Empirical Issues," in Charles Soludo, Osita Ogbu, and Ha-Joon Chang, eds., *The Politics of Trade and Industrial Policy in Africa*. Nairobi: Africa World Press.

Lall, Sanjaya and Erika Kraemer-Mbula. 2005. Industrial Competitiveness in Africa: Lessons from East Asia. Warwickshire, UK: ITDG Publishing.

Layne, Christopher. 1994. "Kant or Cant: The Myth of the Democratic Peace." *International Security* 19: 5–49.

Li, Quan and Rafael, Reuveny. 2003. "Economic Globalization and Democracy: An Empirical Analysis." *British Journal of Political Science* 31(1): 29–54.

Lindert, Peter H. 1989. "Response to Debt Crisis: What is Different About the 1980s?" in Barry Eichengreen and Peter H. Lindert, eds., *The International Debt Crisis in Historical Perspective*. Cambridge, MA: MIT Press (227–275).

Lipset, Seymour M. 1994. "The Social Requisites of Democracy Revisited." *American Sociological Review* 59: 1–22.

Lipson, Charles. 1989. "International Debt and National Security: Comparing Victorian Britain and Postwar America." in Barry Eichengreen and Peter H. Lindert, eds., *The International Debt Crisis in Historical Perspective*. Cambridge, MA: MIT Press.

Little, Ian M. D., Richard N. Cooper, Werner M. Corden, and Sarath Rajapatirana, 1993. *Boom, Crisis and Adjustment: The Macroeconomic Experience of Developing Countries*. Oxford: Oxford University.

Livi-Bacci, Massimo. 2007. *A Concise History of World Population*, 4th ed. Malden, MA: Blackwell.

Londregan, John B. and Keith T. Poole. 1996. "Does High Income Promote Democracy?" *World Politics* 49(1): 1–30.

Lucas, Robert E., Jr. 2000. "Some Macroeconomics for the Twenty-first Century." *Journal of Economic Perspectives* 14(1): 159–168.

Lucas, Robert E., Jr. 2003. "The Industrial Revolution: Past and Future." Annual Report, Federal Reserve Bank of Minneapolis. Http:www.minneapolisfed.org/pubs/region/04-05/essay.cfm.

Lupton, A. 1996. *Stability and Change: Socio-Political Development in North Mesopotamia and Southeast Anatolia, 4000–2700 B.C.* Oxford: British Archaeological Reports.

Maddison, Angus M. 1995. *Monitoring the World Economy, 1820–1992.* Paris: OECD.

Maddison, Angus M. 2001. *The World Economy: A Millennial Perspective.* Paris: OECD.

Maddison, Angus M. 2003. *The World Economy: Historical Statistics.* Paris: OECD.

Maddison, Angus M. 2007. *Historical Statistics for the World Economy: 1–2003 AD.* Http://www.ggdc.net/maddison.

Mankiw, N.G., D. Romer, and D. N. Weil. 1992. "A Contribution to the Empirics of Economic Growth." *Quarterly Journal of Economics* 107: 407–436.

Mansfield, Edward. 1992. "The Concentration of Capabilities and the Onset of War." *Journal of Conflict Resolution* 36: 3–24.

Mansfield, Edward. 1994. *Power, Trade and War.* Princeton, NJ: Princeton University Press.

Mansfield, Edward and Jack Snyder. 1995. "Democratization and the Danger of War." *International Security* 20(1): 5–38.

Marichal, Carlos, 1989. *A Century of Debt Crises in Latin America: From Independence to the Great Depression, 1820–1930.* Princeton, NJ: Princeton University Press.

Marx, Daniel, Jose Echague, and Guido Sandleris. 2006. "Sovereign Debt and the Debt Crisis in Emerging Countires: The Experience of the 1990s," in Chris Jochnick and Fraser A. Preston, eds., *Sovereign Debt at the Crossroads: Challenges and Proposals for Resolving the Third World Debt Crisis.* Oxford: Oxford University Press.

McCallum, Bennett T. 1993. "Unit Roots in Macroeconomic Time Series: Some Critical Issues." *Economic Quarterly* 79: 13–44.

McGowan, Patrick. 1985. "Pitfalls and Promise in the Quantitative Study of the World-System: A Re-analysis of Bergesen and Schoenberg's 'Long Waves' of Colonialism." *Review* 8: 177–200.

McKeown, Timothy. 1991. "A Liberal Trade Order? The Long-Run Pattern of Imports to the Advanced Capitalist States." *International Studies Quarterly* 35(2): 151–172.

Midlarsky, Manus I. 1995. "Environmental Influences on Democracy: Aridity, Warfare and a Reversal of the Causal Arrow." *Journal of Conflict Resolution* 39: 224–262.

Milanovic, Branko. 2005. *Worlds Apart: Global and International Inequality 1950–2000.* Princeton, NJ: Princeton University Press.

Mitchell, Sara McLaughlin, Scott Gates, and Havard Hegre. 1999. "Evolution in Democracy-War Dynamics." *Journal of Conflict Resolution* 43(6): 771–792.

Modelski, George. 1987. *Long Cycles in World Politics.* London: Macmillan.

Modelski, George. 1996. "Evolutionary Paradigm for Global Politics." *International Studies Quarterly* 40(3): 321–342.

Modelski, George and William R. Thompson. 1987. "Testing Coweb Models of the Long Cycle," in George Modelski, ed., *Exploring Long Cycles*. Boulder, CO: Lynne Rienner.

Modelski, George and William R. Thompson. 1988. *Sea Power in Global Politics, 1494–1993*. London: Macmillan.

Modelski, George and Gardner Perry III. 1991. "Democratization in Long Perspective." *Technological Forecasting and Social Change* 39: 22–34.

Modelski, George and William R. Thompson. 1996. *Leading Sectors and World Power: The Coevolution of Global Economics and Politics*. Columbia: University of South Carolina Press.

Modelski, George and Gardner Perry III. 2002. "Democratization in Long Perspective." *Technological Forecasting and Social Change* 69: 259–376.

Modelski, George, Tessaleno Devezas, and William R. Thompson, eds. (2008) *Globalization as Evolutionary Process: Modeling Global Change*. London: Routledge.

Moore, W. H. 1995. "Action-Reaction or Rational Expectations? Reciprocity and the Domestic International Nexus During the Rhodesia Problem." *Journal of Conflict Resolution* 39: 129–167.

Morawetz, David. 1977. *Twenty-Five Years of Economic Development: 1950– 1975*. Washington, DC: World Bank.

Morrow, James, Randolph D. Siverson and Tressa E. Tabares 1998. "The Political Determinants of International Trade: The Major Powers 1907–1990." *American Political Science Review* 92(3): 649–661.

Mott, William H., IV. 1997. *The Economic Basis of Peace: Linkages Between Economic Growth and International Conflict*. Westport, CT: Greenwood Press.

Mousseau, Michael and Yuhang Shi. 1999. "A Test for Reverse Causality in the Democratic Peace Relationship." *Journal of Peace Research* 36(6): 639–663.

Mueller, John. 1989. *Retreat from Doomsday: The Obsolescence of Major War*. New York: Basic Books.

Muller, Anders Riel and Raj Patel. 2004. "Shining India? Economic Liberalism and Rural Poverty in the 1990s." Policy Brief, No. 10, Food First Institute for Food and Development Policy. Http: //www.foodfirst.org/pubs/policy pb10.pdf.

Muller, Edward N. and Mitchell A. Seligson. 1994. "Civic Culture and Democracy: The Question of Causal Relationship." *American Political Science Review* 88(3): 635–652.

Myrdal, Gunnar. 1957. *Rich Lands and Poor: The Road to World Prosperity*. New York: Harper and Row.

Nafziger, Wayne E. 1993. *The Debt Crisis in Africa*. Baltimore, MD: Johns Hopkins University Press.

Newey, Whitney K. and Kenneth D. West 1987. "A Simple Positive Semi-Definite, Heteroscedasticity and Autocorrelation Consistent Covariance Matrix." *Econometrica* 55(4): 703–708.

North, Robert C. 1990. *War, Peace, Survival: Global Politics and Conceptual Synthesis*. Boulder, CO: Westview.

Nye, Joseph S., Jr. 2004. "Hard Power, Soft Power, and 'War on Terrorism,'" in David Held and Mathias Koenig-Archibugi, eds., *American Power in the 21st Century*. Cambridge: Polity.

O'Brien, Patrick K. 2006. "Colonies in a Globalizing Economy, 1815–1948," in Barry K. Gills and William R. Thompson, eds., *Globalization and Global History*. London: Routledge.

O'Brien, S. P. 1996. "Foreign Policy Crisis and the Resort to Terrorism." *Journal of Conflict Resolution* 40: 320–335.

Olson, Mancur. 1982. *The Rise and Decline of Nations: Economic Growth, Stagflation, and Social Rigidities*. New Haven, CT.: Yale University Press.

Oneal, John and Bruce, Russett. 1999. "Assessing the Liberal Peace with Alternative Specifications: Trade Still Reduces Conflict." *Journal of Peace Research* 36(4): 423–442.

Organski, A. F. K. and Jacek Kugler. 1980. *The War Ledger*. Chicago, IL: University of Chicago Press.

Passe-Smith, J. T. 1996. "Convergence and Divergence in the Post-World War II Era," in C. R. Goddard, J. T. Passe-Smith, and J. G. Conklin, eds., *International Political Economy: State-Market Relations in the Changing Global Order*, Boulder, CO: Lynne Rienner.

Passe-Smith, John T. 1998. "The Persistence of the Gap Between Rich and Poor Countries: Taking Stock of World Economic Growth, 1960–1993," in Mitchell A. Seligson and John T. Passe-Smith, eds., *Development and Underdevelopment: The Political Economy of Global Inequality*. Boulder, CO: Lynne Rienner.

Pettis, Michael. 2001. *The Volatility Machine: Emerging Economies and the Threat of Financial Collapse*. Oxford: Oxford University Press.

Pevehouse, Jon C. 2002. "Democratization from the Outside-In? International Organizations and Democratization." *International Organization* 56: 515–549.

Phillips, P. C. B. and P. Perron. 1988. "Testing for a Unit Root in Time Series Regressions." *Biometrika* 65: 335–346.

Pollins, Brian M. 1996. "Global Political Order, Economic Change and Armed Conflict: Coevolving Systems and the Use of Force." *American Political Science Review* 90: 103–117.

Pollins, Brian M. and Kevin P. Murrin. 1999. "Where Hobbes Meets Hobson: Core Conflict and Capitalism, 1495–1985." *International Studies Quarterly* 43: 427–454.

Prebisch, Raul. 1950. *The Economic Development of Latin America and Its Principal Problems*. New York: United Nations Economic Commission for Latin America.

Pritchett, Lant. 1997. "Divergence-Big Time." *Journal of Economic Perspectives* 11(3): 3–17.

Przeworski, Adam, Michael Alvarez, Jose A. Cheibub, and Fernand Limongi. 2000. *Democracy and Development; Political Institutions and Well-Being in the World, 1950–1990*. New York: Cambridge University Press.

Rasler, Karen and William R. Thompson. 1985. "War and the Economic Growth of Major Powers." *American Journal of Political Science* 29: 513–538.

Rasler, Karen and William R. Thompson. 1989. *War and State Making: The Shaping of the Global Powers*. Boston: Unwin Hyman.

Rasler, Karen and William R. Thompson. 1994. *The Great Powers and Global Struggle: 1490–1990*. Lexington: University Press of Kentucky.

Rasler, Karen and William R. Thompson. 2004. "The Democratic Peace and the Sequential, Reciprocal, Causal Arrow Hypothesis." *Comparative Political Studies* 37: 879–908.

Rasler, Karen and William R. Thompson. 2005. *Puzzles of the Democratic Peace: Theory, Geopolitics and the Transformation of World Politics*. New York: Palgrave Macmillan.

Rasler, Karen and William R. Thompson. forthcoming. "Globalization and North–South Inequality, 1870–2003: A Factor for Convergence, Divergence or Both?".

Reiter, Dan. 2001. "Does Peace Nurture Democracy?" *Journal of Politics* 63: 935–948.

Reuveny, Rafael. 2001. "Bilateral Import, Export, and Conflict/Cooperation Simultaneity." *International Studies Quarterly* 45(1): 131–158.

Reuveny, Rafael and Quan Li. 2003. "Democracy and Dyadic Militarized Disputes: A Simultaneous Equations Model, 1950–1992." *International Studies Quarterly* 47(2): 325–346.

Reuveny, Rafael and William R. Thompson. 1999. "Economic Innovation, Systemic Leadership, and Military Preparation for War: The U.S. Case." *Journal of Conflict Resolution* 43(5): 570–595.

Reuveny, Rafael and William R. Thompson. 2001. "Leading Sectors, Lead Economies and Economic Growth." *Review of International Political Economy* 8(4): 689–719.

Reuveny, Rafael and William R. Thompson. 2002. "World Economic Growth, Northern Antagonism, and North–South Conflict." *Journal of Conflict Resolution* 46(4): 484–515.

Reuveny, Rafael and William R. Thompson. 2003. "Exploring the North–South Gap." *Japanese Journal of Political Science* 4(1): 77–102.

Reuveny, Rafael and William R. Thompson. 2004a. "World Economic Growth, Systemic Leadership and Southern Debt Crises." *Journal of Peace Research* 41(1): 5–24.

Reuveny, Rafael and William R. Thompson. 2004b. *Growth, Trade and Systemic Leadership*. Ann Arbor: University of Michigan Press.

Rodrik, Dani and Arvind Subramanian. 2008. "The Primacy of Institutions (and what this does and does not mean)," in Giorgi Secondi, ed., *The Development Economics Reader*. London: Routledge.

Romer, Paul M. 1986. "Increasing Returns and Long-run Growth." *Journal of Political Economy* 94: 1002–1037.

Roodman, David. 2006. "Creditor Initiatives in the 1980s and 1990s," in Chris Jochnick and Fraser A. Preston, eds., *Sovereign Debt at the Crossroads: Challenges and Proposals for Resolving the Third World Debt Crisis*. Oxford: Oxford University Press.

Sachs, Jeffrey D. 2005. *The End of Poverty: Economic Possibilities for Our Time*. New York: Penguin Press.

Sachs, Jeffrey D. 2008. "Institutions Matter, But Not for Everything: The Role of Geography and Resource Endowments in Development Shouldn't be Underestimated," in Giorgio Secondi, ed., *The Development Economics Reader*. London: Routledge.

Sachs, Jeffrey D. and Andrew M. Warner. 1995. "Economic Reform and the Process of Global Interpretation." *Brookings Papers on Economic Activity* 1: 1–118.

Sachs, Jeffrey D., Andrew D. Mellinger, and John L. Gallup. 2001. "The Geography of Poverty and Wealth." *Scientific American* 284(3, March): 71–75.

Sala-I-Martin, Xavier. 2002. *The Disturbing "Rise" of Global Income Inequality*. New York: Columbia University Press.

Schraeder, Peter J. 2002. "Promoting an International Community of Democracies," in Peter J. Schraeder, ed., *Exporting Democracy: Rhetoric vs. Reality.* Boulder, CO: Lynne Rienner.

Schumpeter, Joseph A. 1939. *Business Cycles: A Theoretical, Historical, and Statistical Analysis of the Capitalist Process,* 2 vols. New York: McGraw Hill.

Schwartz, Gideon, 1978. "Estimating the Dimension of a Model." *The Annuals of Statistics* 6(3): 461–464.

Seligson, Mitchell R. and Edward N. Muller. 1987. "Democratic Stability and Economic Crisis: Costa Rica, 1978–1983." *International Studies Quarterly* 31(3): 301–326.

Sims, Christopher A. 1980. "Macroeconomics and Reality." *Econometrica* 48: 1–49.

Sims, Christopher A. 1988. "Bayesian Skepticism on Unit Root Econometrics." *Journal of Economic Dynamics and Control* 12: 463–474.

Singer, Max and Aaron Wildavsky. 1993. *The Real World Order: Zones of Peace, Zones of Turmoil.* New York: Chatham House.

Small, Melvin and J. David Singer. 1982. *Resort to Arms.* Beverly Hills, CA: Sage.

Smith, Adam. 1776/1937. *An Inquiry into the Nature and Causes of the Wealth of Nations,* edited by Edwin Cannan. New York: The Modern Library.

Solow, Robert M. 1956. "A Contribution to the Theory of Economic Growth." *Quarterly Journal of Economics* 70: 65–94.

Stalling, Barbara, 1987. *Banker to the Third World: U.S. Portfolio Investment in Latin America, 1900–1986.* Berkeley: University of California Press.

Stein, Gill J. 1999. *Rethinking World-Systems: Diasporas, Colonies, and Interaction in Uruk Mesopotamia.* Tucson: University of Arizona Press.

Suter, Christian. 1992. *Debt Cycles in the World-Economy: Foreign Loans, Financial Crises, and Debt Settlements, 1820–1990.* Boulder, CO: Westview.

Temple, Jonathan. 1999. "The New Growth Evidence." *Journal of Economic Literature* 37: 112–156.

Thompson, William R. 1988. *On Global War: Historical-Structural Approaches to World Politics.* Columbia, SC: University of South Carolina Press.

Thompson, William R. 1993. "The Consequences of War." *International Interactions* 19: 125–147.

Thompson, William R. 1996. "Democracy and Peace: Putting the Cart Before the Horse?" *International Organization* 50: 141–174.

Thompson, William R. 2000. *The Emergence of the Global Political Economy.* London: UCL Press/Routledge.

Tocqueville, de Alexis. 1835. *Democracy in America,* translated by G. Lawrence. Vol 1–2, edited by J. P. Mayer. Garden City, NY: Anchor Books.

Tomz, Michael. 2007. *Reputation and International Cooperation: Sovereign Debt Across Three Centuries.* Princeton, NJ: Princeton University Press.

United Nations. 2005. *World Population Prospects: The 2004 Revision.* New York: Department of Economic and Social Affairs, Population Division.

United Nations Development Programme. 2001. *Human Development Report: Making Technologies Work for Human Development.* New York: United Nations.

United Nations Development Programme. 2007. *Human Development Report: Fighting Climate Change: Human Solidarity in a Divided World.* New York: United Nations.

Verspagen, Bart. 1998. "The Analysis and Measurement of Economic Growth." *Review of Income and Wealth* 44(1): 143–149.

Vos, Rob, 1994. *Debt and Adjustment in the World Economy: Structural Asymmetries in North–South Interactions*. London: Macmillan.

Wade, Robert H. 2007. "Should We Worry About Income Inequality?," in David Held and Ayse Kaya, eds., *Global Inequality: Patterns and Explanations*. Cambridge: Polity.

Wallerstein, Immanuel. 1974, 1980, 1989. *The Modern World-System*. New York: Academic Press.

Werner, Suzanne. 1996. "Absolute and Limited War: The Possibilities of a Foreign Imposed Regime Change." *International Interactions* 22: 67–88.

Whitehead, Lawrence. 2001. "Three International Dimensions of Democratization," in Lawrence Whitehead, ed., *The International Dimensions of Democratization*. Oxford: Oxford University Press.

Williams, John T. 1993. "Dynamic Change, Specification Uncertainty, and Bayesian Vector Autoregression Analysis." *Political Analysis*, 4: 97–125.

Williams, John T., Michael. D. McGinnis and John C. Thomas. 1994. "Breaking the War-Economy Link." *International Interactions* 20: 169–188.

Wright, Quincy. 1942/1965. *A Study of War*, revised ed. Chicago, IL: University of Chicago Press.

World Bank. 2008. *Global Economic Prospects: Technology Diffusion in the Developing World*. Washington, DC: World Bank.

Index